# HANDBOOK OF
# MODERN JAPANESE GRAMMAR

including
Lists of Words and Expressions
with English Equivalents
for Reading Aid

## 口語日本文法便覧
（日本語特殊表現とその英語相当訳及び例題付）

by

### YOKO MATSUOKA McCLAIN
University of Oregon

1981
## THE HOKUSEIDO PRESS
Tokyo

ISBN 4-590-00570-0


First printing, 1981
Sixteenth printing, 1991

Published by The Hokuseido Press
3-32-4, Honkomagome, Bunkyo-ku, Tokyo

# ACKNOWLEDGMENT

The enthusiasm and earnestness of my students at the Univeristy of Oregon during the past several years gave me the courage, inspiration and moral support to write this book, and I would first like to thank all of them. I am also grateful to those who wrote me from time to time commenting on my previous two books; their kind words often gave me much-needed encouragement. Special thanks go to those who took their valuable time reading the manuscript and offering helpful suggestions: Professors Stephen Kohl and Ryoko Toyama; Messrs. Bruce Batten, John O'Donnell, Michael Powell, Miss Juliet Thorpe, my husband Robert and son Ken.

# PREFACE

This book is intended both as a Japanese grammar reference book and as a reading aid, that is to say, an effective reference tool for those who study Japanese, either in a classroom or on their own. For that reason I have tried to explain the various grammatical points simply and concisely, avoiding the use of most technical terms and, whenever possible, comparing Japanese grammar with that of English for clarity. Reference has sometimes been made to traditional Japanese grammatical explanations, but considerable liberty has also been taken wherever necessary to arrive at satisfactory, as well as easily understood, explanations.

It is clear that the problems of teaching Japanese grammar to English-speaking students are entirely different from those of teaching this grammar to native Japanese students. For example, no Japanese, not even little children, would ask which particle, wa は or ga が, should be used for a certain occasion. Nor would a Japanese wonder which would be the correct way to form a verb and adjective te-form, and so forth. These, however, are some of the most confusing, if not most difficult, problems that non-Japanese students face when they study Japanese. Japanese grammar books written for non-native students must include clear and convincing explanations for these kinds of problems peculiar to the Japanese language. Traditional Japanese grammar sometimes serves well for this purpose, but at other times it tends to hinder students' learning by making the Japanese language appear more complicated than it really is.

Japanese grammar may be complex, but it is not as difficult to learn as many people believe. Once the basic principles are learned, the structure of most sentences can be understood. For example, main verbs are always at the end of a clause or sentence; any element which changes the status of these verbs, such as negative, desiderative, or passive forms, will be attached at the end of the verb; and every modifier, whether an adjective, adverb, or some others, always precedes what it modifies; the position of the rest of the words, such as adverbial phrases, is very flexible, and so forth.

Therefore, in spite of the often-heard remark, "Japanese is an impossible language," it is indeed possible for most students to learn to speak, read, and write modern Japanese. Naturally, the students need to make a conscientious effort, receive effective instruction if possible, and use quality dictionaries and reference books.

My previous two books, *Intermediate Japanese Reading Aids*, Volume I, *Verbs and Verb-following Expressions*, and Volume II, *Particles and Noun-supporting Words and Expressions*, have fortunately been received favorably by many teachers as well as students of Japanese. My original intent was to continue the series with a third volume which would cover adverbs and some other smaller problems peculiar to the Japanese language. Several users of the two volumes have suggested, however, that I should combine the third volume with the first two, making one comprehensive Japanese grammar reference book. I am thankful for this suggestion, because it is a logical step in making my work more useable. The first two volumes have been revised; many additional grammatical points have been included, and Japanese script has been added after the romanized words and sentences to make the book more bilingual. Further, because there are many expressions in Japanese which are difficult, or sometimes even impossible, to find in the dictionaries, I have added, as in the previous two books, alphabetically arranged lists of such expressions at the ends of several appropriate chapters.

In translating Japanese expressions into English, I have tried to show some literal relationships between the original Japanese and the English expressions, while also trying to make the English translations idiomatically sound. Sometimes, however, this was not possible because of the marked differences between the two languages, in which case the literal translation is given in the parentheses immediately after the more idiomatic equivalents.

Readers may find some inconsistencies in the use of *kanji* 漢字 and *kana* 仮名. For example, the word *koto* is usually written in *kanji* in such a case as *sonna koto* そんな事 "such a thing," but it seems to be more common to write it in *hiragana* in such an expression as *koto ni suru* ことにする " to decide." This variation also depends on writers. Although the Japanese government has on several occasions issued guidelines concerning the use of *kanji* and *kana* as well as the readings of *kanji*, it seems that even at present no uniformity exists, and convention in some cases persists, and in others gives way. Words which are often written in *hiragana*, but sometimes in *kanji*, depending on the writer, are first transcribed in *hiragana*, then followed by the corresponding *kanji* in parentheses.

The book now begins with verbs and then goes to adjectives, a special class of verbs in Japanese. It then proceeds to particles, nouns, and the remaining parts of speech. I have adopted this order because I believe that verbs and particles are the most important grammatical elements in Japanese, while nouns and other parts of speech, though they have their own peculiarities, are less complex than verbs and particles. The work is complete with cross references and two indexes, one for verb- and noun- following expressions, and the other for grammatical points.

My sincere hope is that this book will prove to be a useful reference tool for all those who use it.

# CONTENTS

# PARTS OF SPEECH 品詞＜ひんし＞

According to their uses in sentences, Japanese words are divided into seven large classes, which are again subdivided as shown below. Some parts of speech are similar to their English counterparts (e.g. common nouns such as *tsukue* 机 "desk," or interjections such as *ā* ああ "ah"), some are used quite differently, and other parts of speech do not even exist in English. For example, Japanese adjectives can be conjugated and are actually a special class of verbs, and some groups of nouns, called copular nouns or adjectival nouns, have no English equivalents. The characteristics of each part of speech in Japanese will be explained later under separate headings.

1. Verbs 動詞〈どうし〉
   (Regular) Verbs
   Auxiliary Verbs 助動詞〈じょどうし〉
   Auxiliary verbs will be treated as verb suffixes in this book; thus they are included in the section of Verb-following Expressions.

2. Adjectives 形容詞〈けいようし〉
   (Conjugative) Adjectives＝Verbal Adjectives 形容詞
   Non-conjugative Adjectives 連体詞〈れんたいし〉

3. Particles 助詞〈じょし〉

4. Nouns 名詞〈めいし〉
   Nouns 名詞
   Pronouns 代名詞〈だいめいし〉
   Copular Nouns＝Adjectival Nouns 形容名詞〈けいようめいし〉
   Because this sort of noun is always followed by the copula (*da* [*desu*], *de*, *na*, etc.), it is treated as an adjectival verb 形容動詞〈けいようどうし〉 in traditional Japanese grammar, instead of being categorized as a special class of nouns.

5. Adverbs 副詞〈ふくし〉

6. Conjunctions 接続詞〈せつぞくし〉

7. Interjections 感動詞〈かんどうし〉 間投詞〈かんとうし〉

If we examine the above Japanese parts of speech, we notice

that two English parts of speech are missing, namely, articles and prepositions.  Articles, either definite or indefinite, do not exist in Japanese.  Prepositions are sometimes expressed by particles in Japanese, but particles are always post-positional rather than pre-positional as in English.  Moreover, Japanese particles have a much broader usage than English prepositions, as explained in the section "Particles" (pp. 93–140).

# VERBS 動詞＜どうし＞

Because the Japanese sentence often omits the subject, the verb assumes paramount importance for the reader. This chapter deals with various aspects of verbs, beginning with their conjugation. In order to present grammatical points as simply as possible, however, many of these points are included in the section "Verb-following Expressions." These expressions are alphabetically arranged under the six bases of verbs at the end of this chapter (pp. 39–83). For the benefit of those who are not familiar with Japanese verb conjugations, an alphabetical index of verb-following expressions is provided at the end of the book (pp. 253–63), separate from the index of general grammatical points.

The expressions which follow the stems of adjectives as well as of copular nouns are also included in this chapter, since many of these expressions are very similar to verb-following expressions (pp. 83–86). Some peculiarities of Japanese verbs which cannot be briefly explained in the section dealing with Verb-following Expressions (such as directional verbs, miscellaneous conditional patterns, etc.) are presented under separate headings immediately after verb conjugations.

## DICTIONARY FORM OF JAPANESE VERBS

The dictionary form of all Japanese verbs ends with *u*. This form appears as the third base of the verb conjugation on the charts that are presented on pp. 7–16.

## JAPANESE VERBS ARE ROUGHLY DIVIDED INTO THREE CATEGORIES

### I. Vowel-stem verbs

1. *-IRU* verb (Stem consisting of one or more syllables with the final vowel *-I*) 上一段活用〈かみいちだんかつよう〉
   e.g. *miru* (mi/ru) 見る "to see"
   *iru* (i/ru) いる "to be," etc.

2. *-ERU* verb (Stem consisting of one or more syllables with

the final vowel -*E*)　下一段活用〈しもいちだんかつよう〉
e.g.　*taberu* (tabe/ru) 食べる "to eat"
　　　*deru* (de/ru) 出る "to go out," etc.
Exceptions:　The following verbs, though ending with -*iru* or
　　　　　　-*eru*, belong to the consonant-stem verb group.
*hairu* (hair/u) 入る "to enter"
*hashiru* (hashir/u) 走る "to run"
*iru* (ir/u) い(要)る "to need"
*kaeru* (kaer/u) 帰る "to return"
*kagiru* (kagir/u) 限る "to limit"
*kiru* (kir/u) 切る "to cut"
*shiru* (shir/u) 知る "to know," etc.

## II.　Consonant-stem verbs　五段活用〈ごだんかつよう〉

1.　Stem consisting of one or more syllables plus a consonant
　　e.g.　*aru* (ar/u) ある "to be," "to exist," "to have"
　　　　*kaku* (kak/u) 書く "to write"
　　　　*yomu* (yom/u) 読む "to read," etc.

2.　Stem consisting of one or more syllables plus the consonant
-*W* (This -*W* is missing from the dictionary form. Thus the
final *u* is preceded by another vowel.)
　　e.g.　*iu* (iw/ ) 言う "to say"
　　　　*narau* (naraw/ ) 習う "to learn"

3.　Stem consisting of one or more syllables plus the consonant
-*T* (Dictionary form of this group of verbs ends -*TSU*.)
　　e.g.　*matsu* (mat/ ) 待つ "to wait"
　　　　*tatsu* (tat/ ) 立つ "to stand"

4.　Stem consisting of one or more syllables plus the consonant
-*S*
　　e.g.　*dasu* (das/u) 出す "to take out," "to mail"

## III.　Irregular verbs

1.　*suru* する "to do" サ行変格活用〈さぎょうへんかくかつよう〉
2.　*kuru* 来る "to come" カ行変格活用〈かぎょうへんかくかつよう〉
3.　*nasaru* なさる "to do" (honorific form of verb *suru*)
　　*kudasaru* 下さる "to give" (honorific form of verb *kureru*)
　　*ossharu* おっしゃる "to say" (honorific form of verb *iu*)
　　*irassharu* いらっしゃる "to be," "to go," "to come" (honorific

form of the verbs *iru, iku, kuru*)　不規則五段活用〈ふきそくご
だんかつよう〉

4.　*gozaru* ござる "to be" (polite form of the verb *aru*)　不規則
五段活用

Only the 2nd base is used in modern Japanese with the
auxiliary *masu.*

> e.g. Koko ni hon ga *gozaimasu.* ここに本がございます.
> "There is a book here."
> Koko ni hon ga *gozaimasen.* ここに本がございません.
> "There is no book here."
> Koko ni hon ga *gozaimashita.* ここに本がございました.
> "There was a book here." etc.

## CONJUGATIONS OF JAPANESE VERBS

On the following pages, the conjugations of Japanese verbs will
be given.　The six verb bases in traditional Japanese grammar
are slightly different from the ones presented here.　Due to the
change in the *kanazukai* 仮名遣 (*kana* usage) of verb endings, it
seems logical to modify somewhat the traditional conjugation in
order to facilitate the student's learning.

It is essential for students to be well acquainted with these six
bases, since numerous suffixes may be attached to them, creating
broad ranges of meaning.

FUNCTIONS OF EACH BASE (The Japanese term, the arbitrary
　　English term, and the abbreviation are given with each base.)

1.　*First Base* 未然形〈みぜんけい〉—Negative Base ($V_1$)
Negative Base is an arbitrary term, because it refers to
only one of the functions of this base.　However, it may be
helpful to use the term to keep the form in mind, because
it is fairly simple to remember the *nai*-form of most verbs.

2.　*Second Base* 連用形〈れんようけい〉—Continuative Base ($V_2$)
This is one of the most used forms.　It is the form used
in creating compound verb forms.　Verbal nouns are also
derived from it, e.g. *kangae* 考え "thought" from *kangaeru,*
"to think," *kaeri* 帰り "the way back," from *kaeru,* "to return."　The Second Base also functions as a coordinating
conjunction, "and," e.g. *Otōto wa uchi de hon o yomi,*

*watakushi wa toshokan de benkyō shimashita.* 弟は家で本を
読み私は図書館で勉強しました． "My younger brother read a
book at home, and I studied at the library."

3.   *Third Base* {a. 終止形〈しゅうしけい〉—Conclusive Base } (V₃)
             {b. 連体形〈れんたいけい〉—Attributive Base}

The third base is the dictionary form of all verbs. The
classical Japanese verb conjugation divided Conclusive and
Attributive into two separate bases. However, the Japanese
language has experienced fairly extensive grammatical
changes through the centuries, and the conclusive and attributive stems of modern Japanese no longer have separate
forms (Exception: copular *da* [Conclusive], *na* [Attributive].
See p. 15.) Students should remember that the suffixes belong
to the attributive verb functions. This will help to avoid
confusion when students are introduced to classical grammar
later. The attributive form of the verb is followed only by
nouns.

4.   *Fourth Base* 仮定形〈かていけい〉—Conditional (V₄)

The only function of this base in modern colloquial speech
is to take the ending -*ba*, which becomes simple conditional
"if" or "when." (For conditional -*ba*, see pp. 30, 81.)

5.   *Fifth Base* 命令形〈めいれいけい〉—Imperative Base (V₅)

As an imperative form, this is used only in rough speech.
Therefore, the beginner should avoid it. However, this
form is used often enough in sentences before the quotative
*to*, e.g. *Sensei ni kore o shiro to iwaremashita.* 先生にこれを
しろと言われました． "I was told to do this by the teacher."

6.   *Sixth Base* 推量形〈すいりょうけい〉—Tentative Base (V₆)

In traditional Japanese grammar, the tentative verb was
formed from the First Base. However, with use of the new
*kanazukai* since 1946, it seems easier for students to remember this form if it is separated from the First Base
and defined as a new base.

## CONJUGATIONS OF JAPANESE VERBS

**I. Vowel-stem verbs**

1.  *-IRU* verb, *miru* (mi/ru) 見る "to see"

| | stem | base formative | suffix* | arbitrary term for base |
|---|---|---|---|---|
| 1. | mi | | -nai, -zu <br> -rareru <br> -saseru, -sasu <br> -saserareru, etc. | Negative |
| 2. | mi | | -masu <br> -tai <br> -sugiru <br> -yasui, -nikui, etc. | Continuative |
| 3. | mi | ru | a.—(deshō, darō) <br><br> b.  Noun | Conclusive (Dictionary Form) <br> Attributive |
| 4. | mi | re | -ba | Conditional |
| 5. | mi | ro <br> yo | | Imperative |
| 6. | mi | yō | | Tentative |

2.  *-ERU* verb, *taberu* (tabe/ru) 食べる "to eat"

| | stem | base formative | suffix* | arbitrary term for base |
|---|---|---|---|---|
| 1. | tabe | | -nai, etc. | Negative |
| 2. | tabe | | -masu, etc. | Continuative |
| 3. | tabe | ru | a.—(deshō, darō) <br><br> b.  Noun | Conclusive (Dictionary Form) <br> Attributive |
| 4. | tabe | re | -ba | Conditional |
| 5. | tabe | ro <br> yo | | Imperative |
| 6. | tabe | yō | | Tentative |

Exceptions: Some verbs, though ending with *-iru* or *-eru*, belong to the consonant-stem verb group. For some examples, see p. 4.

*For complete suffix list, see pp. 39–83.

## II. Consonant-stem verbs

1. *kaku* (kak/u) 書く "to write"

|    | stem | base formative | suffix* | arbitrary term for base |
|----|------|----------------|---------|-------------------------|
| 1. | kak | a | -nai, -zu <br> -reru <br> -seru, -su, etc. | Negative |
| 2. | kak | i | -masu <br> -tai, etc. | Continuative |
| 3. | kak | u | a.—(deshō, darō) <br><br> b. Noun | Conclusive (Dictionary Form) <br> Attributive |
| 4. | kak | e | -ba | Conditional |
| 5. | kak | e |  | Imperative |
| 6. | kak | ō |  | Tentative |

2. *iu* (iw**) 言う "to say"

|    | stem | base formative | suffix* | arbitrary term for base |
|----|------|----------------|---------|-------------------------|
| 1. | iw | a | -nai, etc. | Negative |
| 2. | i | i | -masu, etc. | Continuative |
| 3. | i | u | a.—(deshō, darō) <br><br> b. Noun | Conclusive (Dictionary Form) <br> Attributive |
| 4. | i | e | -ba | Conditional |
| 5. | i | e |  | Imperative |
| 6. | i | ō |  | Tentative |

*For complete suffix list, see pp. 39–83.

**In modern Japanese, the sound represented in transliteration by "w" disappears before all vowels except "a."

3. *matsu* (mat/) 待つ "to wait"

| | stem | base formative | suffix* | arbitrary term for base |
|---|---|---|---|---|
| 1. | mat | a | -nai, etc. | Negative |
| 2. | mach | i | -masu, etc. | Continuative |
| 3. | mats | u | a.—(deshō, darō)<br><br>b. Noun | Conclusive (Dictionary Form)<br>Attributive |
| 4. | mat | e | -ba | Conditional |
| 5. | mat | e | | Imperative |
| 6. | mat | ō | | Tentative |

4. *dasu* (das/u) 出す "to take out," "to mail"

| | stem | base formative | suffix* | arbitrary term for base |
|---|---|---|---|---|
| 1. | das | a | -nai, etc. | Negative |
| 2. | dash | i | -masu, etc. | Continuative |
| 3. | das | u | a.—(deshō, darō)<br><br>b. Noun | Conclusive (Dictionary Form)<br>Attributive |
| 4. | das | e | -ba | Conditional |
| 5. | das | e | | Imperative |
| 6. | das | ō | | Tentative |

*For complete suffix list, see pp. 39–83.

Note: The negative suffix *nai* is the negative of the verb *aru*, but *nai* is in an adjectival form, and thus conjugates like an adjective (see pp. 88–89). There is no such word as *aranai*.

Regarding the verb *aru* (consonant-stem verb) and *iru* (vowel-stem verb):

Both *aru* and *iru* mean "to be" in the sense of "to exist," but *aru* is used with an inanimate object for its subject, while *iru* is used with an animate object for its subject.

　　e.g.　Koko ni *hon* ga *arimasu*. ここに本があります. "There is a book here (A book exists here)."

Koko ni *hito* ga *imasu.* ここに人がいます. "There are people here (People exist here)."

*Aru* is also used in the sense of "to have," but distinguish this *aru* from *motsu* "to have."

**e.g.** Nōto ga *arimasu* ka. ノートがありますか; "Do you have notebooks (in your possession or to sell)?"

Nōto o *motte imasu* ka. ノートを持っていますか. "Do you have a notebook (in your personal possession)?"

## III.  Irregular verbs

1. *suru* する

|   | stem | base formative | suffix* | arbitrary term for base |
|---|------|----------------|---------|--------------------------|
| 1. | sh<br>s<br>s | i<br>e<br>a | -nai<br>-zu<br>-reru<br>-seru, -su, etc. | Negative |
| 2. | sh | i | -masu<br>-tai<br>-nikui, -yasui, etc. | Continuative |
| 3. | su | ru | a.—(deshō, darō)<br><br>b.  Noun | Conclusive<br>(Dictionary Form)<br>Attributive |
| 4. | su | re | -ba | Conditional |
| 5. | se<br>shi | yo<br>ro |  | Imperative |
| 6. | shi | yō |  | Tentative |

*For complete suffix list, see pp. 39–83.

The verb *suru* is perhaps the most often used verb in the Japanese language. First, it is used as the verb meaning "to do," or "to make** (something) into (something)." e.g. Ima shukudai o *shite imasu.* 今宿題をしています. "I am doing my

---

** Distinguish this "to make" from "to make" in the sense of "to create." e.g. Kyonen kono yōfuku o *tsukurimashita.* 去年この洋服を作りました. "I made this dress last year."

home work now." Kono furui ki o (kitte) maki ni *shimashō*.
この古い木を(伐って)薪にしましょう. "Let's make firewood out
of this old tree (by cutting it)." It is also used as the verb
meaning "to cost." *Kono udedokei wa ichiman-en shimashita.*
この腕時計は一万円しました. "This watch cost ￥ 10,000." It
is also used for the passing of time, e.g. *Ato ni-nen suru to
uchi no kodomo wa daigaku o sotsugyō shimasu.* あと二年す
ると家の子供は大学を卒業します. "In two years our child will
graduate from the university."

   The verb *suru* is attached to many nouns of foreign origin
(whether Chinese or Western), making them into verbs. For
example, *ryokō* 旅行 (travel)+*suru* means "to travel," and
*dansu* ダンス (dance)+*suru* means "to dance." Also *suru* is
used in some special expressions which almost cannot be
translated into English. For example, *Ano uchi wa omoshiroi
katachi o shite imasu* あの家は面白い形をしています. means
"That house has an interesting shape," and *Ano hito wa
aoi me o shite imasu* あの人は青い目をしています. means
"That person has blue eyes." *Kuchi ni suru* 口にする means
"to speak (of)," or sometimes "to eat," and *Ano hito wa
sensei o shite imasu.* あの人は先生をしています. means "He
is a teacher (He serves as a teacher)." (for more usages of
the verb *suru*, see pp. 20–21)

2.  *kuru* 来る "to come"

|    | stem | base formative | suffix* | arbitrary term for base |
|----|------|---------------|---------|------------------------|
| 1. | k | o | -nai<br>-rareru<br>-saseru, -sasu, etc. | Negative |
| 2. | k | i | -masu<br>-tai<br>-nikui, -yasui, etc. | Continuative |
| 3. | ku | ru | a.—(deshō, darō)<br><br>b.  Noun | Conclusive (Dictionary Form)<br>Attributive |
| 4. | ku | re | -ba | Conditional |
| 5. | ko | i |  | Imperative |
| 6. | ko | yō |  | Tentative |

*For complete suffix list, see pp. 39–83.

The character 来 should be read *ko, ki, ku,* according to the varied forms of its conjugation, e.g. 来ない (*ko*nai), 来ます (*ki*masu), 来る (*ku*ru), 来れば (*ku*reba), 来い (*ko*i), 来よう (*ko*yō).

Note: The verbs *iku* and *kuru* are sometimes used in a different way from the English verbs "go" and "come." When one uses *iku*, the direction of the action is always away from the location of the speaker, while with *kuru* the direction of the action is always towards the speaker. Therefore, while in English one can ask, "May I come to your house tomorrow?", in Japanese one has to say, *Ashita otaku ni itte mo ii desu ka*, and never *Ashita otaku ni kite mo ii desu ka*, unless one is at the listener's house, and asks, "May I come here again tomorrow?" *Ashita mo kite ii desu ka*. (See also p. 55 for V*te iku*, pp. 56–57 for V*te kuru*)

3. nasaru なさる (honorific form of *suru*)

|  | stem | base formative | suffix* | arbitrary term for base |
|---|---|---|---|---|
| 1. | nasar | a | -nai, zu, etc. | Negative |
| 2. | nasa** | i | -masu | Continuative |
|  | nasar | i | -tai<br>-yasui, nikui, etc. |  |
| 3. | nasar | u | a.—(deshō, darō)<br><br>b.   Noun | Conclusive (Dictionary Form)<br>Attributive |
| 4. | nasar | e | -ba | Conditional |
| 5. | nasa** | i |  | Imperative |
| 6. | nasar | ō |  | Tentative |

*For complete suffix list, see pp. 39–83.
**r is dropped before -masu and in the imperative form.

4. gozaru ござる (polite form of *aru*)

In modern Japanese, only the following forms are used: gozaimasu ございます; gozaimashita ございました; gozaimasen ございません: gozaimashō ございましょう. (*r* is dropped before -*masu*.)

## CONJUGATION OF SUFFIX *MASU* ます

*Masu* is attached to the second base of all verbs and makes the tone of speech polite. Aside from changing the tone, it has no meaning.

| | stem | base formative | suffix | arbitrary term for base |
|---|---|---|---|---|
| 1. | mas | e | -n | Negative |
| 2. | mash | i | -te, -ta | Continuative |
| 3. | mas | u | a.—(deshō) | Conclusive (Dictionary Form) |
| | | | b. Noun | Attributive |
| 4. | mas | ure | -ba | Conditional |
| 5. | mas<br>mash | e<br>i | | Imperative |
| 6. | mash | ō | | Tentative |

Note: *Te*-form (*mashite*) and Imperative (*mase, mashi*) are used only in a very polite level of speech. Attributive (*masu* before noun) and Conditional (*masureba*) are seldom used in modern Japanese. The forms *masen* (negative present), *mashita* (perfective), *masu* (present), *mashō* (tentative), *masen deshita* (negative perfective) are very common.

## COPULAS, *DA* だ AND *DESU* です (Be-verb)

Copula *da* (informal form) and *desu* (polite form) may both be used as follows:

1. As a predicate verb, they show that the subject (A) equals the complement (B). A complement may be a noun or some other part of speech.

e.g. *Watakushi* wa *gakusei desu.* 私は学生です。
　　　A　　　　　B　　=
"I am a student." (A=B)
*Watakushi* no *jugyō* wa *ni-ji made desu.* 私の授業は
　　　　　　　A　　　　B　　　=
二時までです。 "My classes are until two o'clock."
(A=B)

2.  As a predicate, *da* (*desu*) is sometimes used as a substitute for other predicate verbs.

    e.g.  Boku wa karēraisu *da* (ni suru) kedo, kimi wa nan' ni suru?　僕はカレーライスだけど君は何にする.
    "I'll choose (decide on) curry and rice; how about you?
    Boku wa sushi *da*.　僕はすしだ.　"I'll choose sushi."

Note:  This *da* is used when the meaning is clear from the context as shown above. It often expresses one selection out of many choices.

    Watakushitachi no kurasu wa Amerika-jin ga go-nin *de* (ite) Furansu-jin ga san-nin *desu* (imasu).　私達のクラスはアメリカ人が五人でフランス人が三人です.
    "In our class five are Americans and three are French (There are five American and three French people).

3.  After a place noun, *da* and *desu* mean "is located at (in)" and are used in the same way as *ni arimasu*, or *ni imasu*.

    e.g.  Watakushi no uchi wa *Tokyo desu*. 私の家は東京です.
    =Watakushi no uchi wa *Tokyo ni arimasu*.　"My house is in Tokyo."
    Gakusei wa *kyōshitsu desu*. 学生は教室です. =Gakusei wa *kyōshitsu ni imasu*. "The students are in the classroom."

4.  After *o*-V$_2$, they form the honorific expression.

    e.g.  Ano kata wa okosan ga takusan *oari desu*. あの方はお子さんが沢山おありです. =*oari ni narimasu*.　"He has lots of children."

BUT:  After predicate adjectives, *desu* changes the ending to the polite level.  It should be remembered that this *desu* does not have a verbal function, since Japanese predicate adjectives are not only adjectives but also verbs.  Because predicate adjectives are the informal verb ending form, *da* is redundant, as shown in the following example.

    e.g.  Kono uchi wa *ōkii* (informal ending). この家は大きい.
    "This house is large."
    Kono uchi wa *ōkii desu* (polite ending). この家は大きいです. "This house is large."

Wrong:

    Kono uchi wa *ōkii* <u>da</u>. (*Da* is redundant and cannot be used after adjectives.)

**5.**  *darō* (*deshō*) after V₃ or V*ₜₐ* shows probability.

  e.g.  Kare wa mō sugu Amerika e iku *darō*.   彼はもうす
    (直)ぐアメリカへ行くだろう.  "He will probably go
    to America soon."

  *darō* (*deshō*) after V₃ or V*ₜₐ* also indicates a light question,
  when the statement ends with a rising tone.

    e.g.  Ashita irassharu *deshō·* 明日いらっしゃるでしょう.
    "You are going tomorrow, aren't you?"

## CONJUGATIONS OF COPULAS, *DA* AND *DESU*

  Conjugations of both *da* and *desu* are highly irregular.

**1.**  *da* だ

|   | stem | base formative | suffix | arbitrary term for base |
|---|------|----------------|--------|--------------------------|
| 1. | — | | | |
| 2. | de<br>dat | | <br>-ta | Continuative |
| 3. | da<br><br>na | | | Conclusive<br>(Dictionary Form)<br>Attributive |
| 4. | nar | a | -ba | Conditional |
| 5. | — | | | |
| 6. | dar | ō | | Tentative |

*da=de aru*

|          | present        | perfective        | tentative          |
|----------|----------------|-------------------|--------------------|
| positive | da: de aru     | datta: de atta    | darō: de arō       |
| negative | de wa* nai     | de wa* nakatta    | de wa* nai darō    |

*A more colloquial form of *de wa* では is *ja* じゃ

2.   *desu*  です

| | stem | base formative | suffix | arbitrary term for base |
|---|---|---|---|---|
| 1. | — | | | |
| 2. | desh | i | -te*, -ta | Continuative |
| 3. | des | u | | Conclusive (Dictionary Form) |
| | (na) | | | Attributive |
| 4. | (nara) | | | Conditional |
| 5. | — | | | |
| 6. | desh | ō | | Tentative |

*\*Te*-form (*deshite*) is not commonly used.  *De* often takes its place.

*desu*=*de arimasu*

| | present | perfective | tentative |
|---|---|---|---|
| positive | desu : <br> de arimasu | deshita : <br> de arimashita | deshō : <br> de arimashō |
| negative | de wa* arimasen <br><br> de wa* nai desu | de wa* arimasen <br> deshita <br> de wa nai deshita | de wa* arimasen <br> deshō <br> de wa nai deshō |

\*A more colloquial form of *de wa* is *ja*.

Differences in usage:  *da*   used in informal prose; informal men's speech

  *de aru*   impersonal; used in formal writing such as newspaper and scholarly articles

  *desu*   polite conversational

  *de arimasu*  used in such occasions as formal lectures and speeches

## HOW TO FORM *TA*-FORM AND *TE*-FORM OF VERBS

In classical Japanese *tari*-form (modern day *ta*-form) and *te*-form were formed by adding *tari* and *te* directly to the second base ending of all verbs.  This is still true with vowel-stem verbs (for use of *ta*-form and *te*-form, see pp. 51–59).

**I.  Vowel-stem verbs**—simply add *ta* or *te* to the stem, i.e. to the second base.

| third base (dic. form) | stem | | *ta*-form | *te*-form |
|---|---|---|---|---|
| iru いる | i | simply add *ta* or *te* | ita いた | ite いて |
| miru 見る | mi | | mita 見た | mite 見て |
| deru 出る | de | | deta 出た | dete 出て |
| taberu 食べる | tabe | | tabeta 食べた | tabete 食べて |

**II.  Consonant-stem verbs**—This group of verbs went through various changes through the years.  The formation of the modern *te*-form can be divided into four categories as shown below, and the one exception (the verb *iku*) that follows.

| | third base (dic. form) | stem | final stem consonant change | *ta*-form | *te*-form |
|---|---|---|---|---|---|
| 1. | yomu 読(む) | yom | *m* changes to *n*: add *da* or *de* | yonda ⎫ | yonde ⎫ |
| | yobu 呼(ぶ) | yob | *b* changes to *n*: add *da* or *de* | yonda ⎬ (んだ) | yonde ⎬ (んで) |
| | shinu 死(ぬ) | shin | *n* remains: add *da* or *de* | shinda ⎭ | shinde ⎭ |
| 2. | iu 言(う) | iw* | *w* changes to *t*: add *ta* or *te* | itta ⎫ | itte ⎫ |
| | matsu 待(つ) | mat | *t* remains: add *ta* or *te* | matta ⎬ (った) | matte ⎬ (って) |
| | wakaru 分(る) | wakar | *r* changes to *t*: add *ta* or *te* | wakatta ⎭ | wakatte ⎭ |
| 3. | kaku 書(く) | kak | *k* changes to *i*: add *ta* or *te* | kaita (いた) | kaite (いて) |
| | isogu 急(ぐ) | isog | *g* changes to *i*: add *da* or *de* | isoida (いだ) | isoide (いで) |
| 4. | dasu 出(す) | das | add *ta* or *te* to the 2nd base | dashita (した) | dashite (して) |

Note: Generally, if the final consonant is voiced, the *t*-sound of *ta* and *te* is changed to a *d*-sound, *da* and *de*.

*Exceptions: Some classical verbs ending with *u* う which are still in occasional use (e.g. *tou* 問う) becomes *touta* 問うた.

## III.　Exception

| | iku　行く | ik | k changes to t:<br>add ta or te | itta　行った | itte　行って |
|---|---|---|---|---|---|

## IV.　Irregular verbs

| 1. | kuru 来る | add ta or te to the 2nd base | kita　来た | kite　来て |
|---|---|---|---|---|
| 2. | suru　する | add ta or te to the 2nd base | shita　した | shite　して |

## TENSES OF JAPANESE VERBS

Japanese verb forms have two main tenses, the present and the perfective (which denotes completion of action and often equals the past tense in English). There is no future tense form, and the present tense form serves that function. For example, such English expressions as "I eat," "I shall eat," "I will eat," and "I am going to eat," can all be expressed in Japanese by *Watakushi wa tabemasu.* 私は食べます. though in actuality such expressions as *Tabeyō to omotte imasu.* 食べようと思っています. or *Taberu to omoimasu.* 食べると思います. are more likely to be used. The Japanese present tense also expresses habitual action: *Ii undō shita ato de wa itsumo yoku tabemasu.* いい運動した後ではいつ(何時)もよく食べます. "After exercising well, we always eat a lot."

One has to keep in mind, however, that the present tense of the Japanese verb often implies an instantaneous action of the presnt rather than a prolonged action. For example, while in English we can use a simple present tense and say, "I live in Tokyo now," in Japanese one has to use V$_{te}$ *iru* form and say, *Watakushi wa ima Tokyo ni sunde imasu.* 私は今東京に住んでいます. as long as some duration is involved in the action of the verb. The form V$_{te}$ *iru* (*ita*) is mainly used for the tense equivalent to the English (1) present (past) progressive (for an action occurring at the moment), and (2) present (past) perfect (for an action that began in the past and continues into the present). There are several other verbs besides *sumu* which are usually used in the V$_{te}$ *iru* form.

e.g. *motsu* "to have"　Okane o *motte imasu* ka.　お金を持ってい
　　　　ますか. "Do you have money?"

Iie, *motte imasen.* いいえ持っていません.
"No, I don't." (See p. 10 for more about *motsu*)

**shiru** "to know"   Watakushi wa ano hito o *shitte imasu.* 私はあの人を知っています. "I know him (I came to know him, and I still know him)."

but in negative:   Watakushi wa *shirimasen.* 私は知りません. "I don't know."

Probability is expressed by adding *darō* (*deshō*) after the dictionary form (V₃) for the present and the future tenses, and after the perfective form (V*ₜₐ*) for the past.

e.g. present:   Yamamoto-san wa *ima* Tokyo ni sunde iru *deshō.* 山本さんは今東京に住んでいるでしょう. "Mr. Yamamoto probably lives in Tokyo now."

future:   Jonson-san wa *mō sugu* Nihon ni tatsu *deshō.* ジョンソンさんはもうす(直)ぐ日本に発(立)つでしょう. "Mr. Johnson will probably leave for Japan very soon."

past:   Suzuki-san wa *mō* Nihon e kaetta *deshō.* 鈴木さんはもう日本へ帰ったでしょう. "Mr. Suzuki has probably gone back to Japan already."

Note:   As shown in the above examples, the form *darō* (*deshō*) is usually used for the probability of the action of the third person. For a sentence whose subject is first person, such as "I'll probably go tomorrow," one will most likely say in Japanese, *Ashita wa tabun iku to omoimasu.* 明日は多分行くと思います. or simply *Ashita wa tabun ikimasu.* 明日は多分行きます. without *darō* (*deshō*) at the end.

## SPECIFICITY OF JAPANESE VERBS IN DESCRIBING AN ACTION

The Japanese verb is sometimes more specific in describing the action it represents than is the English verb. That is, in Japanese one may have to use several different verbs for a certain action for which only one verb can be used in English. One good example is the English verb "to wear." In English we can say, "I wear a dress," "I wear a hat," "I wear a pair of shoes," and so forth. But in Japanese one has to change the verb, depending on which part of the body the clothing will be put on.

| | |
|---|---|
| I wear a dress. | Yōfuku o *kimasu.*　洋服を着ます.<br>(put on the body) |
| I wear a hat. | Bōshi o *kaburimasu.*　帽子をかぶ(被)りま<br>す. (put on the head) |
| I wear a pair of shoes. | Kutsu o *hakimasu.*　靴をは(履)きます.<br>(put on footwear) |
| I wear gloves. | Tebukuro o hamemasu (shimasu). 手袋を<br>はめます. (*hameru* also means to insert) |
| I wear a ring. | Yubiwa o *hamemasu (shimasu).*<br>指輪をはめます. |
| I wear a tie. | Nekutai o *shimemasu (shimasu).*　ネクタ<br>イを締めます. (*shimeru* means to tie) |
| I wear glasses. | Megane o *kakemasu.* 眼鏡をかけます.<br>(*kakeru* means to hang) |
| I wear a shawl. | Shōru o *kakemasu.* ショールをかけます. |
| I wear a scarf. | Sukāfu o *makimasu.* スカーフをまきます.<br>(*maku* means to wrap around) |
| I wear a badge. | Batji o *tsukemasu.* バッジをつけます.<br>(*tsukeru* also means to attach) |
| I wear a wrist watch. | Udedokei o *shimasu.* 腕時計をします. |

Another good example is the English verb "to play," which has more than half a dozen counterparts in Japanese.

| | |
|---|---|
| Children play in the yard. | Kodomo wa niwa de *asobimasu.*　子供は<br>庭で遊びます. |
| I play the piano. | Piano o *hikimasu.* ピアノを弾きます.<br>(use the verb *hiku* for the musical in-<br>strument which requires mainly the<br>manipulation of fingers) |
| I play the drum. | Taiko o *tatakimasu.*　太鼓をたたきます.<br>(use the verb *tataku* "beat" for the mu-<br>sical instrument which requires beating) |
| I play the flute. | Fue o *fukimasu.* 笛を吹きます.<br>(use the verb *fuku* for the musical in-<br>strument which requires blowing) |
| We play cards. | Torampu o *shimasu.* トランプをします. |
| I play a record. | Rekōdo o *kakemasu.* レコードをかけます. |
| I play the role of<br>Hamlet. | Hamuretto no yaku o *enjimasu.* ハムレ<br>ットの役を演じます. |

| They are playing *Hamlet* at the theatre. | Ano gekijō de Hamuretto o *jōen shite imasu.* あの劇場でハムレットを上演しています. |
|---|---|
| We play* tennis. | Tenisu o *shimasu*\*. テニスをします. |

*This verb is applicable to most other sports as well.

Note: The verb *asobu* means primarily "to amuse oneself."  e.g. Kodo-motachi ga *yakyū o shite asonde* imasu. 子供達が野球をして遊んでいます. "Children are enjoying themselves, playing baseball." *Toranpu o shite asonde imasu.* トランプをして遊んでいます. "They are enjoying a card game."

## TRANSITIVE VERBS 他動詞〈たどうし〉 and INTRANSITIVE VERBS 自動詞〈じどうし〉

As the Chinese characters show, *tadōshi* literally means "other-moving word," while *jidōshi* means "self-moving word." They roughly correspond to English transitive and intransitive verbs. Many Japanese verbs exist in *tadōshi* and *jidōshi* pairs which have the same verbal base, but have different endings (cf. English verbs, "lay" and "lie"). Special attention should be paid to the use of these verbs.  Compare the following three sentences:

1. Mado ga *aite imasu.* 窓があ(開)いています. "The window is open." (No agent is involved.) *Jidōshi-te* followed by the auxiliary verb *iru* is used in descriptive sentences.

   *aite* is a *te*-form of *aku* (*jidōshi*, meaning "to be open")

   More examples:
   Jidōsha ga *tomatte imasu.* 自動車がとまっています. "The car is parked."
   Hito ga *atsumatte imasu.* 人が集まっています. "People are gathered."
   Machigai ga *naotte imasu.* 間違いが直っています. "Mistakes are corrected."

2. Mado ga *akete arimasu.* 窓があ(開)けてあります. "The window is open." (The window has been opened by someone, and is still open.) *Tadōshi-te* followed by the auxiliary verb *aru* is used in descriptive sentences.

   *akete* is a *te*-form of *akeru* (*tadōshi*, meaning "to open")

   More examples:
   Jidōsha ga *tomete arimasu.* 自動車が止めてあります. "The car is parked."

Hon ga *atsumete arimasu*. 本が集めてあります. "The books are gathered."

Machigai ga *naoshite arimasu*. 間違いが直してあります. "Mistakes are corrected."

The difference between the above two constructions is that in (1) no agent is implied, but in (2) the action has been done by someone and the state resulting from the action still continues. Often the translation of the two sentences, *Mado ga aite imasu*, and *Mado ga akete arimasu*, comes out the same in English. "The window is open."

3.    Mado o *akete imasu*. 窓をあ(開)けています. "He is opening the window." $V_{te}$ (both *jidōshi* and *tadōshi*)+*iru* is used as the progressive form.

More examples:

Watakushi wa machigai o *naoshite imasu*. 私は間違いを直しています. (*tadōshi*+*iru*) "I am correcting the mistakes."

Watakushi wa *hashitte imasu*. 私は走っています. (*jidōshi*+*iru*) "I am running."

However, $V_{te}$+*iru* has a different use with some motion verbs (*iku, kuru, kaeru*, etc.)

Tanaka-san ga *kite imasu*. 田中さんが来ています.
(motion verb+*iru*) "Mr. Tanaka is here. (Mr. Tanaka came and is still here.)"

Tanaka-san ga *kite imashita*. 田中さんが来ていました.
"Mr. Tanaka was here."

Gakkō ni *itte imasu*. 学校に行っています.
(motion verb+*iru*) "He is at school. (He went to school and is still there.)"

Uchi e *kaette imasu*. (motion verb+*iru*) 家へ帰っています.
(motion verb+*iru*) "He is home. (He came home and is still home.)"

## A PARTIAL LIST OF TADŌSHI-JIDŌSHI PAIRS

| *Tadōshi* | *Jidōshi* |
|---|---|
| ageru 上(揚, 挙)げる "to raise" | agaru 上(揚, 挙)がる "to rise" |
| akeru あ(開, 明)ける "to open" | aku あ(開, 明)く "to be open" |

| *Tadōshi* | *Jidōshi* |
|---|---|
| amasu 余す "to save, to leave over" | amaru 余る "to remain, to be left over" |
| ateru 当てる "to hit" | ataru 当たる "to be hit" |
| atsumeru 集める "to gather" | atsumaru 集まる "to be gathered" |
| azukeru 預ける "to entrust to someone" | azukaru 預かる "to take charge of" |
| dasu 出す "to put out, to serve, to take out" | deru 出る "to come out, to appear" |
| fuku 吹く "to breathe" | fuku 吹く "to blow" (same as tadōshi) |
| fuyasu 殖やす "to increase" | fueru 殖える "to be increased" |
| hajimeru 始める "to begin" | hajimaru 始まる "to begin" |
| horobosu 滅ぼす "to defeat" | horobiru 滅びる "to perish, to be ruined" |
| ireru 入れる "to put in, to insert" | hairu 入る "to enter, to be put in" |
| kaesu 返(帰)す "to give back, to return" | kaeru 返(帰)る "to return" |
| kudaku 砕く "to break" | kudakeru 砕ける "to be crushed" |
| machigaeru 間違える "to err" | machigau 間違う "to be in error" |
| mageru 曲げる "to bend" | magaru 曲がる "to be bent" |
| masu 増す "to increase" | masu 増す "to increase" (same as tadōshi) |
| mazeru 混ぜる "to mix" | mazaru 混ざる "to be mixed" |
| mitsukeru 見つ(付)ける "to look for, to find" | mitsukaru 見つ(付)かる "to be found" |
| moyasu 燃やす "to burn" | moeru 燃える "to be burnt" |
| mukeru 向ける "to turn towards" | muku 向く "to turn one's head" |
| nagasu 流す "to let flow" | nagareru 流れる "to flow" |
| naosu 直す "to correct" | naoru 直る "to be mended" |
| natsukeru なつ(懐)ける "to make someone attached to oneself" | natsuku なつ(懐)く "to become attached to" |
| nokosu 残す "to leave" | nokoru 残る "to be left" |
| okosu 起こす "to raise" | okiru 起きる "to get up" |
| otosu 落す "to drop" | ochiru 落ちる "to fall" |
| oeru 終える "to finish" | owaru 終る "to end" |
| sageru 下げる "to lower, to hang" | sagaru 下がる "to go down, to be hanged" |

| *Tadōshi* | *Jidōshi* |
|---|---|
| shimeru 閉(締)める "to close," "to tighten up" | shimaru 閉(締)まる "to be closed," "to be tightened up" |
| shizumeru 静(鎮)める "to calm" | shizumaru 静(鎮)まる "to calm down" |
| shizumeru 沈める "to sink" | shizumu 沈む "to sink" |
| sodateru 育てる "to bring up" | sodatsu 育つ "to grow up" |
| sugosu 過ごす "to pass" | sugiru 過ぎる "to pass by" |
| susumeru 進める "to advance" | susumu 進む "to advance" |
| tateru 立(建)てる "to erect, to build" | tatsu 立(建)つ "to stand, to be built" |
| tomeru 止(留)める "to stop" | tomaru 止(留)まる "to stop" |
| tsukeru つ(付)ける "to attach, to light" | tsuku つ(付)く "to stick to, to be lit" |
| tsumeru 詰める "to stuff" | tsumaru 詰まる "to be stuffed" |
| tsunageru つなげる "to connect" (tsunagu) | tsunagaru つながる "to be connected" |
| tsutaeru 伝える "to convey" | tsutawaru 伝わる "to be transmitted" |
| ukaberu 浮かべる "to float" | ukabu 浮かぶ "to float" |
| umeru 埋める "to bury" | umaru 埋まる "to be buried" |
| watasu 渡す "to pass over, to hand over" | wataru 渡る "to go over, to cross over" |
| yaku 焼く "to bake, to roast" | yakeru 焼ける "to be baked" |

## DIRECTIONAL VERBS

There are six verbs (three pairs) for "giving" and "receiving." The correct usage of these depends on the interrelationships (superior *meue* 目上—inferior *meshita* 目下 relationship according to Japanese tradition) between the first, the second, and the third persons.

Special attention should be given to the third person when one's immediate family is involved. That is, one should always consider all immediate family members (not only one's own children and younger siblings, but also older siblings, spouse, and even parents) inferior to the person to whom one is speaking if that person is not a family member.

Examples of each instance will be given below:

**I.**   $\begin{cases} kureru \text{ くれる} \\ kudasaru \text{ 下さる} \quad \text{(honorific form of } kureru) \end{cases}$ "to give"

| Subject (*Giver*) | Verb | Indirect object (*Recipient*) |
|---|---|---|

$\begin{rcases} \text{you} \\ \text{he(they)} \end{rcases}$   give(s)   $\begin{cases} \text{to me (us)} \\ \text{to the one who is close to me} \\ \text{to you who are close to me} \end{cases}$

*Never* I (we)

**1.**   When the giver is inferior to the recipient, use *kureru*.

*Otōto* ga *watakushi* ni *kuremashita.* 弟が私にくれました。
"My younger brother gave it to me."

**2.**   When the giver is superior to the recipient, use *kudasaru*.

*Sensei* ga *watakushi* ni *kudasaimashita.* 先生が私に下さいました。"The teacher gave it to me."

*Sensei* ga *watakushi no otōto* ni *kudasaimashita.* 先生が私の弟に下さいました。"The teacher gave it to my brother."

*Sensei* ga *anata* ni *kudasaimashita* ka. 先生があなたに下さいましたか。"Did the teacher give it to you?"

*Sensei* ga *watakushi no haha* ni *kudasaimashita.* 先生が私の母に下さいました。"The teacher gave it to my mother."

**3.**   When the giver is a direct family member, and one is speaking to a non-family person, use *kureru*.

*Chichi* ga *watakushi* ni *kuremashita.* 父が私にくれました。"My father gave it to me."

When the giver is a direct family member, but one is speaking to another member of the family, e.g. to one's sisters or brothers, one may say:

*Otō-san* ga *watakushi* ni *kudasaimashita.* お父さんが私に下さいました。"Father gave it to me."

**II.**   $\begin{cases} yaru \text{ やる} \\ ageru \text{ 上げる} \quad \text{(honorific of } yaru) \end{cases}$ "to give"

| Subject (*Giver*) | Verb | Indirect object (*Recipient*) |
|---|---|---|

$\begin{rcases} \text{I (we)} \\ \text{you} \\ \text{he (they)} \end{rcases}$   give(s)   $\begin{cases} \text{to you} \\ \text{to him (them)} \end{cases}$

**1.** *yaru*

The verb *yaru* should be used with discretion, since this

directional verb indicates that the recipient is decisively inferior to the giver; that is, the recipient is one's own child,
younger sibling, pet, or even a plant.

*Watakushi* wa *otōto* ni okashi o *yarimashita.* 私は弟にお菓
子をやりました. "I gave a cake to my younger brother."
*Chichi* wa *inu* ni gohan o *yarimashita.* 父は犬にごはんをや
りました. "Father fed the dog."
*Haha* wa *hana* ni mizu o *yarimashita.* 母は花に水をやりま
した. "Mother gave water to the flower."

2. *ageru*

In other cases of giving except the above, *ageru* should be
used.

*Anata* wa *sensei* ni ringo o *agemashita* ka. あなたは先生に
リンゴ(林檎)を上げましたか. "Did you give an apple to
the teacher?"
*Watakushi* wa *haha* ni hon o *agemashita.* 私は母に本を上
げました. "I gave a book to my mother."
*Sensei* wa *gakusei* ni enpitsu o *agemashita.* 先生は学生に鉛
筆を上げました. "The teacher gave the student a pencil."
*Gakusei* wa *sensei* ni hon o *agemashita.* 学生は先生に本を上
げました. "The student gave the teacher a book."

III. $\begin{cases} \textit{morau} \text{ もら(貰)う} \\ \textit{itadaku} \text{ いただ(戴,頂)く} \quad \text{(honorific of } \textit{morau}) \end{cases}$ "to receive"

| Subject (Recipient) | Verb | from whom (Giver) |
|---|---|---|
| I (we) | | from* you |
| you | receive(s) | from him (them) |
| he (they) | | |

* this *from* is expressed by the Japanese particles *ni* or *kara*

1. When the recipient is superior to the giver, use *morau.*
*Watakushi* wa kore o *imōto* ni (kara) *moraimashita.*
私はこれを妹にもらいました. "I received this from my
younger sister."

2. When the recipient is inferior to the giver, use *itadaku.*
*Gakusei* wa kore o *sensei* ni (kara) *itadakimashita.* 学生
はこれを先生にいただきました. "The student received
it from the teacher."

3. If the giver is a member of the recipient's immediate

family, the recipient uses *morau* when reciting the story
to a non-family member.

*Watakushi* wa kore o *haha* ni (kara) *moraimashita.*

私はこれを母にもらいました. "I received this from my
mother."

When the giver is the recipient's immediate family
member, but the recipient is reciting the story of receiving to his own family member, the recipient may say:

*Watakushi* wa kore o *okā-san* ni (kara) *itadakimashita.*

私はこれをお母さんにいただきました. "I received this
from Mother."

## DIRECTIONAL VERBS AS AUXILIARIES

Each of the above directional verbs may occur as auxiliaries
following the *Verb te*-form. The direction of the action is the
same as in the case of the independent directional verb.

I. $V_{te}$ ⎰ *kureru* くれる
　　 ⎱ *kudasaru* 下さる

(Implication—Someone is kind enough to do something
for someone else)

*Haha* ga *watakushi* ni kono hon o *katte kuremashita.* 母
が私にこの本を買ってくれました. "My mother bought
this book for me. (My mother was kind enough to
buy this book for me.)"

*Sensei* ga *watakushi no otōto* ni hon o *yonde kudasaimashita.* 先生が私の弟に本を読んで下さいました. "My
teacher read the book to my younger brother. (My
teacher was kind enough to read the book for my
younger brother.)"

II. $V_{te}$ ⎰ *yaru* やる
　　 ⎱ *ageru* 上げる

(Implication—Someone is doing somebody else a favor.)

*Watakushi* wa *imōto* ni *hon* o *yonde yarimashita.* 私は
妹に本を読んでやりました. "I read a book to my younger
sister. (I did a favor for my sister by reading a book.)"

*Sensei* ga *Yamamoto-kun* o *tetsudatte agemashita.* 先生が
山本君を手伝って上げました. "The teacher helped Mr.
Yamamoto. (The teacher did a favor for Mr. Yamamoto
by helping him.)"

III. V*le* $\begin{cases} \text{morau } もら(貰)う \\ \text{itadaku } いただ(戴, 頂)く \end{cases}$

(Implication—Someone is the recipient of someone else's kindness. Usually someone asks for someone else's favor before he receives it.)

*Imōto* ni yōfuku o *tsukutte moraimashita.* 妹に洋服を作ってもらいました. "I was fortunate that my younger sister made a dress for me."

*Watakushi no otōto* wa *sensei* ni hon o *yonde itadakimashita.* 私の弟は先生に本を読んでいただきました. "My younger brother was fortunate that the teacher read a book to him."

## CAUSATIVE VERB *TE*-FORM PLUS A DIRECTIONAL AUXILIARY VERB

The direction of the action is the same as in the case of the independent directional verb.

This pattern means, "to do someone the favor of letting him do something," or "to permit someone to do something"

| | | | | |
|---|---|---|---|---|
| Vowel-stem V₁ | $\begin{cases}\text{sasete*}\\\text{sashite}\end{cases}$ | $\begin{cases}\text{kureru}\\\text{kudasaru}\end{cases}$ | yaru<br>ageru | $\begin{cases}\text{morau}\\\text{itadaku}\end{cases}$ |
| Consonant-stem V₁ | $\begin{cases}\text{sete*}\\\text{shite}\end{cases}$ | $\begin{cases}\text{kureru}\\\text{kudasaru}\end{cases}$ | yaru<br>ageru | $\begin{cases}\text{morau}\\\text{itadaku}\end{cases}$ |

Irregular

| | | | | |
|---|---|---|---|---|
| *suru* | $\begin{cases}\text{sasete*}\\\text{sashite}\end{cases}$ | $\begin{cases}\text{kureru}\\\text{kudasaru}\end{cases}$ | yaru<br>ageru | $\begin{cases}\text{morau}\\\text{itadaku}\end{cases}$ |
| *kuru* | $\begin{cases}\text{kosasete*}\\\text{kosashite}\end{cases}$ | $\begin{cases}\text{kureru}\\\text{kudasaru}\end{cases}$ | yaru<br>ageru | $\begin{cases}\text{morau}\\\text{itadaku}\end{cases}$ |

* *Sasete* and *sete* forms are more refined than the *sashite* and *shite* forms respectively.

e.g. Imōto ga jitensha ni *norasete kuremashita.* 妹が自転車に乗らせてくれました. "My younger sister let me ride her bicycle."

Sensei ga watakushi ni benkyō o *tsuzukesasete kudasaimashita.* 先生が私に勉強を続けさせて下さいました. "My teacher permitted me to continue my studies."

Imōto ni bōru o *nagesasete yarimashita.* 妹にボールを投

げさせてやりました. "I let my younger sister throw my ball."

Tanaka-san ni watakushi no okashi o *tabesasete age-mashita.* 田中さんに私のお菓子を食べさせて上げました. "I let Mr. Tanaka eat my cake."

Chichi ni *oyogasete moraimashita.* 父に泳がせてもらいました. "I was permitted, by my father, to swim."

Sensei ni *kosasete itadakimashita.* 先生に来させていただきました. "I was permitted, by my teacher, to come."

## OTHER VERBS OF DIRECTIONAL RESTRICTIONS

Besides the three pairs of directional verbs just discussed, there are several Japanese verbs which also have certain restrictions of direction in their usage. For example, when the following verbs are used, care has to be taken as to whom the words are directed.

*kawaigaru* 可愛がる "to pet," "to treat with love," directed to *meshita* from *meue* (see p. 24). e.g. Ano sensei wa hontō ni yoku ukemochi no kodomotachi o *kawaigarimasu.* あの先生は本当によく受持ちの子供たち(達)を可愛がります. "That teacher really treats the children in her room nicely."

*shitau* 慕う "to adore," directed to *meue* from *meshita.* e.g. Dakara kodomotachi mo kanojo o taihen *shitatte imasu.* だから子供たちも彼女を大変慕っています. "Therefore, the children adore her, too."

*tattobu* 尊ぶ=tōtobu "to revere," directed to *meue* from *meshita.* e.g. Ano rōjin wa kono machi de hijō ni *tattobarete imasu.* あの老人はこの町で非常に尊ばれています. "That old man is highly respected in this town."

*uyamau* 敬う "to respect," directed to *meue* from *meshita.* e.g. Wareware wa oya o *uyamawanakereba* naranai. 我々は親を敬わなければならない. "We must respect our parents."

## CONDITIONALS

The following four conditional forms are often used interchangeably, as indicated in the parentheses, but the *-tara* conditional has the least restriction in its usage.

I. V₃ *to* type conditional

(In most cases the resultant part is an objective state-ment.) The verb before *to* is always in the dictionary form, and its tense always follows that of the principal clause.

1. "when"

   a. habitual occurrence

   Natsu ga *kuru to* yoku yama ni ikimashita. 夏が来るとよく山に行きました. (not inter-changeable with *-ba, -tara,* or *nara*) "When summer came, we often went to the mountains."

   b. specific occurrence

   Mado o *akeru to* (=*aketara*) yuki ga futte ima-shita. 窓をあ(開)けると雪が降っていました. (not interchangeable with *-ba* or *nara*) "When I opened the window, it was snowing."

   Note: The clause following V₃ *to* conditional is often unexpected.

2. "if"

   Kore o *nakusu to* (=*nakushitara*) taihen desu. これ をなくすと大変です. (not interchangeable with *-ba* or *nara*) "If I lose this, I'll be in trouble."

II. *-ba* type conditional

(In most cases the resultant part involves one's will or determination, or is an inevitable occurrence to the con-ditional part.)

"if"

Anata ga *ikeba* (=*iku nara*) watakushi mo ikimasu. あなたが行けば私も行きます. (not interchangeable with either *to* or *-tara*) "If you go, I will go too." *Takakereba* (=*takakattara, takai nara*) kaimasen. 高 ければ買いません. (not interchangeable with *to*) "If it is expensive, I won't buy it." Ashita yuki *nara* (=*dattara*) ikimasen. 明日雪なら 行きません. (not interchangeable with *da to*) "If it snows tomorrow, I won't go." (*Nara*(ba) is the conditional of the copula *da*; see p. 15 for con-jugations of copula.)

III. *-tara* type conditional
"if"

> Sensei ni *kiitara* (=*kikeba*, *kiku to*) wakarimasu yo.
> 先生に聞いたらわか(分)りますよ. (not interchange-
> able with *nara*) "If you ask your teacher, you'll
> understand it."
>
> Ashita ame *dattara* (=*nara*) ikimasen. 明日雨だった
> ら行きません. (not interchangeable with *da to*)

Note: When the resultant clause is either imperative or interrogative, use the *-tara* conditional. Avoid using the *to*
or *-ba* conditionals.

Shitte *itara* (=*iru nara*), oshiete kudasai. 知っていたら教
えて下さい. "If you know it, please tell me."
Ame ga *futtara*, omukae ni ikimashō ka. 雨が降ったら
お迎えに行きましょうか. "If it rains, shall I come and
get you?"

The following three sentences are so similar in meaning that native speakers may not be able to make clear
distinctions. However, slight differences may be de-
tected.

> *Samui to* atatakai yōfuku o kimasu. 寒いと暖かい洋
> 服を着ます. "Whenever it is cold, we wear warm
> clothes." —habitual occurrence: resultant clause
> is an objective statement.
>
> *Samukereba* atatakai yōfuku o kimasu. 寒ければ暖
> かい洋服を着ます. "If it is cold, we'll wear warm
> clothes." —resultant clause involves will, and is
> an inevitable occurrence to the conditional part.
>
> *Samukattara* atatakai yōfuku o kimasu. 寒かったら
> 暖かい洋服を着ます. "If it is cold, we wear warm
> clothes." —plain conditional

IV. $V_3$ [*no, n'*] *nara*=no (n') *dattara*
(Because *nara* is a short form of *naraba*, the conditional
form of the copula *da*, $V_3$ *nara* is frequently interchangeable
with *-ba* conditional (see II, 1), but the subject of the
*nara* conditional clause is usually someone (or something)
other than *I*.) *Nara* conditional clause is often followed
by an imperative clause.

"if," "in case that"

Issho ni ikitai *nara*, sugu shitaku o shinasai.　一緒
に行きたいなら，す(直)ぐ仕度をしなさい．　"If you
want to go with me, get ready right away."
cf.　*Anata* ga *iku nara*, watakushi mo ikimasu.
あなたが行くなら私も行きます．"If you go,
I'll go, too."
*Watakushi* ga *ikeba* (not iku nara), anata mo
ikimasu ka. 私が行けばあなたも行きますか.
"If I go, will you go too?"
Yomitai *nara*, kashite agemashō. 読みたいなら貸し
てあ(上)げましょう．"If you want to read it, I'll
lend it to you."
Samui *nara*, sētā o kinasai. 寒いならセーターを着な
さい. "If you're cold, put on a sweater."

## TOKI　時

"when"

1. Span of time

*Yasumi no toki*, benkyō shimasen.　(Noun+*no toki*) 休み
の時勉強しません．"When it is a holiday, I don't study."
*Isogashii toki*, konai de kudasai. (Adj$_3$+*toki*) 忙しい時来
ないで下さい．"Please don't come when I am busy."
*Chiisakatta toki* (=chiisai\* *toki*) (Adj$_{ta}$/Adj$_3$+*toki*)　Tokyo
ni sunde imashita.　小さかった時東京に住んでいました.
"I lived in Tokyo when I was little."
Hana ga *kirei na toki* kōen ni ikimashō. (Copular noun+
*na toki*) 花がきれい(綺麗)な時，公園に行きましょう．
"Let's go to the park when the flowers are pretty."
Chichi ga *genki na* (=*datta*) *toki*, yoku issho ni dekake-
mashita. 父が元気な時，よく一緒にでかけました．"When
my father was well, we often went out together."
Nihon ni *iru\** (=*ita*) *toki* Nihongo o naraimashita. (V$_3$/V$_{ta}$
*toki*) 日本にいる時日本語を習いました．"When I was in
Japan, I learned Japanese."

2. Specific time

Tegami o *kaku toki* pen ga irimasu.　(V$_3$+*toki*) 手紙を書

---

\* The present tense of adjectives or verbs can be used even though the
occurrence was in the past, and in fact this usage may be more common.

く時ペンがい(要)ります. "When we write a letter, we need a pen."

Gohan o tabete *ita toki*, tomodachi ga kimashita. (V*ta*+ *toki*) ごはん(御飯)を食べていた時，友達が来ました. "When we were eating, our friend came."

Note: Special attention should be paid when the verb which precedes *toki* is a motion verb such as *iku*, *kuru*, or *kaeru*.

Nihon e *iku toki* tomodachi ni aimasu. 日本へ行く時友達に会います. "On the way to Japan, I'll see my friend."

Nihon ni *itta toki*, tomodachi ni aimasu. 日本に行った時友達に会います. "When I go to (After I arrive in) Japan, I'll see my friend." Use the perfective form even if the action will occur in the future.

Nihon ni *iku toki*, tomodachi ni aimashita. 日本に行く時友達に会いました. "On the way to Japan, 1 met my friend."

Nihon ni *itta toki*, tomodachi ni aimashita. 日本に行った時友達に会いました. "When I went to (After I arrived in) Japan, I met my friend.

# SUBJUNCTIVE

## I. "if"

### 1. Hypothetical

$$to \begin{cases} suru\ to & すると \\ shitara & したら \\ sureba & すれば \\ suru\ nara & するなら \end{cases}$$

Kyoto ni *iku to suru to* itsu ikimasu ka. (V₃ *to suru to*) 京都に行くとするといつ(何時)行きますか. "If you were to go to Kyoto, when would you go?"

Kinō Nihon o *deta to shitara* ima wa mō Amerika ni iru hazu desu. (V*ta to shitara*) 昨日日本を出たとしたら，今はもうアメリカにいるはず(筈)です. "If (presumably) he left Japan yesterday, he should be in the United States already."

### 2. Contrary to fact

#### a. present

Yasui mono *nara* (=*dattara*) kau no ni (kau n' desu ga)... 安い物なら買うのに... "If it were a cheap thing, I would buy it (but I won't buy it, because it is not cheap)."

*Yasukereba* (=*yasukattara*) kau no ni (kau n'
desu ga)... 安ければ買うのに...    "If it
were cheap, I would buy it (but I won't buy
it, because it is not cheap)."

    b. past

*Yasui mono nara* (=*dattara*) katta deshō. 安
い物なら買ったでしょう。 "If it had been a
cheap thing, he would have bought it."

*Yasukereba* (=*yasukattara*) katta n' desu ga
... 安ければ買ったんですが... "If it had
been cheap, I would have bought it."

II. "I wish..."

    1. wish for present

Kyō otenki *nara* (=*dattara*) ii no ni (n' desu ga)...
今日お天気ならいいのに... "I wish the weather
were good today (but it isn't)."

    2. wish for future

Ashita otenki *nara* (*dattara*) ii n' desu ga... 明日
お天気ならいいんですが... "I hope the weather
will be good tomorrow (but I have some doubts)."
—Do not use *no ni* for future.

Ashita otenki *nara* ii desu ne. 明日お天気ならいいで
すね。 "It would be nice if the weather were good
tomorrow, wouldn't it?"

    3. wish for past

Kinō otenki *nara* (=*dattara*) yokatta no ni (n' desu
ga)... 昨日お天気ならよかったのに... "It would
have been nice if the weather had been good
yesterday."

## MISCELLANEOUS CONDITIONAL PATTERNS

*te wa* is the conditional form meaning "if," which is always followed by a negative idea.

  I. Prohibition

    1. *te (de) wa komarimasu* "We'll be in trouble, if you
do..."

Sonna koto o *itte wa komarimasu*. (V*te wa komari*-

*masu*) そんなことを言っては困ります．"We'll be in trouble, if you say such a thing."

*Ōkikute wa komarimasu.* (Adj*te wa komarimasu*) 大きくては困ります．"We'll be in trouble, if it is big."

Konna *mono de wa komarimasu.* (Noun *de wa komarimasu*) こんな物では困ります．"We'll be in trouble, if it is this kind of thing."

2. *te (de) wa ikemasen* "You may not...," "You must not ..."(literally, "if you do..., it can't go [it won't do]").

Sonna koto o *itte wa ikemasen.* (V*te wa ikemasen*) そんなことを言ってはいけません．"You must not say such a thing."

*Chiisakute wa ikemasen.* (Adj*te wa ikemasen*) 小さくてはいけません．"It must not be small."

Sonna *mono de wa ikemasen.* (Noun *de wa ikemasen*) そんな物ではいけません．"It must not be such a thing."

3. *te (de) wa dame desu* "You must not...," "It is not good if ..."

*Tabete wa dame desu.* (V*te wa dame desu*) 食べては駄目です．"You must not eat. (It is not good if you eat.)"

*Chiisakute wa dame desu.* (Adj*te wa dame desu*) 小さくては駄目です．"It's not good if it's small."

Chiisai *no de wa dame desu.* (Noun *de wa dame desu*) 小さいのでは駄目です．"It's not good if it's a small one."

II. Obligation

1. *nakereba ikemasen.* "*You* must do..." (literally, "if you don't..., it can't go").

Kyō benkyō *shinakereba ikemasen.* (V*nakereba ikemasen*) 今日勉強しなければいけません．"You must study today."

*Akakunakereba ikemasen.* (Adj*nakereba ikemasen*) 赤くなければいけません．"It must be red."

2. *nakereba narimasen.* "*I* must do..." (literally, "if I don't..., it won't become").

Sensei to *hanasanakereba narimasen.* V*nakereba* *nari-masen*) 先生と話さなければなりません. "I must talk with my teacher."

3. *nakereba dame desu.* "You must do..." (literally, "if you don't..., it is not good").

Kyō kore o *shinakereba dame desu.* (V*nakereba* *dame desu*) 今日これをしなければ駄目です. "You have to do this today."

"*Akakunakereba dame desu.* (Adj*nakereba* *dame desu*) 赤くなければ駄目です. "It has to be red."

## III. Denial of Obligation

1. *nakute mo ii desu.* "You do not have to. ." (literally, "even if you don't..., it is all right").

Kono hon wa *yomanakute mo ii desu.* (V*nakute* *mo ii desu*) この本は読まなくてもいいです. "You don't have to read this book."

2. *nakute mo kamaimasen.*

*Ikanakute mo kamaimasen.* (V*nakute* *mo kamaimasen*) 行かなくても構いません. "It doesn't matter if you don't go."

## IV. Permission

1. *te mo kamaimasen.* "It does not matter even if you do..."

*Kaite mo kamaimasen.* (V*te* *mo kamaimasen*) 書いても構いません. "It doesn't matter even if you write."

*Kitanakute mo kamaimasen.* (Adj*te* *mo kamaimasen*) 汚くても構いません. "It doesn't matter even if it's dirty."

Chiisai *hon de mo kamaimasen.* (Noun *de mo kamai-masen*) 小さい本でも構いません. "It doesn't matter if it is a small book."

2. *te mo ii desu.* "You may do..."

*Kaette mo ii desu.* (V*te* *mo ii desu*) 帰ってもいいです. "You may go home."

*Kaette mo ii desu ka.* 帰ってもいいですか. "May I go home?"

Answer: positive—*Hai, kaette mo ii desu.* はい, 帰ってもいいです. "Yes, you may go home."

negative—*Iie, kaette wa ikemasen.* い
いえ，帰ってはいけません.
"No, you may not go home."

*Chiisakute mo ii desu.* (Adj*te mo ii desu*) 小さくて
もいいです. "It's all right if it is small."

Chiisai *uchi de mo ii desu.* (Noun *de mo ii desu*)
小さい家でもいいです. "It is all right even if it is
a small house."

## V. Suggestion (not a conditional pattern)

*hō ga ii desu.* "It is better that you do..."

Sono hon o yonda *hō ga ii desu* yo. (V*ta hō ga ii
desu*) その本を読んだ方がいいですよ. "It is better
to read that book."

Sorosoro kekkon suru (=shita) *hō ga ii desu* yo.
(V₃/V*ta hō ga ii desu*) そろそろ結婚する方がいいで
すよ. "It is better to marry soon."

Ōkii *hō ga ii desu* yo. (Adj₃ *hō ga ii desu*) 大きい
方がいいですよ. "It is better to have a big one."

Note: *Hō ga ii* is not a conditional pattern, but it is easy to
remember it with other conditional patterns. *Hō ga ii*
can be preceded either by the third base or the *ta*-form
of the verb.

## AUXILIARY VERBS  助動詞＜じょどうし＞

Auxiliary verbs are verbs that give additional meanings to main verbs. They are included in the section of "Verb-following Expressions" (pp. 39–86), because they all may be attached to the end of the main verb or adjective. Some of the functions of very common auxiliary verbs are negative, desiderative, passive, perfective, potential, and causative. All these forms conjugate the same as main verbs or adjectives. Some auxiliary verbs are in verb forms (e.g. *rareru* and *saseru*), and others are in adjective forms (e.g. *nai, tai* or *rashii*).

# VERB-FOLLOWING EXPRESSIONS

The phases of the Japanese verb are shown by adding a variety of suffixes. A broad range of meaning can be derived by supplying the appropriate endings or combination of endings. Some endings, such as *-nai* ない or *-tai* たい, are adjectival in nature, and thus take further endings whenever necessary (e.g. *Ikitaku nakatta.* 行きたくなかった. "I didn't want to go.").

The expressions are alphabetically arranged under six bases of the verbs, adjectives, and copular nouns, in order to be easily accessible as a reading aid. As mentioned in the section, "How to Form *Ta*-form and *Te*-form," on p. 16, both *ta*-form and *te*-form were formerly made from the second base of the verb. Therefore, the expressions which follow *ta*-form or *te*-form are listed in this volume under second base.

Some endings used in very familiar speech have not been included. If one learns the meaning and use of the endings listed in this book, one will be able to deal with most problems of verbs which appear in modern Japanese writing.

Informal endings of the verb (Dictionary form) are used for the headings of the verb-following expressions, but in the accompanying examples, both polite (*masu, desu* type of endings) and informal (*de aru, da, miru, taberu, yomu, kaku* type of endings) are used.

First base, second base, third base, fourth base, fifth base, and sixth base of the verb, adjective, and copular noun, are hereafter abbreviated $V_1$, $V_2$, $V_3$, $V_{ba}$ ($V_4+ba$), $V_{imperative}$ ($V_5$), $V_{tentative}$ ($V_6$), Adj. and Cop. n., respectively. In the headings, the word in the parentheses ( ) shows that it is interchangeable with the previous word, e.g. *iku to (ni) shite mo : iku **to** shite mo* or *iku **ni** shite mo*, and the word in the brackets [ ] shows that it can be added after the previous word, e.g. *ka shira[n]: ka shira* or *ka shiran*.

I. **Expressions which follow the First Base** 未然形〈みぜんけい〉 **of the verb.**

*-mai* まい (tentative negative) follows the 1st base of vowel-stem verbs and irregular verbs *suru* and *kuru*. *-mai* follows the 3rd base of consonant-stem verbs (see p. 68 for more *-mai*). It has two functions:

1. negative will, e.g. *Sonna koto wa mō shimai to kesshin shita.* そんな事はもうしまいと決心した. "I decided not to do such a thing any more."

2. negative probability, e.g. *Sonna koto wa mō shimai.* そんな事はもうしまい. "Perhaps he won't do such a thing any more."

-*n'* ん (tentative)=-*mu* speaker's conjecture, e.g. *Sō naran to negau.* そうならんと願う. "I hope it will turn out to be so." (negative)= -*nai*=-*nu*, e.g. *Sō wa ikan.* そうはいかん. "It won't work out that way."

-*nai* ない (informal negative ending) conjugates as an adjective: *naku* for *ku*-form, and *nakereba* for conditional, *nakatta* for perfective, e.g. *Tabenai.* 食べない. "I don't eat." "I won't eat."

-*nai bakari de wa nai* ないばかりではない not only does he not..., e.g. *Ano hito wa tabako o nomanai bakari de wa naku, osake mo nomimasen.* あの人はタバコ(煙草)をのまないばかりではなくお酒も飲みません. "Not only does he not smoke cigarettes, he doesn't drink *sake* either."

-*nai dake de wa nai* ないだけ(丈)ではない =-*nai bakari de wa nai*, e.g. *Kono kodomo wa gohan o tabenai dake de wa naku, mizu mo nomimasen.* この子供はごはん(御飯)を食べないだけではなく，水も飲みません. "Not only does this child not eat rice, he does not drink water either."

-*nai de* ないで =-*zu ni* instead of, without...ing, e.g. *Kyō gakkō ni ikanai de uchi ni imashita.* 今日学校に行かないで家にいました. "Without going to school, I stayed home today."

-*nai de hoshii* ないで欲しい =-*nai de morai tai* I do not want you to do..., e.g. *Sonna koto wa shinai de hoshii.* そんな事はしないで欲しい. "I do not want you to do such a thing."

-*nai de kudasai* ないで下さい. please don't, e.g. *Tabenai de kudasai.* 食べないで下さい. "Please don't eat."

-*nai de morai tai* ないでもら(貰)いたい =-*nai de hoshii Ano hito ni wa sore ni tsuite hanasanai de morai tai.* あの人にはそれについて話さないでもらいたい. "I do not want you to talk about it to him."

-*nai de sumu* ないで済む get by without doing something, e.g. *Kyō sensei ga yasunda no de benkyō shinai de sumimashita.* 今日先生が休んだので勉強しないで済みました. "Because our teacher was absent today, we got by without studying."

*-nai hazu wa nai* ないはず(筈)はない  there is no reason not to...,
it's likely that..., e.g. *Ano hito ni kore ga wakaranai hazu wa
arimasen.* あの人にこれが分らないはずはありません. "There is no
reason for him not to understand this." "It is likely that he
understands this."

*-nai hō ga ii* ない方がいい  it is better not to do..., e.g. *Kyō wa
ikanai hō ga ii desu yo.* 今日は行かない方がいいですよ. "It's better not to go today."

*-nai kawari ni* ないかわりに  instead of, e.g. *Nihon e ikanai kawari
ni Furansu e ikimasu.* 日本へ行かないかわりにフランスへ行きます.
"Instead of going to Japan, I'll go to France."

*-nai koto wa nai* ないことはない  It's not that I don't..., e.g. *Eiga
o minai koto wa arimasen ga amari minai no desu.* 映画を見ない
ことはありませんがあま(余)り見ないのです. "It's not that I don't
see movies; I don't see them very often."

*-nai mae ni* ない前に  =*-nai uchi ni* before..., e.g. *Ame ga
furanai mae ni dekakemashō.* 雨が降らない前にでかけましょう.
"Before it rains, let's go out."

> Note: The Japanese expression is negative, but the English idea is
> positive. This expression is used only when the speaker wishes
> the verb before *-nai mae ni* not to occur until he finishes the
> action after *-nai mae ni*, in order to avoid inconvenience. (cf.
> *mae ni*, p. 67)

*-nai nara* ないなら  if not, e.g. *Anata ga ikanai nara watakushi
mo ikimasen.* あなたが行かないなら私も行きません. "If you don't
go, I won't go either."

*-nai shi...nai* ないし...ない  not only does (he) not..., (he) does not
...either, e.g. *Yamamoto-san mo konai shi Kimura-san mo konai
desu.* 山本さんも来ないし木村さんも来ないです. "Not only is Mr.
Yamamoto not coming, Mr. Kimura isn't coming either."

*-nai to* ないと  unless..., if not..., e.g. *Ashita no asa hayaku
okinai to shichi-ji no kisha ni maniaimasen yo.* 明日の朝早く起き
ないと七時の汽車に間に合いませんよ. "Unless you get up early tomorrow morning, you won't be on time for the seven-o'clock
train."

*-nai to wa kagiranai* ないとは限らない  it is not impossible, it may
be..., e.g. *Sonna koto mo okoranai to wa kagiranai.* そんな事もお

こらないとは限らない. "It may be that such a thing could happen too."

*-nai uchi ni* ない内に =*-nai mae ni* before..., e.g. *Samuku naranai uchi ni niwa o kirei ni shinakereba narimasen.* 寒くならない内に庭をきれい(綺麗)にしなければなりません. "Before it gets cold, we have to clean up the yard."

*-nai wake wa (ga) nai* ないわけはない there is no reason not to ..., e.g. *Ano hito ga ikanai wake wa nai desu yo.* あの人が行かないわけはないですよ. "There is no reason for him not to go, you know."

*-nai wake de wa nai* ないわけではない it doesn't mean that I don't ..., e.g. *Nihongo ga hanasenai wake de wa nai ga, amari umaku wa hanasemasen.* 日本語が話せないわけではないが, あまりうま(旨)くは話せません. "It doesn't mean that I can't speak Japanese; but I can't speak it too well."

*-nai wake ni [wa] ikanai* ないわけにはいかない can't very well not do something, e.g. *Tetsudawanai wake ni wa ikimasen deshita.* 手伝わないわけにはいきませんでした. "I couldn't very well not help them."

*-nai yō ni* ないように in order not to, e.g. *Gakkō ni okurenai yō ni hayaku okimasu.* 学校に遅れないように早く起きます. "I get up early in order not to be late for school."

*-nakatta* なかった (perfective of *nai*)

*-nakattara* なかったら (negative conditional) if not..., e.g. *Kyō owaranakattara mō ososugimasu yo.* 今日終らなかったらもう遅すぎますよ. "If you don't finish it today, it will be too late."

*-nakereba* なければ =*-nakattara*

*-nakereba ikenai* なければいけない *you* must (often used with the second person), e.g. *Yoku benkyō shinakereba ikemasen yo.* よく勉強しなければいけませんよ. "You must study hard!" See p. 35 for more examples.

*-nakereba naranai* なければならない *I* must (often used with the first and third person), e.g., *Ashita shiken ga aru kara, kyō benkyō shinakereba narimasen* 明日試験があるから今日勉強しなければなりません. "Because I have a test tomorrow, I have to study hard today." See pp. 35-36 for more examples.

*-nakute* なくて because not..., e.g. *Chikagoro gohan ga taberarenakute komatte imasu.* 近頃ごはん(御飯)が食べられなくて困っています. "Lately I haven't been able to eat, and I am having

trouble (because of it)."

*-nakute mo* なくても even if you don't..., e.g. *Neko wa nannichi-kan mo tabenakute mo shinanai sō desu.* 猫は何日間も食べなくても死なないそうです. "I heard that cats won't die, even if they don't eat for many days."

*-nakute mo ii* なくてもいい need not, do not have to, e.g. *Sono hon wa yomanakute mo ii desu.* その本は読まなくてもいいです. "You don't have to read that book." See pp. 36–37 for more examples.

*-nakuto mo* なくとも =*-nakute mo*

*-neba naranai* ねばならない =*-nakereba naranai* (*-neba* is the conditional form of *nu*)

*-nu* ぬ (negative suffix) frequently contracted to *-n* as in *arimasen*.

*-rareru* られる this form is attached to vowel-stem verbs, e.g. *taberareru*, and to the irregular verb *kuru*, 来る *korareru*, and has three separate functions. It will generally be clear from the context which meaning is intended.

1. sign of passive, e.g. *Watakushi wa kyō haha ni shikarare-mashita.* 私は今日母に叱られました. "I was scolded by my mother today (and I suffered from it)." In Japanese passive voice, the subject often suffers from the action expressed by the passive verb. The agent which takes "by" in English is expressed by the particle *ni* in Japanese (See p. 122).

   Note: a. Directional verbs are not made into passive forms.
   b. Intransitive verbs can be made into passive forms in Japanese. *Kyō isogashii no ni tomodachi ni korarete komatta.* 今日忙しいのに友達に来られて困った. "I was busy today, but my friend came and I had trouble."

2. as an honorific, e.g. *Sensei ga taberaremashita.* 先生が食べられました. "The teacher ate it." (See pp. 217–23)

3. as a potential, e.g. *Anata wa Nihon no tabemono ga tabe-raremasu ka.* あなたは日本の食物が食べられますか. "Can you eat Japanese food?"

*-reru* れる this form is attached to consonant-stem verbs, e.g. *Yomareru*, and to the irregular verb *suru*, する *sareru*, and has two separate functions.

1. sign of passive, e.g. *Minna ni warawaremashita.* 皆に笑わ
   れました. "I was laughed at by everybody."

2. as an honorific, e.g. *Sensei ga warawaremashita.* 先生が笑
   われました. "The teacher laughed (or smiled)."

   Note: A consonant-stem verb has a different potential form, e.g. *wa-
   raeru* "can laugh," *yomeru* "can read," *kakeru* "can write," etc.
   The irregular verb *suru* has a potential form, *dekiru* "can do."

   The verb *iku* has two potential forms, *ikeru* (regular) and *ikareru* (irregular), "can go," both commonly used. *Ikareru*, besides
   being used as the potential form, has a slang usage, meaning
   "be touched in the head," e.g. Aitsu wa konogoro mattaku *ika-
   rete iru* na. あいつはこの(此)頃全くいかれているな. "Something
   is really wrong with that guy('s head) lately."

   The verb *miru* has two potential forms, *mieru* (irregular), and
   *mirareru* (passive form): the former means "is visible," and is
   more commonly used. e.g. Kono mado kara Fuji-san ga *miemasu.* この窓から富士山が見えます. "Mt. Fuji is visible (We can
   see Mt. Fuji) from this window." *Mirareru*, besides being used
   as the potential form, has a slang usage, meaning "can bear
   to look at," e.g. Kare no kaita e wa mazukute totemo *mirareta*
   mono ja nai. 彼のかいた絵はまずくてとても見られたものじゃない.
   "His painting is so bad that you just can't look at it."

   The verb *kiku* has two potential forms, *kikeru* (regular) and
   *kikoeru* (irregular); the latter means "is audible." e.g. Nihonjin
   no ōku wa *eru* to *āru* no chigai ga *kikemasen.* 日本人の多くはエ
   ルとアールの違いが聞けません. "Many Japanese cannot hear the
   difference between "l" and "r." Ii ongaku ga *kikoemasu.* いい音
   楽が聞こえます. "Good music is audible."    "I can hear good
   music."

*-saserareru* させられる  =*-sasareru* (causative-passive) vowel-stem
verb, *tsuzukesaserareru* (*tsuzukesasareru*). It has two functions:

1. is caused (forced) to, e.g. *Tsumaranai shigoto o tsuzukesase-
   raremashita.* つまらない仕事を続けさせられました. "I was
   forced to continue a boring job."

2. high form of honorific, e.g. *Heika ga sore o tsuzukesaserareta.*
   陛下がそれを続けさせられた. "His Majesty deigned to continue
   it." (See p. 218)

*-saseru* させる  =*-sasu* (causative), both forms are attached to
vowel-stem verb, *tabesaseru* (*tabesasu*), makes one do..., e.g.
*Kodomo ni gohan o tabesasemashita.* 子供にごはん(御飯)を食べさ
せました. "I made my child eat," or "I fed my child."

*-sasete ageru* させて上げる　=-*sashite ageru* -*sasete* form is more refined and preferred. Allow someone to do something, e.g. *Tomodachi ni tsuzukesasete agemashita.* 友達に続けさせて上げました. "I allowed my friend to continue."

*-sasete itadaku* させていただく　=-*sashite itadaku* be permitted to do something, e.g. *Oishii mono o tabesasete itadakimashita.* おいしいものを食べさせていただきました. "I was permitted to eat the tasty food."

*-sasete kudasaru* させて下さる　=-*sashite kudasaru* allow me to do something, e.g. *Sensei ga kurabesasete kudasaimashita.* 先生が較べさせて下さいました. "My teacher allowed me to compare."

*-sasete kureru* させてくれる　=-*sashite kureru* meaning same as above, e.g. *Chichi ga sakuban dekakesasete kuremashita.* 父が昨晩出か(掛)けさせてくれました. "My father allowed me to go out last night."

*-sasete morau* させてもら(貰)う　=-*sashite morau* meaning same as -*sasete itadaku*, e.g. *Mado o akesasete moratte ii desu ka.* 窓を開けさせてもらっていいですか. "Am I permitted to (may I) open the window?"

*-sasete yaru* させてやる　=-*sashite yaru* meaning same as -*sasete ageru*, e.g. *Kodomo ni okashi o tabesasete yarimashita.* 子供にお菓子を食べさせてやりました. "I allowed my child to eat candy."

-*serareru* せられる　=-*sareru* causative-passive, these forms, attached to consonant-stem verb, *yomaserareru* (*yomasareru*), have two functions:

1. is caused (forced) to, e.g. *Tsumaranai hon o yomasaremashita.* つまらない本を読まされました. "I was forced to read an uninteresting book."

2. high form of honorific, e.g. *Heika ga sore o yomaserareta.* 陛下がそれを読ませられた. "His Majesty read it." (See p. 218)

-*seru* せる (-*su*) (causative), these forms attached to consonant-stem verb, *yomaseru* (*yomasu*), e.g. *Imōto ni hon o yomasemashita.* 妹に本を読ませました. "I made my younger sister read a book."

*-sete ageru* せて上げる　=-*shite ageru* -*sete* form is more refined

---

* For a more detailed explanation on the use of causative verb *te*-form plus directional verbs, see pp. 28–29.

and preferred. Allow someone to do something, e.g. *Kono hon o yomasete agemasu.* この本を読ませて上げます. "I'll allow you to read this book."

*\*-sete itadaku* せていただく  =*-shite itadaku* be permitted to do something, e.g. *Sensei ni ikasete itadakimashita.* 先生に行かせていただきました. "I was permitted to go by my teacher."

*\*-sete kudasaru* せて下さる  =*-shite kudasaru* allow me to do something, e.g. *Sensei ga watakushi ni kakasete kudasaimashita.* 先生が私に書かせて下さいました. "My teacher allowed me to write."

*\*-sete kureru* せてくれる  =*-shite kureru* meaning same as above, e.g. *Otōto ga watakushi ni hon o tsukawasete kuremashita.* 弟が私に本を使わせてくれました. "My younger brother allowed me to use his book."

*\*-sete morau* せてもら(貰)う  =*-shite morau* meaning same as *-sete itadaku*, e.g. *Tarō ni norasete moraimashita.* 太郎に乗らせてもらいました. "I was permitted by Tarō to ride."

*\*-sete yaru* せてやる  =*-shite yaru* meaning same as *-sete ageru*, e.g. *Tarō ni yomasete yarimashita.* 太郎に読ませてやりました. "I allowed Tarō to read."

*-zaru o enai* ざるを得ない  cannot help...ing, e.g. *Okorazaru o enakatta.* 怒らざるを得なかった. "I couldn't help being angry."

*-zu* ず  another negative ending, the same as *-nai*

*-zu jimai* ずじまい(仕舞)  end up without...ing, e.g. *Kyō wa amari isogashikute ichinichi-jū tabezu jimai datta.* 今日はあま(余)り忙しくて一日中食べずじまいだった. "I was so busy all day today that I had no time to eat (I ended up without eating)."

*-zu ni* ずに  =*nai de* without...ing, e.g. *Gohan o tabezu ni nete imasu.* ごはん(御飯)を食べずに寝ています. "He is sleeping without having eaten dinner."

*-zu ni [wa] okanai* ずにお(措)かない  cannot help but to..., e.g. *Kono hon wa dokusha o miryō sezu ni wa okanai.* この本は読者を魅了せずにはおかない. "This book cannot help but fascinate the reader."

*-zu shite* ずして  =*-zu ni*=*nai de*

---

\* For a more detailed explanation on the use of causative verb *te*-form plus directional verbs, see pp. 28–29.

II. **Expressions which follow the Second Base** 連用形〈れんようけい〉 **of the verb.** Some of the words listed below may also be used as independent verbs.

*-agaru* 上がる (*jidōshi*, see pp. 21-24)

1. ... up, e.g. *Tachiagarimashita.* 立上がりました. "I stood up."

2. finish, e.g. *Sakubun ga kakiagarimashita.* 作文が書き上がりました. "The composition is finished."

*-ageru* 上げる (*tadōshi*, see pp. 21-24)

1. up, e.g. *Bōto o mizusoko kara hikiagemashita.* ボートを水底からひき上げました. "We pulled the boat up out of the water."

2. finish...ing, e.g. *Sono shigoto o shiagemashita.* その仕事を仕上げました. "I finished doing that work."

*-asaru* あさ(漁)る  do something in a frenzy, e.g. *Kyō Kanda de hon o kaiasarimashita.* 今日神田で本を買いあさりました. "Today I bought books in a frenzy in Kanda."

*o-asobasu* お V₂ 遊ばす  high form of honorific, e.g. *Osuwari asobashimashita.* お坐り遊ばしました. "She sat down."

*-bae* ば(栄)え  shown (heard) to advantage, e.g. *Ano tenrankai wa mibae ga shita.* あの展覧会は見栄えがした. "That exhibition was much to look at." *Kikibae no shinai ongaku* 聞き栄えのしない音楽 "music not pleasing to hear"

*o-da* お V₂ だ (colloquial honorific)=*o* V₂ *ni naru Anata wa gakkō no oshigoto mo oari da shi, kodomo-san mo oari da kara oisogashii deshō.* あなたは学校のお仕事もおありだし子供さんもおありだからお忙しいでしょう. "Perhaps you are busy, since you not only have your schoolwork, but you have children, too."

*-dasu* 出す

1. ... out, e.g. *Oshidashimasu.* 押し出します. "I push it out."

2. start...ing [involuntarily], e.g. *Arukidashimashita.* 歩き出しました. "I started walking."

   Note: The latter usage is the more common.

*-de ga aru* でがある  be substantial, e.g. *Kono hon wa yomide ga arimasu.* この本は読みでがあります. "It takes one a long time to read this book through."

*-dōshi* どうし  keep...ing, e.g. *Asa kara ban made kyō wa tachi-dōshi deshita.* 朝から晩まで今日は立ちどうしでした. "Today I kept standing from morning till night."

*-enai* え(得)ない  is not possible, e.g. *Sonna koto wa arienai.* そんな事は有り得ない. "Such a thing can't be possible." positive of *-enai, uru*, p. 59.

*-gachi* がち  tend to..., e.g. *Amari atsui no de namakegachi ni narimasu.* あま(余)り暑いので怠けがちになります. "Because it is too hot, we tend to get lazy."

*-gai* 甲斐  worth...ing, e.g. *Ano ko wa nan' de mo yoku oboeru kara, oshiegai ga aru.* あの子は何でもよく覚えるから教え甲斐がある. "Because that child can learn everything well, it is worth teaching him."

*-gatai* がた(難)い  difficult to=*nikui* (*-gatai* is more literary)

*-ge* げ  seeming condition of others, e.g. *Totemo imi arige na kao o shite watakushi o mimashita.* とても意味ありげな顔をして私を見ました. "He looked at me with a face that seemed to hold some meaning."

*-hajimeru* 始める  start...ing, e.g. *Tabehajimemasu.* 食べ始めます. "We start eating."

*-hatasu* 果たす  finish, ...up, e.g. *Okane o sukkari tsukaihatashita.* お金をすっかり使い果たした. "I used up all my money."

*-hateru* 果てる  end up, be finished, e.g. *Kyō wa isogashikute tsukarehatete shimaimashita.* 今日は忙しくて疲れ果ててしまいました. "I was so busy that I was exhausted."

*o-itasu* お V₂ 致す  humble form, e.g. *Odenwa o okake itashimashita.* お電話をおかけ致しました. "I called you." (See p. 218)

*-kaesu* 返す  re-...ing, do again, e.g. *Yomikaeshimashita.* 読みかえしました. "I read it again." *Iikaesu* 言いかえす. "talk back."
Note: *kaesu* means to return (*tadōshi*, see pp. 21-24), (cf. V₂ *naosu*, p. 50).

*-kakeru* かける  start...ing [but soon interrupted], e.g. *Benkyō shikaketa tokoro e tomodachi ga kimashita.* 勉強しかけたところへ友達が来ました. "When I started studying, my friend came."

*-kaneru* 兼ねる  be hard to, e.g. *Mōshikanemasu ga...* 申し兼ねますが... "It's hard to say, but..."

*-kata* 方  manner, way, how to, e.g. *Ano hito no Nihongo no hanashikata wa sukoshi okashii desu.* あの人の日本語の話し方は少しおかしいです. "His way of speaking Japanese is a little funny." *Shikata ga nai.* 仕方がない "Nothing can be done about it." "It can't be helped." (cf. V₂ *yō*, p. 60)

*-kireru* 切れる  run out of, e.g. *Kinō uridashita no ni, mō urikire-te shimaimashita.* 昨日売り出したのに，もう売り切れてしまいました. "Although they just started selling it yesterday, it is already sold out."

*-kiru* きる  be through, completely, e.g. *Kyō wa ichinichi-jū iso-gashikute tsukarekitte shimaimashita.* 今日は一日中忙しくて疲れきってしまいました. "I was so busy all day today that I am now all tired out."

*-komu* 込む

1. in, into, e.g. *Hon ni kakikomimashita.* 本に書き込みました. "I wrote in the book." *Pūru ni tobikomimashita.* プールに飛び込みました. "I jumped into the pool."

2. to settle firmly in the state of preceding V₂, e.g. *Kare wa soko ni suwarikonda.* 彼はそこに坐り込んだ. "He sat down there (and did not move)."

*o-kudasai* お V₂ 下さい  polite imperative, e.g. *Onomi kudasai.* お飲み下さい. "Please drink."

*o-kudasaimase* お V₂ 下さいませ  more polite imperative than above. *Okake kudasaimase.* おかけ下さいませ "Would you please sit down."

*-masu* ます  (polite suffix), see p. 13. e.g., *Ikimasu.* 行きます. "I will go."

*-mo...mo suru* も...もする  do both...and..., e.g. *Ano hito wa Nihongo o yomi mo kaki mo shimasu.* あの人は日本語を読みも書きもします. "He reads Japanese and writes it as well."

*-mo shinai* もしない  don't even do, e.g. *Mi mo shinakatta.* 見もしなかった. "She didn't even look at it."

*-mo sureba* V₂ *mo suru* もすれば V₂ もする  do both...and..., not only...but also..., e.g. *Ano hito wa yoku tabe mo sureba nomi mo shimasu.* あの人はよく食べもすれば飲みもします. "He not only eats a lot, but drinks a lot, too."

*-mono* 物  thing, e.g. *tabemono* 食物 "thing to eat," "food"

*-nagara* ながら  simultaneous state or action of the same person (cf. V₃ *aida*, p. 60)

1. while, e.g. *Rajio o kikinagara tabako o nomimasu.* ラジオを聞きながらタバコ（煙草）をのみます. "While I am listening to the radio, I smoke."

2.  though, e.g. *Shitte inagara nani mo iimasen deshita.* 知って
    いながら何も言いませんでした。 "Although he knew, he didn't
    tell me anything."

*-naosu* 直す re-..., e.g. *Kakinaoshimasu.* 書き直します。 "I'll re-
write it." (*naosu* means "to correct," cf. V₂ *kaesu*, p. 48)

*-nareru* 慣れる get used to...ing, e.g. *Kakinareru to kanji mo
yasashiku narimasu.* 書きなれると漢字も易しくなります。 "When
you get used to writing, *Kanji* gets easy, too."

*-nasai* なさい imperative, e.g. *Kakinasai.* 書きなさい。 "Write."
Often attach honorific *o* before the verb, *Oyominasai.* お読みな
さい。 "Read!"

*-ni* に+verb of motion, indicates purpose, e.g. *Eiga o mi ni ikimashō.* 映画を見に行きましょう。 "Let's go to see the movie."

*-ni kakaru* にかかる start...ing, [with some effort] e.g. *Kare wa
sassoku hahaoya o nagusame ni kakatta.* 彼は早速母親を慰めにか
かった。 "He started comforting his mother right away."

*o-ni naru* お V₂ になる honorific form. e.g. *Sensei ga okaki ni narimashita.* 先生がお書きになりました。 "Teacher wrote." (See p. 218)

*-nikui* にく(難)い difficult to, e.g. *Kono hon wa yominikui desu.*
この本は読みにくいです。 "This book is difficult to read." *yominikui hon* 読みにくい本 "a book which is difficult to read." (Opposite of *-yasui*, p. 60)

*-otosu* 落す fail to, e.g. *Machigai o miotoshimashita.* 間違いを見落
しました。 "I failed to see the mistakes."

*-owaru* 終る finish...ing, e.g. *Iiowaru.* 言い終る。 "I finish saying." Though the verb *owaru* is a jidōshi (p. 23), as a suffix it is
used like a *tadōshi*.

*-sae sureba* さえすれば emphatic, if only, e.g. *Okane ga ari sae
sureba kotoshi Nihon e iku n' desu ga...* お金がありさえすれば
今年日本へ行くんですが... "If only I had money, I would go to
Japan this year, but..."

*-shidai* 次第 as soon as, e.g. *Tabeshidai ikimashō.* 食べ次第行き
ましょう。 "Let's go as soon as we finish eating."

*-sō da* そうだ, *-sō na* そうな look as if it will (seems imminent),
e.g. *Ame ga furisō desu.* 雨が降りそうです。 "It looks like rain."
*Ame ga furisō na soramoyō desu.* 雨が降りそうな空模様です。
"The sky looks like it will rain."

*-sō mo nai* そうもない  =*-sō ni nai* it looks as if one won't even do..., e.g. *Ano hito wa kyō kisō mo arimasen.* あの人は今日来そうもありません. "It looks as if he won't even come today."

*-sō ni naru* そうになる  almost..., e.g. *Kesa pūru de oboresō ni narimashita.* 今朝プールで溺れそうになりました. "This morning I almost drowned in the pool."

*-sobireru* そびれる  fail to..., lose a chance to..., e.g. *Daiji na koto o iisobiremashita.* 大事な事を言いそびれました. "I missed a chance to say an important thing."

*-sokonau* 損なう  fail to do..., e.g. *Kōen o kikisokonatta.* 講演を聞き損った. "I missed hearing the lecture."

*-sugiru* 過ぎる  over-..., e.g. *Kinō tabesugimashita.* 昨日食べすぎました. "I overate yesterday."

*-sugiru kirai ga aru* す(過)ぎるきらい(嫌)がある  there is a tendency to over-..., e.g. *Ano hito wa hanashisugiru kirai ga aru.* "She has tendency to talk too much." あの人は話しすぎるきらいがある.

*-ta (-da)* た  informal perfective ending, e.g. *Hon o yonda.* 本を読んだ. "I read a book." *Nihongo de sakubun o kaita.* 日本語で作文を書いた. "I wrote a composition in Japanese." *Ta*-form is also used as a noun modifier. e.g. *kinō mita eiga* 昨日見た映画 "the movie that I saw yesterday."

> Note: For formation of *ta (da)*-form, see pp. 16–18; when to use *ta*-form, see Noun Modifier, pp. 189–190; informal level, pp. 215–16.

*-ta (-da) ato de* た後で  after...ing, e.g. *Gohan o tabeta ato de dekakemashō.* ごはん(御飯)を食べた後で出か(掛)けましょう. "Let's go out after eating dinner." Note the use of *ta*-form before *ato de*, even if the time referred to is the future.

*-ta (-da) baai [wa]* た場合  =*-tara* conditional, if, in case..., e.g. *Ame ga futta baai wa ikimasen.* 雨が降った場合は行きません. "If it rains, we won't go." For V₃ *baai*, p. 60.

*-ta (-da) bakari* たばかり  has just, e.g. *Ima kita bakari desu.* 今来たばかりです. "I have just come now." For V₃ *bakari*, p. 60.

*-ta (-da) bakari ni* たばかりに  just because, e.g. *Byōki datta bakari ni nakayoshi no tomodachi no kekkonshiki ni deraremasen deshita.* 病気だったばかりに仲良しの友達の結婚式に出られませんでした. "Just because I was ill, I couldn't attend my good friend's wedding."

*-ta* (*-da*) *ga saigo* たが最後   =*-tara saigo* once you do..., e.g. *Itta ga saigo, kaette kimasen.* 行ったが最後帰って来ません. "Once he goes, he'll never come back."

*-ta* (*-da*) *kiri* たきり  just did..., and...(implies finality) e.g. *Okane o karita kiri mada kaesanai.* お金を借りたきりまだ返さない. "He just borrowed money and has not returned it yet."

*-ta* (*-da*) *koto ga aru* たことがある  experience up to the present, e.g. *Nihon ni itta koto ga arimasu ka.* 日本に行ったことがありますか. "Have you ever been to Japan?"  For V₃ *koto ga aru*, p. 66.

*-ta* (*-da*) *koto ga atta* たことがあった  past experience, e.g. *Sore made Nihon ni itta koto ga arimasen deshita.* それまで日本に行ったことがありませんでした. "Until then I had never been to Japan." For V₃ *koto ga atta*, p. 66.

*-ta* (*-da*) *koto ni suru* たことにする  assume, e.g. *Koko ni ita koto ni shimashō.* ここにいたことにしましょう. "Let's assume that we were here."  For V₃ *koto ni suru*, p. 66.

*-ta* (*-da*) *mama* たまま (儘) as it is, e.g. *Omotta mama o itte kudasai.* 思ったままを言って下さい. "Please tell me just as you think."

*-ta* (*-da*) *mono da* たものだ  habitual occurrence in the past, e.g. *Chiisai toki watakushi wa yoku otōto to kenka shita mono desu.* 小さい時私はよく弟とけんか (喧嘩) したものです. "I often used to fight with my little brother when I was little."  For V₃ *mono da*, see p. 68.

*-ta* (*-da*) *oboe ga aru* た覚えがある  remember that..., e.g. *Sonna koto o yonda oboe wa arimasen.* そんなことを読んだ覚えはありません. "I don't remember if I read about such a thing."

*-ta* (*-da*) *tameshi ga* (*wa*) *nai* た例がない  have never..., e.g. *Ano hito wa okotta tameshi ga arimasen.* あの人は怒った例がありません. "He has never been mad."

*-ta* (*-da*) *tokoro* [*da*] たところ  =*-ta* (*-da*) *bakari* have just, e.g. *Ima kita tokoro desu.* 今来たところです. "I have just come." For V₃ *tokoro*, pp. 77-78. *tokoro* emphasizes the situation, while *bakari* emphasizes the time.

*-ta* (*-da*) *tokoro de* たところで  even though, e.g. *Yonda tokoro de wakaranai deshō.* 読んだところで分らないでしょう. "Even if he reads it, he will not understand it."

*-ta* (*-da*) *tokoro ga* たところが  =*-ta* (*-da*) *ga*  when (often the fol-

lowing clause expresses something contrary to normal expectations), e.g. *Osashimi o tabeta tokoro ga oishii deshita.* おさしみを食べたところがおいしいでした. "When I ate raw fish, it tasted good—to my surprise."

*-ta (-da) tsumori* 〔*da*〕 たつも(積)り   I am under the impression that ..., e.g. *Tegami o dashita tsumori desu ga...*  手紙を出したつもりですが... "I am under the impression that I mailed the letter, but..." For V₃ *tsumori*, p. 78.

*-ta (-da) ue de* た上で  after...ing, upon...ing, e.g. *Hanashita ue de kimemashō.* 話した上で決めましょう. "Let's decide after talking it over."

*-tagaru* たがる  wish of someone else other than the speaker, want to, e.g. *Kodomo wa itsu mo okashi o tabetagarimasu.* 子供はいつ(何時)もお菓子を食べたがります. "Children are always wanting to eat candies."

*-tai* たい  desiderative, want to..., e.g. *Ikitai desu.* 行きたいです. "I want to go."

> Note: *-tai* conjugates as an adjective; *taku* for *ku*-form, *takereba* for conditional, *takatta* for perfective. *-tai* cannot be used as an independent word. It is always used as a verb suffix. cf. *hoshii*, p. 107.

*-takute* たくて  *te*-form of *tai*

*-takute tamaranai* たくてたまらない  See *-kute tamaranai*, see p. 85.

*-tamae* 給え  an imperative suffix used by men on a friendly level in modern Japanese, e.g. *Ano hon o yomitamae.* あの本を読み給え. "Read that book."

*-tara (-dara)* たら  colloquial conditional, if, when, e.g. *Ashita ame ga futtara ikimasen.* 明日雨が降ったら行きません. "If it rains tomorrow, I won't go." For more details on conditionals, see pp. 29-32.

(interrogative word)-*tara (dara) ii ka wakaranai* たらいいかわか(分)らない. =(interrogative) V*ba ii ka wakaranai*  don't know (what, etc.) to do..., e.g. *Dō shitara ii ka wakaranai.* どうしたらいいかわからない. "I don't know what to do." *Doko e ittara ii ka wakaranai.* どこ(何処)へ行ったらいいかわからない. "I don't know where to go."

*-tara (-dara) saigo* たら最後 = *-ta (-da) ga saigo*

*-tari (-dari)* たり

1. with two (or more) *tari*, action in alternation, now doing this, now doing that, e.g. *Kinō asondari benkyō shitari shima-shita.* 昨日遊んだり勉強したりしました. "Yesterday I played and studied."

   Note: Last *tari* (*dari*) is usually followed by the verb *suru*, which itself does not mean anything.

2. one *tari*, representative or typical actions, do such things as ..., e.g. *Natsu wa umi ni oyogi ni ittari shimasu.* 夏は海に泳ぎに行ったりします. "During the summer we do such things as go to the seashore to swim."

   Note: *tari* (*dari*) is usually followed by the verb *suru*.

*-te (-de)* て for the formation of *te*-form, see pp. 16–18. *Te*-form has no tense of its own; it usually follows the tense of the final verb.

1. conjunction for sequence of actions, and, e.g. *Toshokan ni itte, benkyō shimashita.* 図書館に行って勉強しました. "We went to the library, and studied."

2. conjunction for simultaneous actions, while, e.g. *Hon o yonde waratte imasu.* 本を読んで笑っています. "He is laughing while reading."

3. how the action of the main verbs is performed, e.g. *Densha ni notte ikimashita.* 電車に乗って行きました. "I went by (riding a) train." *Aruite gakkō ni ikimasu.* 歩いて学校に行きます. "We go to school on foot."

4. because, the cause of the main verb, e.g. *Koko wa ichinen-jū atatakakute totemo sumiyasui desu.* ここは一年中暖かくてとても住みやすいです. "Because this place is warm all year, it is very easy to live here." This usage is similar to the English participial phrase, "*Being warm,* it is an easy place for people to live."

5. sentence-ending in colloquial women's speech, (1) Mild imperative, e.g. *Ashita kite (ne).* 明日来て. "Come tomorrow, OK?" (2) I understand that..., e.g. *Ano kata mō Osaka e irasshatta n' desutte.* "I heard that she has already gone to Osaka." Other than this usage, *te*-form does not come at the end of the sentence.

6. after, often used before the time word, e.g. *Kurisumasu no yasumi ga owatte sugu shiken ga aru kara yasumi-chū mo isogashii.* クリスマスの休みが終ってすぐ試験があるから休み中も忙しい. "Even during the vacation I am busy, because we'll have exams right after the Christmas vacation is over."

*\*-te (-de) ageru* てあ(上)げる （Ⅰ） do a favor in doing something, e.g. *Tomodachi ni hon o yonde agemashita.* 友達に本を読んであげました. "I read a book (did a favor in reading a book) to my friend." (cf. *-te yaru*, p. 59)

*-te (-de) aru* てある  *tadōshi+te aru*, describes an action which has occurred and is still in force, e.g. *Mado ga akete arimasu.* 窓があ(開)けてあります. "The window is open (The window has been opened and is still open)." See pp. 21–22.

*-te (-de) bakari iru* てばかりいる  always, e.g. *Tabete bakari imasu.* 食べてばかりいます. "He is always eating."

*-te (-de) hoshii* て欲しい  =*-te moraitai*  want someone to do something, e.g. *Ano hito ni atte hoshii n' desu.* あの人に会ってほしいんです. "I want you to meet him." *-nai de hoshii*, see p. 40.

(interrogative word) *-te (-de) ii [no] ka wakaranai* ていいか分らない don't know how (what, etc.), e.g. *Muzukashii ji o dō shite mitsukete ii ka wakaranai.* 難しい字をどうして見つけていいか分らない. "I don't know how to find difficult characters."

*-te (-de) iku* て行く  (opposite of *-te kuru*, p. 56)

1. direction of the action when it is away from the location of the speaker, e.g. *Sō iinagara heya o dete ikimashita.* そう言いなが(乍)ら部屋を出て行きました. "Saying that, he went out of the room." *Kyō kodomo o gakkō ni tsurete ikimashita.* 今日子供を学校に連れて行きました. "I took my child to school today." *Obentō o motte ikimashō.* お弁当を持って行きましょう. "Let's take our lunch." *tsurete iku* is used to take a person or pet along, while *motte iku* is used to carry some object along.

2. verb of learning or performing a skill+*te iku* refers to the performance of an action from the present or some future point in time onwards, e.g. *Kore kara sō shite ikimasu.* これからそうして行きます. "I'll do it that way from now on." (cf. *-te kuru*, p. 57.)

---

\* For a more detailed explanation on the use of *te*-form+directional verbs, see pp. 27–28.

*-te (-de) irai* て以来 since..., e.g. *Nihon ni itte irai Nihon ga suki ni narimashita.* 日本に行って以来日本が好きになりました. "Since I went to Japan, I came to like Japan."

*-te (-de) iru* ている

1. *tadōshi+te iru* progressive form, continuative action, doing something, e.g. *Tegami o kaite imasu.* 手紙を書いています. "I am writing a letter." See p. 22.

2. *jidōshi+te iru* descriptive meaning, e.g. *Mado ga shimatte imasu.* 窓が閉まっています. "The window is closed." See p. 21.

*\*-te (-de) itadaku* ていただ(戴, 頂)く (to be fortunate) to receive someone's favor, e.g. *Sensei ni eigo o oshiete itadakimashita.* 先生に英語を教えていただきました. (I am fortunate that) my teacher taught me English." (cf. *-te morau*, p. 58).

*-te (-de) kara* てから after, e.g. *Gohan o tabete kara, gakkō e ikimasu.* ごはん(御飯)を食べてから学校へ行きます. "After eating a meal, I go to school."

*-te (-de) koso* てこそ only when, e.g. *Sonna muzukashii kyoku ga utsukushiku hikete koso, idai na ongakuka to ieru.* そんな難しい曲が美しく弾けてこそ偉大な音楽家と言える. "Only when he can play such difficult music beautifully, can we say he is a great musician."

*-te (-de) kudasai* て下さい mild imperative, e.g. *Yonde kudasai.* 読んで下さい "Please read." *-nai de kudasai*, p. 40.

*\*-te (-de) kudasaru* て下さる (he) is kind to do something for (me), e.g. *Sensei ga watakushi ni hon o kashite kudasaimashita.* 先生が私に本を貸して下さいました. "My teacher was kind enough to lend me a book." (cf. *-te kureru*, see below)

*-te (-de) kure* てくれ abrupt imperative used by men, *Kore o shite kure.* これをしてくれ. "Do this (for me)."

*\*-te kureru* てくれる same as *-te kudasaru* e.g. *Imōto ga yōfuku o tsukutte kuremashita.* 妹が洋服を作ってくれました. "My younger sister made a dress for me. (My younger sister was kind enough to make me a dress.)"

*-te (-de) kuru* て来る

1. verb of motion+*te kuru* direction of the action when it is towards the speaker, e.g. *Heya ni haitte kimashita.* 部屋に入って来ました. "He came into the room." (cf. *-te iku*, p. 55).

2. verb of learning or performing a skill+*te kuru*, refers to the performance of an action beginning at any point in the past and continuing as far as the present, but not beyond, e.g. *Ima made sō naratte kimashita.* 今までそう習って来ました. "I have learned it that way up to now." (cf. -te iku, p. 55).

3. some *jidōshi*+*te kuru* begin to..., *Ame ga futte kimashita.* 雨が降って来ました. "It has begun to rain."

*-te (-de) made* てまで even going to the extent of..., e.g. *Hito no okane o tsukatte made sonna koto ga shitai desu ka.* 人のお金を使ってまでそんなことがしたいですか. "Do you want to do such a thing, even at the expense of other people (even going to the extent of using other people's money)?"

*-te (-de) mieru* て見える appears as if, e.g. *Kono yōfuku o kiru to futotte miemasu.* この洋服を着ると太って見えます. "When I wear this dress, I look fat (it appears as if I were fat)."

*-te (-de) miru* てみる

1. try doing something, e.g. *Furansugo o benkyō shite mimashita ga muzukashisugimashita.* フランス語を勉強してみましたが難しすぎました. "I tried studying French, but it was too difficult."

2. to do something and see what happens, e.g. *Kono hon o yonde mimashō ka.* この本を読んでみましょうか. "Shall we read this book (and see what kind of a book it is)?"

*-te (-de) mo* ても even if, e.g. *Anata ga itte mo watakushi wa ikimasen.* あなたが行っても私は行きません. "Even if you go, I won't go."

(interrogative word)-*te (-de) mo* ても no matter how (what, etc.), e.g. *Ano hito wa donna ni tabete mo ōkiku narimasen.* あの人はどんなに食べても大きくなりません. "No matter how much he eats, he doesn't get big."

*-te (-de) mo ii* てもいい you may, e.g. *Sore o tabete mo ii desu yo.* それを食べてもいいですよ. "You may eat it." (see pp. 36–37)

*-te (-de) mo kamawanai* ても構わない It doesn't matter even if you do..., e.g. *Yamete mo kamaimasen.* やめても構いません. "Even if you quit, it doesn't matter." (see p. 36)

---

\* For a more detailed explanation on the use of *te*-form+directional verbs, see pp. 27–28.

*-te (-de) mo* V*nakute mo* ても V なくても   whether or, e.g. *Konna koto wa shite mo shinakute mo kamaimasen.* こんなことはしてもしなくても構いません. "It doesn't matter whether you do such a thing or not."

*-te (-de) moraitai* てもら(貰)いたい  =*-te hoshii* want someone to do something, e.g. *Kodomo ni hayaku ōkiku natte moraitai desu.* 子供に早く大きくなってもらいたいです. "I want my child to grow fast." *-nai de morai tai,* p. 40.

\*-*te (-de) morau* てもら(貰)う ( I ) am fortunate to receive someone's favor, e.g. *Ane ni yōfuku o tsukutte moraimashita.* 姉に洋服を作ってもらいました. ("I am fortunate that) my sister made a dress for me." (cf. *-te itadaku,* p. 56)

*-te (-de) naranai* てならない  =*-te (-de) shiyō ga nai.*

*-te (-de) nokeru* てのける   manage to do, e.g. *Hidoku muzukashii shigoto o umaku shite noketa.* ひどく難しい仕事をうま(旨)くしてのけた. "I managed to do a very difficult job well."

*-te (-de) oku* ておく

1. do something for future use, e.g. *Tomodachi ga kuru kara okashi o katte okimasu.* 友達が来るからお菓子を買っておきます. "I'll buy cakes because my friend will come."

2. leave it or let it go at that, e.g. *Sō kotaete okimashita.* そう答えておきました. "I answered thus, and let it go at that."

*-te (-de) ori* ており  =*-te ita* (conjunctive) is doing..., and e.g. *Chichi wa ima Tokyo ni ryokō shite ori, haha wa Kyoto ni nokotte orimasu.* 父は今東京に旅行しており，母は京都にのこっております. "Father is traveling in Tokyo now, and Mother remains in Kyoto."

*-te (-de) sae* V*ba* てさえ V ば   only if, e.g. *Yoku benkyō shite sae okeba daijōbu desu.* よく勉強してさえおけば大丈夫です. "Only if you study hard now will everything be all right."

*-te (-de) shimau* てしまう   completion or finality of an action, e.g. *Wasurete shimaimashita.* 忘れてしまいました. "I completely forgot about it."

*-te (-de) shiyō (shō) ga nai* て仕様(しよう)がない  =*-te naranai* couldn't help...ing, e.g. *Nakete shiyō ga nakatta.* 泣けて仕様がなかった. "I couldn't help crying hard."

*-te (-de) wa* ては   conditional form of the pattern, if A, then a negative consequence.  Examples are below.  See also pp. 34-35.

*-te (-de) wa ikenai* てはいけない   (prohibition) literally, it can't go if you do something, therefore, you may not, e.g. *Mite wa ikemasen.* 見てはいけません. "You may not look." See p. 35.

*-te (-de) wa irarenai* てはいられない   be unable to bear..., e.g. *Totemo mite wa irarenakatta.* とても見てはいられなかった. "I couldn't bear to look at it."

*-te (-de) wa komaru* ては困る   we will be in difficulty if you do..., *Sonna koto o shite wa komarimasu.* そんなことをしては困ります. "You distress me (inconvenience me) by doing such a thing." See pp. 34-35 for more examples.

*-te (-de) wa naranai* てはならない   (prohibition) we must not, e.g. *Nihongo no kurasu de wa eigo o tsukatte wa naranai no desu.* 日本語のクラスでは英語を使ってはならないのです.  "We must not use English in our Japanese class."

\*-*te (-de) yaru* てやる   (I) do a favor in doing something, e.g. *Kodomo ni hon o katte yarimashita.* 子供に本を買ってやりました. "I did a favor in buying a book for my child." (cf. *-te ageru*, p. 55)

*-tsukusu* 尽くす   finish up, e.g. *Motte iru mono o zenbu uritsukushimashita.* 持っているものを全部売り尽くしました. "I sold everything that I had."

*-tsutsu* つつ  =*-nagara*   while, though, e.g. *Warui to shiritsutsu sasete shimaimashita.*   悪いと知りつつさせてしまいました.   "Although I knew it was wrong, I let him do it."

*-tsuzukeru* 続ける   continue...ing, e.g. *Benkyō shitsuzukeru.* 勉強し続ける. "He continues studying."

*-uru* 得る   be possible to..., e.g. *Sonna koto ga ariuru hazu ga nai.* そんなことがあり得るはず(筈)がない "Such a thing cannot possibly occur."  negative of *uru*, *enai*, see p. 48.

*-wa shimai* はしまい   (negative tentative), e.g. *Sonna mono wa mi wa shimai.* そんなものは見はしまい. "Perhaps he won't look at such a thing."

*-wa shinai* はしない   (emphatic negative), e.g. *Sonna mono wa ari*

---

\* For a more detailed explanation on the use of *te*-form + directional verbs, see pp. 27-28.

*wa (arya) shinai.* そんなものはありはしない．  "There isn't any such thing."

-*yasui* やす(易)い  is easy to... (opposite of -*nikui*, p. 50) e.g. *Kono pen wa kakiyasui desu.* このペンは書きやすいです．  "This pen is easy to write with." *kakiyasui pen* 書きやすいペン "a pen which is easy to write with."

-*yō* よう(様)  way of... ing, e.g. *Sonna mono wa tabeyō ga nai.* そんなものは食べようがない．  "There is no way to eat such a thing." (cf. V₂ *kata*, p. 48) V₂ *yō* is often used with verbs *aru* or *nai*.

## III. Expressions which follow the *Third Base* 終止形〈しゅうしけい〉, 連体形〈れんたいけい〉 of the verb and some adjectives.

-*aida* 間  while, all the time when, e.g. *Haha ga kaimono ni itte iru aida, watakushi wa hon o yonde imashita.* 母が買物に行っている間，私は本を読んでいました．"While my mother was out shopping, I was reading a book."

> Note: In a sentence using -*aida*, subjects for the principal clause and the subordinate clause are usually different. For the same subject, it is more common to use V₂ *nagara*, see p. 49.

-*baai* 場合  when, in the case of..., e.g. *Nihon ni iku baai, hikōki de ikimasu.* 日本に行く場合，飛行機で行きます．"When we go to Japan, we'll go by airplane." For V*ₜₐ* *baai*, see p. 51.

-*bakari* ばかり

1. only, e.g. *Taberu bakari de shigoto wa shimasen.* 食べるばかりで仕事はしません．"He only eats, and doesn't do the work."

2. be about to..., e.g. *Taberu bakari no tokoro e Toda-san ga kimashita.* 食べるばかりのところへ戸田さんが来ました．"Mr. Toda came just at the time when we were about to eat." For V*ₜₐ* *bakari*, p. 51.

3. to the extent that..., practically, almost, e.g. *Kanashikute mune ga sakeru bakari deshita.* 悲しくて胸が裂けるばかりでした．"I was so sad that my heart almost broke."

-*bakari de wa nai* ばかりではない  not only that..., e.g. *Nihon e itta bakari de wa naku Taiwan e mo ikimashita.* 日本へ行ったばかりではなく台湾へも行きました．"Not only did he go to Japan, but he also went to Taiwan."

*-bekarazaru* ベ(可)からざる  (precedes noun) that which should not be...ed, e.g.  *Sore wa yurusubekarazaru koto da.* それは許すべからざることだ. "It is a thing which should not be permitted."

*-bekarazu* ベ(可)からず negative of *bekari* (*beshi*), prohibition in *bungotai* (literary form) don't, must not, e.g. *Hairu bekarazu.* 入るべからず. "Don't enter!"

*-beki* べき attributive form of *beshi* of *bungotai* (literary form) meaning must, should, e.g. *Kore wa dare mo ga yomu beki hon da.* これは誰もが読むべき本だ. "This is a book everyone should read." *Beki* is also used before the copula *da* (*desu*). *Ashita iku beki desu.* 明日行くべきです. "You should go tomorrow."

> Note: For the verb *suru* both *suru beki* and *su beki* (*ru* is omitted) are used. e.g. *Konna koto wa ima subeki koto de wa nai.* こんなことは今すべきことではない. "This kind of thing should not be done now."

*-dake* だけ(丈)

1.  as much as, e.g. *Taberareru dake tabete kudasai.* 食べられるだけ食べて下さい. "Please eat as much as you can eat."

2.  only, just, e.g. *Taberu dake de shigoto wa shimasen.* 食べるだけで仕事はしません. = *Taberu bakari de shigoto wa shimasen.* "He only eats, and does no work."

*-dake atte* だけあって  =-*dake ni*

*-dake de wa nai* だけではない  =*bakari de wa nai*

*-dake ni* だけに  =-*dake atte* as might be expected, e.g. *Ano otoko wa itsumo okashina koto o jiman suru dake ni doko ka tarinai.* あの男はいつ(何時)もおかしな事を自慢するだけにどこか足りない. "That he is somewhat weak in the head might be expected from the fact that he is always bragging about strange things."

*-darō* だろう  =-*deshō* probably, e.g. *Ima kare wa uchi ni iru darō.* 今, 彼は家にいるだろう. "He is probably home now."

*-deshō* でしょう  =-*darō*  See p. 14 for more *darō* (*deshō*).

*-dokoro de wa nai* どころではない  =-*dokoro no hanashi de wa nai* =-*dokoro no sawagi de wa nai* emphatic, far from..., e.g. *Isogashikute kaimono ni iku dokoro de wa nakatta.* 忙しくて買物に行くどころではなかった. "I was so busy that I couldn't go shopping (far from having time to go shopping)."

*-dokoro ka* どころか far from...but, not at all...but, e.g. *Kyō*

*wa amari isogashikute hon o yomu dokoro ka, gohan o taberu hima mo arimasen deshita.* 今日はあま(余)り忙しくて本を読むどころかごはん(御飯)を食べる暇もありませんでした. "I was so busy today that not only was I unable to read (far from having time to read), but I didn't even have time to eat."

*-furi o suru* ふ(振)りをする　pretend, e.g. *Kare wa watakushi o mite mo itsumɔ minai furi o shimasu.* 彼は私を見てもいつも見ないふりをします. "He always pretends not to see me, even if he does see me."

*-ga* が　conjunctive particle, but, however, e.g. *Kinō wa samukatta ga kyō wa atatakai.* 昨日は寒かったが今日は暖かい. "It was cold yesterday, but it is warm today."

> Note: Sometimes *-ga* may lose all adversative implication, in which case it is best to translate it as "and."

*-ga mono wa nai* がものはない　there is no need to..., e.g. *Kufū suru ga mono wa nai.* 工夫するがものはない. "There is no need to think it out."

*-goto ni* ごと(毎)に　every time (with each occurrence, progressive increase or decrease), e.g. *Otanjōbi ga kuru goto ni hitotsu toshi o torimasu.* お誕生日が来るごとに一つ年をとります. "Every time a birthday comes, we get one year older."

*-hazu* はず(筈)　(normal expectation) supposed to, expected to, e.g. *Kyō iku hazu desu.* 今日行くはずです. "He is supposed to go today."

*-hazu ga (wa) nai* はず(筈)がない　it is not likely that..., there is no reason to expect that, e.g. *Ano hito ga sonna koto o iu hazu ga nai.* あの人がそんなことを言うはずがない. "There is no reason to expect that he would say such a thing." (*-nai hazu wa nai*, p. 41)

*-hazumi ni* はずみに　=*-hyōshi ni* in the act of, e.g. *Kaidan o oriru hazumi ni ashi o suberasemashita.* 階段を降りるはずみに足を滑らせました. "He slipped in the act of descending the stairs."

*-hi ni wa* 日には　if, in case, e.g. *Ā shigoto bakari shite iru hi ni wa tsukarekitte byōki ni natte shimau darō.* ああ仕事ばかりしている日には疲れきって病気になってしまうだろう. "If he works like that all the time, he will probably be exhausted and become ill."

*-hō* 方　literally "direction," side, one as compared with or opposed to another, e.g. *Chikatetsu de iku hō ga basu de iku yori zutto*

*hayai desu yo.* 地下鉄で行く方がバスで行くよりずっと早いですよ.
"It is much faster to go by subway than to go by bus."

> Note: It is convenient to remember that when *hō* is used, adjectives
> should be translated as comparative.  e.g. *Kono hō ga ii desu.*
> この方がいいです. "This is better."

*-hō ga ii* (*yoi*) 方がいい  it is better to..., e.g. *Kyō iku hō ga ii
desu yo.* 今日行く方がいいですよ. "It is better to go today." (*-nai
hō ga ii*, see p. 41)

*-hodo* ほど(程)  =*-kurai*  to the extent that, so much so that...,
e.g. *Ano hito wa suteru hodo okane ga arimasu.* あの人は捨てる
ほどお金があります. "He has so much money that he can afford
to throw it away (He has money to the extent that he throws
it away)."

*-hodo no koto wa nai* ほど(程)のことはない  there is no need to, it's
not worth...ing, e.g. *Sonna ni okoru hodo no koto wa nai deshō.*
そんなに怒るほどのことはないでしょう. "It's not worth being so
mad about, is it?"

*-hoka* [*wa*] *nai* 他はない  =*-yori hoka* [*wa*] *nai*, see. p. 81.

*-hyōshi ni* 拍子に  =*-hazumi ni*  in the act of, e.g. *Tachiagaru
hyōshi ni ocha o koboshimashita.* 立ち上がる拍子にお茶をこぼしま
した. "In the act of standing up, I spilled the tea."

*-igai* [*ni, wa*] 以外  except that..., e.g. *Tanaka-san ga kuru igai
wa dare mo konai deshō.* 田中さんが来る以外は誰も来ないでしょう.
"Except for Mr. Tanaka (Except that Mr. Tanaka comes), perhaps
nobody will come."

*-ijō* [*wa*] 以上  so long as..., e.g. *Ikite iru ijō wa nani ka shinakereba
naranai.* 生きている以上は何かしなければならない. "So long as we
live we have to do something."

*-ka* か

1. interrogative particle, e.g. *Ashita gakkō ni ikimasu ka.* 明日
学校に行きますか. "Do you go to school tomorrow?"

> Note: Traditionally there was no question mark in Japanese, but
> around 1887 it made its first appearance, and in contemporary
> Japanese it is quite frequently used.

2. rhetorical question, e.g. *Ano hito ga sonna koto o suru mono
desu ka.* あの人がそんなことをするものですか. "He won't do
such a thing!" "Do you think he would do such a thing?

No, he wouldn't!"

3.  uncertainty, e.g. *Tanaka-san ga itsu kuru ka shirimasen.*
    田中さんがいつ(何時)来るか知りません. "I don't know when
    Mrs. Tanaka will come."

*-ka dō ka* かどうか  =*-ka* V*ₙₐᵢ* *ka*  whether or not, e.g. *Iku ka dō
ka shirimasen.* 行くかどうか知りません. "I don't know whether
he is going or not."

*-ka dō ka ni yotte* かどうかによって  =*-ka* V*ₙₐᵢ* *ka ni yotte*

*-ka mo shirenai* かもしれない. =*-ka mo shirenu*  may, possibly,
literally, cannot know even whether, e.g. *Ashita iku ka mo shire-
masen.* 明日行くかもしれません. "I may go tomorrow."

*-ka mo shirenu* かもしれぬ  =*-ka mo shirenai*

*-ka* V*ₙₐᵢ* *ka* か V ないか  =*-ka dō ka*  *Iku ka ikanai ka shirimasen.*
行くか行かないか知りません. "I don't know whether he is going
or not."

*-ka* V*ₙₐᵢ* *ka ni yotte* か V ないかによって  depending on whether…
or not, e.g. *Ano hito ga iku ka ikanai ka ni yotte kimemasu.*
あの人が行くか行かないかによって決めます. "I will decide, depend-
ing on whether or not he goes."

*-ka shira[n]* かしら  I wonder if…, e.g. *Ano hito wa Nihongo
ga yoku hanaseru ka shira(n).* あの人は日本語がよく話せるかしら.
"I wonder if he can speak Japanese well?" (Used by women.)

*ka to omou to* かと思うと  =*-ka to omottara*  when I thought that
…, as soon as, e.g. *Kita ka to omou to mō itte shimaimashita.*
来たかと思うともう行ってしま(了)いました. "As soon as he came,
he left."

*kagiri* かぎり  as far as, e.g. *Watakushi no shitte iru kagiri kare
wa shōjikimono desu.* 私の知っているかぎり，彼は正直者です. "As
far as I know, he is an honest man."

*-kankei jō* 関係上  due to the fact that…, e.g. *Koko wa natsu de
mo kikō ga samui kankei jō, shokubutsu ga yoku sodachimasen.*
ここ(此処)は夏でも気候が寒い関係上植物がよく育ちません. "Due to
the fact that it is cold here even in summer, plants do not grow
well."

*-kara* から  because, since (places emphasis on the result, cf. *-no
de*, p. 72) e.g. *Mō sugu iku kara matte ite kudasai.* もうす(直)
ぐ行くから待っていて下さい. "Please wait for me, because I will

come (go) very soon."

*-kara koso* からこそ (emphatic) precisely because, e.g. *Watakushi ga iku kara koso, kare mo iku n' desu.* 私が行くからこそ彼も行くんです. "Precisely because I go, he goes too."

*-kara ni wa* からには now that, since, if, e.g. *Yaru kara ni wa ii shigoto o shinasai.* やるからにはいい仕事をしなさい. "If you do it at all, do a good job." *Kimi ga iu kara ni wa hontō ni chigainai.* 君が言うからには本当に違いない. "If you say so, it must be true."

*-kara to itte* からと言って just because, e.g. *Tsukareta kara to itte nete bakari iru wake ni mo ikimasen.* 疲れたからと言って寝てばかりいるわけにもいきません. "Just because I am tired, I can't very well sleep all the time."

*-kawari ni* かわりに in place of, in exchange for, e.g. *Kyō wa gakkō e iku kawari ni machi e ikimashita.* 今日は学校へ行くかわりに町へ行きました. "Instead of going to school, I went to town today."

*-keredomo* けれども =*-keredo* but, however, more colloquial than *-ga*, e.g. *Ano hito wa okane ga aru keredomo kechi de chittomo tsukaimasen.* あの人はお金があるけれども，けちでちっとも使いません. "He has money, but he is stingy and doesn't spend it at all."

*-ki ga aru* 気がある have a mind to..., e.g. *Anata ni sore o suru ki ga areba shite mo ii desu.* あなたにそれをする気があればしてもいいです. "If you have a mind to do that, you may do it."

*-ki ga suru* 気がする have a feeling that..., feel like...ing, e.g. *Kyō wa gakkō e iku ki ga shimasen.* 今日は学校へ行く気がしません. "I don't feel like going to school today."

*-ki ni naru* 気になる come to feel like...ing, e.g. *Atatakaku natte kita no de, niwa de hataraku ki ni natte kimashita.* 暖かくなってきたので，庭で働く気になってきました. "Since it's getting warm, I am beginning to feel like working in the yard."

*-kirai ga aru* きらい(嫌)がある =*-sugiru kirai ga aru*, p. 51.

*-koto* こと literally "thing" in the abstract sense (cf. *-mono*, p. 68)

1. causes the verb which precedes it to be changed into a noun, e.g. *Oyogu koto ga suki desu.* 泳ぐことが好きです. "I like swimming."

Note: *Koto* often is interpreted as "fact" or "act." *Koto* is interchangeable with *no*, in this usage, except when *koto* is used in set phrases (see the following several expressions).

2. exclamation, emphatic ending, e.g. *Ano hito wa yoku taberu koto.* あの人はよく食べること. "How that man eats!"

3. with verbal adjective of time, for a period =*-aida* e.g. *Nagai koto ome ni kakarimasen deshita.* 長いことお目にかかりませんでした. "I haven't seen you for a long time."

*-koto ga aru* ことがある there are occasions when..., e.g. *Nihon ni iku koto ga arimasu ka.* 日本に行くことがありますか. "Do you have occasion to go to Japan?" For V*ₜₐ koto ga aru*, see p. 52.

*-koto ga atta* ことがあった there were occasions when..., e.g. *Mukashi wa yoku Nihon ni iku koto ga arimashita.* 昔はよく日本に行くことがありました. "Formerly there were many occasions when I went to Japan." For V*ₜₐ koto ga atta*, see p. 52.

*-koto ga dekiru* ことができ(出来)る it is possible to, can..., e.g. *Nihongo o hanasu koto ga dekimasu ka.* 日本語を話すことができますか =*Nihongo ga hanasemasu ka.* "Can you speak Japanese?"

*-koto ni (to) naru* ことになる it is decided that..., it is arranged that..., it has come about that..., e.g. *Otōto ga Amerika ni kuru koto ni narimashita.* 弟がアメリカに来ることになりました. "It is arranged that my brother will come to America."

*-koto ni (to) natte iru* ことになっている this is the practice, it is customary that..., e.g. *Mainichiyō ane no uchi ni iku koto ni natte imasu.* 毎日曜姉の家に行くことになっています. "It is customary that I go to my sister's every Sunday."

*-koto ni (to) shite iru* ことにしている make it a practice to..., e.g. *Mainichi sukoshi sanpo suru koto ni shite imasu.* 毎日少し散歩することにしています. "I make it a practice to take a short walk every day."

*-koto ni suru* ことにする decide, e.g. *Kotoshi no natsu Nihon ni iku koto ni shimashita.* 今年の夏日本に行くことにしました. "I decided to go to Japan this summer." For V*ₜₐ koto ni suru*, see p. 52.

*-koto to omou* ことと思う =*-to omou* I think that, e.g. *Kyō Yamada-san ga kuru koto to omoimasu.* 今日山田さんが来ることと思います. "I think Mr. Yamada comes today."

*-koto wa* V₃ ことは V₃=V₃ *ni wa* V₃ repetition of the same verb,

as far as ... is concerned, it is all right, but ..., e.g. *Taberu koto wa tabemasu ga amari suki de wa arimasen.* 食べることは食べますがあま(余)り好きではありません. "I eat it all right, but I don't particularly like it."

*-kurai* くらい(位)  =*-gurai*=*-hodo*  to the extent that ..., even, so much so that ..., e.g. *Sonna hanashi mo aru kurai desu.* そんな話もあるくらいです. "There is even such a story (It is to the extent that even such a story exists)." *Ano hito wa Nihonjin to machigaerareru kurai Nihongo ga jōzu desu.* あの人は日本人と間違えられるくらい日本語が上手です. "He is so good in Japanese as to be mistaken for a Japanese person (He is good in Japanese to the extent that he is mistaken for a Japanese person)."

*-kuse ni* くせ(癖)に  although, always followed by a negative idea or feeling of contempt (cf. *-no ni*, p. 73) e.g. *Yomanakatta kuse ni, yonda yō na koto o itte imashita.* 読まなかったくせに読んだようなことを言っていました. "Even though he did not read it, he talked as if he had."

*-ma mo naku* 間もなく  without having time to do ..., e.g. *Kesa nani o suru ma mo naku uchi o denakereba narimasen deshita.* 今朝何をする間もなく家を出なければなりませんでした.   "Without having time to do anything, I had to leave home this morning."

*-made* まで  until, e.g. *Anata ga kuru made matte imasu.* あなたが来るまで待っています. "I'll be waiting until you come."

*-made mo nai* までもない  goes without ... ing, e.g. *Sonna koto wa iu made mo nai (koto) desu.* そんなことは言うまでもないことです. "It is needless to say such a thing."

*-made ni* までに  by e.g. *Kare ga kuru made ni owatte iru to omoimasu.* 彼が来るまでに終っていると思います. "I think it will be finished by the time he comes."

*-mae ni* 前に  (sequence of action) before. Use of *mae* and *mae ni* are sometimes interchangeable, but *ni* often pinpoints the time more definitely. That is, without *ni* the period before may be more indefinite, but with *ni* emphasis is on the time just before, e.g. *Nihon ni iku mae ni Nihongo o naraimashita.* 日本に行く前に日本語を習いました. "I learned Japanese before I went to Japan." *Amerika ni kuru mae Nihon ni sunde imashita.* アメリカに来る前日本に住んでいました. "Before I came to America, I was living in Japan."

*-mai* まい (tentative negative) opposite of tentative forms, *-ō, -yō* (see Sixth Base, tentative, pp. 82–83); follows the 3rd base of consonant-stem verbs. *-mai* follows the 1st base of vowel-stem verbs (see pp. 39–40). The irregular verbs *suru* and *kuru* may take this ending with both the 1st and 3rd base with no change in meaning (see pp. 39–40).

1. negative tentative, e.g. *Sonna hon wa yomumai.* そんな本は読むまい. "Perhaps he won't read such a book."

2. negative will, e.g. *Konna mono wa mō kakumai to omotte imasu.* こんなものはもう書くまいと思っています. "I am thinking I won't write such things any more."

*-mai shi* まいし  =*-nai kara* (emphatic) because (he) is not ..., e.g. *Kodomo de wa arumai shi konna yasashii koto ga wakaranai hazu wa arimasen.* 子供ではあるまいし，こんなやさしいことがわか(分)らないはず(筈)はありません. "Because he is not a child, he should (There is no reason for him not to) understand such an easy thing."

*-mama ni* まま(儘)に  just as, e.g. *Omou mama ni kakemasen.* 思うままに書けません. "I can't write just as I think (want)." For V*ₜₐ mama*, p. 52.

*-mitai* みたい  =*-yō* appears as if, e.g. *Kodomotachi wa mina yoku nete iru mitai desu.* 子供たちは皆よく寝ているみたいです. "It seems as if all the children are sleeping well."

*-mono* もの  literally "thing" 物  or "person" 者  in the concrete sense (cf. *koto*, pp. 65–66).

1. person, e.g. *Watakushi wa Tanaka to iu mono desu.* 私は田中という者です. "I am Tanaka (I am a person called Tanaka)."

2. thing, e.g. *Nani ka taberu mono ga arimasu ka.* 何か食べるものがありますか "Is there anything we can eat?"

3. obligation, e.g. *Kodomo wa hayaku neru mono desu.* 子供は早く寝るものです. "A child should go to bed early."

4. reason, e.g. *Mada kodomo da mono...* まだ子供だもの... "Because he is still only a child..."

5. emphatic, e.g. *Anna hon wa yomeru mono de wa nai.* あんな本は読めるものではない. "You can't read that kind of book!" For V*ₜₐ mono*, see, p. 52.

*-mono de mo nan' de mo nai* ものでも何でもない  nothing of that

sort, e.g. *Taberu mono de mo nan' de mo nai.* 食べるものでも
何でもない. "It is not food or anything of that sort."

*-mono (mon') de wa (ja) nai* ものではない   should not, e.g. *Sonna koto
o suru mono de wa arimasen.* そんなことをするものではありませ
ん. "You shouldn't do such a thing."

*-mono no* ものの   although, e.g. *Itsu mo sō shiyō to omou mono no
nakanaka dekimasen.* いつ(何時)もそうしようと思うもののなかなか
(中々)できません. "Although I always think I would like to do
that, I can never do it."

*-n'* ん   short form of *-no*, see pp. 71–72.

*-na* な

1.  (prohibition) e.g. *Sonna hon wa yomu na.* そんな本は読むな.
    "Don't read such a book!" Informal negative imperative,
    used only by men.

2.  sentence ending used by men, e.g. *Sonna hon wa yomitaku
    nai na.* そんな本は読みたくないな. "I don't want to read
    such a book, you know."

*-nā* なあ   (exclamation) how! e.g. *Kare wa hontō ni atama ga ii
nā.* 彼は本当に頭がいいなあ. "How bright he is!"

*-Vₙₐᵢ ni yotte* Vないによって   =*-ka dō ka ni yotte* depending on
whether..., e.g. *Anata ga sore o suru shinai ni yotte watakushi
mo dō suru ka kimemasu.* あなたがそれをするしないによって私も
どうするか決めます. "I'll decide what to do depending on whether
you do it or not."

*-nara(ba)* なら   (conditional) if, e.g. *Anata ga iku nara, watakushi
mo ikimasu.* あなたが行くなら，私も行きます. "If you go, I'll go
too." For more *nara*, see pp. 31–32.

*-nara* V₃ *de* なら V₃ で   (emphatic conditional) e.g. *Suru nara suru
de ii shigoto o shinasai.* するならするで，いい仕事をしなさい. "If
you do it, do a good job."

*-nari* なり

1.  as soon as, e.g. *Asa okiru nari uchi o demashita.* 朝起きる
    なり家を出ました. "As soon as I got up, I left home."

2.  just as, =*-tōri Chichi no iu nari ni shite imasu.* 父の言うな
    りにしています. "I am doing just as my father says."

*-nari* V₃ *nari* なり V₃ なり   either... or, e.g. *Iku nari tomaru nari
suki na yō ni shinasai.* 行くなり泊まるなり好きなようにしなさい.

"Either leave or stay, do as you like."

*-ne* ね (final particle) implies that the speaker wants the hearer to agree; n'est-ce pas? e.g. *Kyō wa otenki ga ii desu ne.* 今日はお天気がいいですね. "It's a beautiful day, isn't it?"

*-ni atatte* に当って　=*-ni atari* at the time when, e.g. *Kono shigoto o suru ni atatte hitokoto iitai koto ga arimasu.* この仕事をするに当って一言言いたいことがあります. "As we begin this work, there is one thing I want to say."

*-ni chigainai* に違いない　there is no doubt that, it is certain that, e.g. *Ano hito wa Amerika-jin de aru ni chigainai.* あの人はアメリカ人であるに違いない. "There is no doubt that he is an American."

*-ni kagiru* に限る　is limited to, is the best, e.g. *Nihongo o narau nara Nihon e iku ni kagirimasu.* 日本語を習うなら日本へ行くに限ります. "If you want to study Japanese, it is best to go to Japan."

*-ni koshita koto wa nai* にこ(越)したことはない　nothing can be better than..., e.g. *Shite miru ni koshita koto wa nai.* してみるにこしたことはない. "There is nothing like trying it." "It is best to try doing it."

*-ni mo kakawarazu* にもかかわ(拘)らず　in spite of the fact that..., e.g. *Isshōkenmei benkyō suru ni mo kakawarazu, ano gakusei wa amari yoku dekinakute, kinodoku desu.* 一生懸命勉強するにもかかわらず, あの学生はあま(余)りよく出来なくて気の毒です. "In spite of the fact that he studies hard, that student does not do too well, and I feel sorry for him."

*-ni oyobi* におよ(及)び　=*-ni oyonde*=*ni atatte*

*-ni shiku wa nai* に如くはない　nothing like, nothing as good as, e.g. *Yōjin suru ni shiku wa nai.* 用心するに如くはない. "It is best to be cautious."

*-ni shinobinai* に忍びない　do not have the heart to..., cannot allow oneself to..., e.g. *Miru ni shinobinai.* 見るに忍びない. "I don't have the heart to look at it."

*-ni shiro* にしろ　even if, e.g. *Nihon ni iku ni shiro sonna ni sugu ni wa ikimasen.* 日本に行くにしろそんなにす(直)ぐには行きません. "Even if I go to Japan, I won't go that soon."

*-ni shiro* V*nai ni shiro* にしろ V ないにしろ　whether...or, e.g. *Iku ni shiro ikanai ni shiro tomokaku shirasete kudasai.* 行くにしろ行かないにしろと(兎)もかく(角)報(知)らせて下さい. "Whether you

go or not, please let us know anyway."

*-ni shita tokoro de* にしたところで  even if, e.g. *Uchi o kau ni shita tokoro de takai uchi wa kaimasen.* 家を買うにしたところで高い家は買いません. "Even if I buy a house, I won't buy an expensive one."

*-ni shitagatte* に従って  in proportion to, e.g. *Toshi o toru ni shitagatte chichi wa yasashiku natta.* 年をとるに従って父は優しくなった. "With age (as he grew older), my father became gentle."

*-ni shite mo* にしても  =*-ni shita tokoro de* even if, e.g. *Nihon ni iku to shite mo kotoshi wa ikimasen.* 日本に行くとしても今年は行きません. "Even if I go to Japan, I won't go this year."

*-ni suginai* にす(過)ぎない  nothing but, no more than, e.g. *Ichinichi ni ichi-pēji o yomu ni suginai.* 一日に一ページを読むにすぎない. "He reads no more than one page a day."

*-ni tsuite* について  concerning, e.g. *Kono shigoto o suru ni tsuite, hajime ni iwanakereba naranai koto ga arimasu.* この仕事をするについて, 初めに言わなければならないことがあります. "As for doing this job, I have something that I must say first."

*-ni tsurete* につれて  in accordance with, in proportion to, e.g. *Kodomo ga ōkiku naru ni tsurete hima ga dekimasu.* 子供が大きくなるにつれて暇ができ(出来)ます. "The older our children get, the more time we can have."

*-ni wa* には  in order to, e.g. *Daigaku ni iku ni wa okane ga kakarimasu.* 大学に行くにはお金がかかります. "It takes money to go to a university." *Kono hon o ireru ni wa ano hako wa chiisasugimasu.* この本を入れるにはあの箱は小さす(過)ぎます. "That box is too small to put this book in."

*-ni wa* V₃ にはV₃ =*-koto wa* V₃ repetition of the same verb, as far as...is concerned, e.g. *Hon ga aru ni wa arimasuga, ii hon wa arimasen.* 本があるにはありますがいい本はありません. "There are books all right, but there are not any good books."

*-ni [wa] oyobanai* に及ばない  unnecessary to do..., e.g. *Ashita kuru ni wa oyobimasen.* 明日来るには及びません. "It's unnecessary for you to come tomorrow."

*-no* の  nominalizes the preceding verb

1.  one who, e.g. *Asoko ni iru no ga Yamada-san desu.* あそこにいるのが山田さんです. "The one who is there is Mr. Yamada."

2. fact that, e.g. *Muzukashii no ga shinpai desu.* 難しいのが心配です. "The fact that it is difficult worries me."

3. time when, e.g. *Ano hito ga kita no wa gogo sanji deshita.* あの人が来たのは午後三時でした. "The time when he came was three o'clock in the afternoon."

Sentence-ending particle:

1. colloquial substitute for *ka*, e.g. *Iku no.* 行くの. "Are you going?"

2. women's speech, e.g. *Iku no.* 行くの. "I am going."

*-no da* のだ =-*n' da* it is a fact that..., e.g. *Ashita iku no (n')desu.* 明日行くのです. "We'll go tomorrow (It is a fact that we'll go tomorrow)."

> Note: *-no da* is a simple sentence-ending phrase, and often does not have to be translated.

*-no de* ので since, because, literally "fact being that"...(emphasis on the reason, cf. *-kara*). Do not use *no de* when the resultant part is interrogative, imperative, or tentative. In these cases use *kara* (See p. 64). e.g. *Ashita shiken ga aru no de kyō isogashii desu.* 明日試験があるので今日忙しいです. "Because I have an exam tomorrow, I am busy today."

*-no de ii* のでいい it is all right with the one that..., e.g. *Soko ni aru no de ii desu.* そこにあるのでいいです. "It is all right with the one that is there."

*-no de mo nan' de mo nai* のでも何でもない not doing anything of that sort, e.g. *Benkyō shite iru no de mo nan'de mo nai.* 勉強しているのでも何でもない. "I am not studying or doing anything like that."

*-no de wa nai* のではない it is not the fact that..., negative of *-no da*, e.g. *Kare wa seijika ni naru no de wa arimasen.* 彼は政治家になるのではありません. "He won't become a politician (It is not the fact that he will become a politician)."

*-no de wa nai darō ka* のではないだろうか I wonder if...not, e.g. *Ano koto o shitte iru no de wa nai darō ka.* あの事を知っているのではないだろうか. "I wonder if he doesn't know that."

*-no de wa naku(te)* のではなく it is not the fact that..., but, e.g. *Ano hito wa seijika ni naru no de wa naku, gakusha ni naru sō desu.* あの人は政治家になるのではなく、学者になるそうです. "I

understand that he won't become a politician, but will be a scholar."

*-no ni* のに

1. in order to, in the process of doing..., e.g. *Tegami o kaku no ni kami ga irimasu.* 手紙を書くのに紙がい(要)ります. "We need paper in order to write letters."

2. although, e.g. *Kono kodomo wa atama wa ii no ni chittomo benkyō shimasen.* この子供は頭はいいのにちっとも勉強しません. "Although this child is bright, he doesn't study at all."

3. (at the end of a sentence) expresses regret or impatience, e.g. *Koko ni ireba aeru no ni...* ここにいれば会えるのに... "We could see him if only he were here (too bad he isn't)."

*-no ni taishite* のに対して as opposed to, in contrast to, e.g. *Otōto ga yoku benkyō suru no ni taishite ani wa zenzen shimasen.* 弟がよく勉強するのに対して兄は全然しません. "In contrast to the younger brother who studies hard, the elder brother doesn't study at all."

*-no wa betsu to shite* のは別として =*-no wa tomokaku* to say nothing of

*-no wa tomokaku [to shite]* のはと(兎)もかく(角) =*-no wa tonikaku [to shite]* to say nothing of..., setting aside..., e.g. *Senshū no shiken no warukatta no wa tomokaku, konshū no wa motto yoku benkyō shite ii oten o totte kudasai.* 先週の試験の悪かったのはともかく、今週のはもっとよく勉強していいお点をとって下さい. "Your test last week was bad, but setting that aside, you should study harder and do well on this week's test."

*-nomi narazu* のみならず not only...but, e.g. *Ano hito wa yoku benkyō suru nomi narazu atama mo ii.* あの人はよく勉強するのみならず頭もいい. "Not only does he study hard, but he is very intelligent."

*-osore ga aru* 恐れがある there is the risk that..., be in danger of..., e.g. *Ano hōhō wa shippai suru osore ga aru.* あの方法は失敗する恐れがある. "That method is in danger of failing."

*-rashii* らしい =*yō da* it seems that, gives every appearance of (*rashii* comes from the classical *rashi*, auxiliary verb meaning "to conjecture.") e.g. *Ano hito wa Nihongo ga yomeru rashii*

*desu.* あの人は日本語が読めるらしいです． "It seems that he can read Japanese."

**-sa** さ (sentence-ending particle) indeed, you know, e.g. *Sonna koto wa shitte iru sa.* そんなことは知っているさ． "I certainly know such a thing." Used by men.

**-sai** 際 when, e.g. *Sono shigoto o suru sai [wa] watakushi ni mo mae motte sōdan shite kudasai.* その仕事をする際私にも前もっ(以)て相談して下さい． "When you do that work, please also consult me ahead of time."

**-saichū ni** 最中に in the midst of, e.g. *Niwa de shokuji o shite iru saichū ni ame ga futte kimashita.* 庭で食事をしている最中に雨が降って来ました． "In the midst of eating dinner in the garden, it started raining."

**-sei da** せい(所為)だ it is because..., e.g. *Ano hito no seiseki no warui no wa chittomo benkyō shinai sei desu.* あの人の成績の悪いのはちっとも勉強しないせいです． "It is because he doesn't study at all that his grades are bad."

**-sei ka** せい(所為)か perhaps because =*-kara ka* e.g. *Kyō ichinichi-jū isogashikatta sei ka totemo tsukaremashita.* 今日一日中忙しかったせいかとても疲れました． "Perhaps because I was busy all day, I got very tired."

**-shi** し not only, but also, and, e.g. *Nihongo mo yomeru shi, Furansugo mo yomemasu.* 日本語も読めるしフランス語も読めます． "Not only can he read Japanese, but he can also read French."

**-sō da** そうだ I understand that..., e.g. *Tanaka-san wa Furansu-go ga hanaseru sō desu.* 田中さんはフランス語が話せるそうです． "I understand that Mr. Tanaka can speak French."

**-tabi ni** たび(度)に each time, e.g. *Haha ga uchi ni kuru tabi ni, okashi o motte kite kuremasu.* 母が家に来るたびにお菓子を持って来てくれます． "Every time my mother comes to our house, she brings us cakes."

**-tame ni** ため(為)に

1. purpose, in order to, e.g. *Hon o yomu tame ni toshokan ni ikimasu.* 本を読むために図書館に行きます． "In order to read books, I go to the library."

2. reason, because, e.g. *Ame ga futte iru tame ni uchi ni imasu.* 雨が降っているために家にいます． "I am staying home because it is raining."

*-to* と

1. (conditional) if, when, e.g. *Miru to wakarimasu.* 見るとわか
   (分)ります. "If you see it, you'll understand."
2. Whenever, if a certain condition occurs, something happens,
   e.g. *Haru ga kuru to atatakaku narimasu.* 春が来ると暖か
   くなります. "Whenever spring comes, it gets warm."
3. (time sequence) e.g. *Uchi e kaeru to haha ga kite imashita.*
   家へ帰ると母が来ていました. "When I returned home, my
   mother was there." (The part after *to* conditional was not
   expected.)

For a more detailed explanation on conditional forms, see pp.
29–32.

4. (sign of closing quotation) no clear distinction is made in
   Japanese between indirect and direct quotation. *-to* may
   be separated by several other words from the verb of
   speaking or hearing, or thinking (examples below).

*-to ieba ieru* と言えば言える  if you want, you can say..., e.g. *Ano
hito wa benkyōka da to ieba ieru deshō.* あの人は勉強家だと言え
ば言えるでしょう. "If you want, perhaps you can say that he is
a hard worker."

*-to iu* と言う

1. say that..., e.g. *Sumisu-san ga Tokyo ni iku to iimashita.*
   スミスさんが東京に行くと言いました.  "He said that Mr.
   Smith would go to Tokyo," or "Mr. Smith said that he
   would go to Tokyo."
2. which is called, who is called, e.g. *Yamamoto-san to iu
   hito o shitte imasu ka.* 山本さんという人を知っていますか.
   "Do you know Mr. Yamamoto (a man who is called Mr.
   Yamamoto)?"
3. defined as, e.g. *'Hōken-jidai' to iu kotoba o shitte imasu ka?*
   「封建時代」という言葉を知っていますか.  "Do you know the
   word defined as 'feudalism'?"

*-to iu hanashi da* とい(言)う話だ  =*-to iu koto da*

*-to iu koto da* ということだ I hear that..., I understand that...,
e.g. *Ano hito wa mukashi gakkō no sensei datta to iu koto desu.*
あの人は昔学校の先生だったということです.  "I understand that he
was a school teacher before."

*-to iu koto dake de wa* ということだけ（丈）では　=*-to iu dake no koto de wa*　if it is only because..., e.g. *Atama ga ii to iu koto dake dewa nakanaka shusse wa muzukashii.* 頭がいいということだけではなかなか（中々）出世は難しい。 "If it is only because one has (one has nothing but) a good brain, one can't succeed in life easily."

*-to iu yō ni* というように　in such a manner that..., e.g. *Ani ga ikeba otōto mo iku to iu yō ni ano kyōdai wa naka ga ii desu.* 兄が行けば弟も行くというようにあの兄弟は仲がいいです。 "Those brothers are close in such a manner that if the older brother goes, the younger one goes, too."

*-to iwan bakari* (*ni*) といわんばかり（に）as if to say, e.g. *Mō kori-gori* (*da*) *to iwan bakari ni atama o futte ita.* もうこりごり（だ）と言わんばかりに頭を振っていた。 "He was shaking his head as if to say that he had had enough."

*-to ka* とか　followed by verbs such as *iu, kiku*

1. something to the effect, e.g. *Sumisu-san ga Nihon ni iku to ka kikimashita.* スミスさんが日本に行くとか聞きました。 "I heard Mr. Smith is going to Japan, or something like that."

2. ...or..., e.g. *Kō suru to ka ā suru to ka nani o itte iru no ka wakarimasen.* こうするとかああするとか何を言っているのかわか（分）りません。 "Doing this, doing that—I don't understand what he is saying. (He had better make up his mind what he is going to do.)"

*-to kiku* と聞く　I hear that..., e.g. *Yamamoto-san wa kyō byōki da to kikimashita.* 山本さんは今日病気だと聞きました。 "I heard that Mr. Yamamoto is sick today."

*-to mieru* と見える　it looks as if, e.g. *Yamada-san wa totemo tsukarete iru to miete kaoiro ga amari yoku arimasen deshita.* 山田さんはとても疲れていると見えて顔色が余りよくありませんでした。 "It looked as if Mr. Yamada was very tired, and his complexion was not very good."

*-to mo* とも

1. (conjunction) even if..., e.g. *Ikani takusan hon o yomu to mo, sore o konasu koto ga dekinakereba yaku ni tatanai.* いか（如何）に沢山本を読むともそれをこなすことができ（出来）なければ役に立たない。 "Even if you read lots of books, unless

you can digest them, it won't be useful."

**2.** (sentence-ending phrase) of course, e.g. *Benkyō suru to mo.* 勉強するとも. "Of course I will study!" Used by men.

*-to mo nashi ni* ともなしに  =*-to mo naku* does not mean to do something, e.g. *Miru to mo nashi ni mimashita.* 見るともなしに見ました. "I didn't mean to look, but I just happened to see it."

*-to no koto da* とのことだ  =*-to iu koto da* I am told that..., e.g. *Ano hito wa Nihon e iku to no koto desu.* あの人は日本へ行くとのことです. "I am told that he is going to Japan."

*-to shite* として  granted that..., deciding to, e.g. *Kono uchi o kau to shite, ikura kurai dasu tsumori desu ka?* この家を買うとしていく(幾)らくらい出すつも(積)りですか. "If you decide to buy this house, how much do you intend to pay?"

*-to (-ni) shite mo* としても  =*to shita tokoro de* even if, e.g. *Ashita iku to shite mo gozenchū ni wa ikimasen.* 明日行くとしても午前中には行きません. "Even if we go tomorrow, we won't go in the morning."

*-to shitara* としたら
*-to sureba* とすれば
*-to suru to* とすると

(hypothesis) if, e.g. *Moshi Nihon ni iku to shitara (-to sureba, -to suru to), taitei rainen deshō.* もし日本に行くとしたらたいてい(大抵)来年でしょう. "If we ever go to Japan, perhaps it will be next year."

*-to wa ie* とは言え  =*-to wa itte mo* even if..., e.g. *[Ikura] isogashii to wa ie, sono kurai no koto wa shite kurete mo ii no ni* ... 忙しいとは言え, そのくらい(位)のことはしてくれてもいいのに ... "Even if he is busy, I wish he would do that much for me, but (he won't)."

*-to [wa] kagiranai* と限らない  it does not necessarily mean that ..., e.g. *Nihonjin dakara ii Nihongo ga hanaseru to wa kagiranai.* 日本人だからいい日本語が話せるとは限らない. "Just because a person is Japanese, it doesn't necessarily mean that he can speak good Japanese." (*-nai to wa kagiranai*, see pp. 41-42)

*-to wa nashi ni* とはなしに  =*-to mo nashi ni*

*-toki* [*ni*] 時に  See pp. 32-33 for the use of *toki*. See also p. 67. *mae ni*, for the difference between *toki* and *toki ni*.

-*tokoro* [*da*] ところ

1. location, the place where, e.g. *Koko wa gohan o taberu tokoro desu.* ここはごはん(御飯)を食べる所です. "This is the place where we eat our meals."

2. point of time, the time when, e.g. *Ima uchi o deru tokoro desu.* 今, 家を出るところです. "We are about to leave home." For V$_{ta}$ *tokoro*, see p. 52.

3. situation, in the situation, e.g. *Ima benkyō shite iru tokoro desu.* 今, 勉強しているところです. "I am studying now (Now I am in the situation of studying)."

4. extent, so far as  =-*kagiri* e.g. *Watakushi no shitte iru tokoro de wa ano hito wa kekkon shite imasen.* 私の知っているところではあの人は結婚していません. "As far as I know, he is not married."

5. thing, e.g. *Anata no iu tokoro wa mottomo desu.* あなたの言うところはもっと(尤)もです. "What you say is reasonable."

-*tokoro no* ところの (relative pronoun) used mainly to translate relative pronouns in foreign languages into Japanese, it often sounds awkward, e.g. *Kore wa ima jibun ga yonde iru tokoro no hon de aru.* これは今自分が読んでいるところの本である. "This is the book which I am now reading." See also p. 189.

-*tōri* 通り  =-*nari* just as, e.g. *Sensei no iu tōri ni shinasai.* 先生の言うとおりにしなさい. "Do as your teacher says."

-*totan ni* とたん(途端)に  no sooner than, e.g. *Ano hito wa toko ni tsuku (tsuita) totan ni nete shimaimasu.* あの人は床に就くとたんに寝てしまいます. "No sooner does he go to bed than he falls asleep."

-*tsuide ni* ついで(序)に  while doing A, [we] will also do B. e.g. *Toshokan de rekishi no hon o yomu tsuide ni chiri no hon mo yomimashita.* 図書館で歴史の本を読むついでに地理の本も読みました. "While at the library to read a history book, I also read a geography book."

-*tsumori* [*da*] つも(積)り  shows intention, e.g. *Ashita iku tsumori desu.* 明日行くつもりです. "I intend to go tomorrow." For V$_{ta}$ *tsumori*, see p. 53.

-*uchi ni* うちに  while, while A is in progress, B will occur, e.g.

*Haha ga kaimono ni itte iru uchi ni, okashi o tsukurimashita.*
母が買物に行っているうちにお菓子を作りました. "While my mother
was gone shopping I made a cake." *-nai uchi ni,* p. 42.

*-ue ni* 上に

1. in addition to, e.g. *Ano hito wa Nihongo ga dekiru ue ni
   Chūgokugo mo dekiru.* あの人は日本語ができ(出来)る上に中
   国語もできる. "In addition to being able to speak Japanese,
   he can speak Chinese, too."

2. when, e.g. *Shōbai o itonamu ue ni taihen taisetsu da.* 商売
   を営む上に大変大切だ. "When you manage business it is very
   important."

*-wake [da]* わけ

1. it means that..., e.g. *Kare ga shita to iu wake desu ne.*
   彼がしたと言うわけですね. "It means that he did it, right?"

2. reason why, e.g. *Nihon ni ita kara Nihongo ga yoku hana-
   seru wake desu.* 日本にいたから日本語がよく話せるわけです.
   "Because he was in Japan, that is why he can speak
   Japanese well."

   > Note: *-wake da* is a sentence-ending form, which often does not
   > have a distinct meaning, and thus cannot be translated into
   > English.

*-wake de wa nai* わけではない   it doesn't mean that..., e.g. *Akui
de suru wake de wa arimasen.* 悪意でするわけではありません.
"It doesn't mean that I do it out of spite." *-nai wake de wa nai,*
see p. 42.

*-wake ni [wa] ikanai* わけにいかない   can't very well do something,
this won't pass, e.g. *Sonna koto o suru wake ni wa ikimasen.*
そんなことをするわけにはいきません. "I can't very well do such a
thing." *-nai wake ni ikanai,* see p. 42.

*-wari ni* 割に   in proportion to, considering, e.g. *Sūgaku ga kirai
da to iu wari ni yoku dekimasu.* 数学が嫌いだという割によくでき
(出来)ます. "Considering that he says. he doesn't like mathematics, he is good in it." *Kare wa toshi ga ikanai wari ni monowa-
kari ga ii.* 彼は年がいかない割に物わかりがいい. "He understands
things well for his young age."

*-ya [ina ya]* や   as soon as, e.g. *Uchi e kaeru ya toko ni tsukimashita.* 家へ帰るや床に就きました. "As soon as I got home, I went

to bed."

*-yara* やら  expresses uncertainty, e.g. *Shimizu-san wa itsu Nihon ni kaeru yara wakaranai.*  清水さんはいつ(何時)日本に帰るやらわか(分)らない.  "We don't know when Mr. Shimizu will go back to Japan."

*-yara...yara* やら...やら  what with..., e.g. *Benkyō suru yara, uchi o kirei ni suru yara, anata wa zuibun isogashii desu ne.*  勉強するやら家をきれい(綺麗)にするやらあなたは随分忙しいですね.  "What with studying and cleaning the house too, you are pretty busy, aren't you?

*-yō da* よう(様)だ, *-yō na* よう(様)な  for attributive form; it looks like, as if (but is not necessarily); *yō* means appearance, e.g. *Ame ga futte iru yō desu.*  雨が降っているようです.  "It looks like rain."  *Dare demo dekiru yō na yasashii shiken deshita.*  誰でもでき(出来)るような易しい試験でした.  "It was an easy examination which it seems, everyone could pass."

*-yō ni* ように

1.  just as, e.g. *Amerika ni Nihongo o hanaseru hito ga takusan iru yō ni, Nihon ni mo Eigo o hanaseru hito ga takusan imasu.*  アメリカに日本語を話せる人が沢山いるように日本にも英語を話せる人が沢山います.  "Just as there are many people who can speak Japanese in the United States, there are lots of people in Japan who can speak English."

2.  in order that..., *Shujin ga benkyō dekiru yō ni ashita wa kodomo to ichinichi-jū gaishutsu suru tsumori desu.*  主人が勉強できるように明日は子供と一日中外出するつもりです.  "In order that my husband can study tomorrow, I intend to go out all day with my child."

3.  something like, e.g. *Nani ka sonna koto o itte ita yō ni oboete imasu.*  何かそんなことを言っていたように覚えています.  "I remember he said something like that."

4.  wish for others, e.g. *Ii kurisumasu o sugosaremasu yō ni...*  いいクリスマスを過ごされますように...  "I wish you (will have) a nice Christmas."

*-yō ni iu* ように言う  (indirect command) e.g. *Gakusei ni sono hon o yomu yō ni iimashita.*  学生にその本を読むように言いました.  "I told the students to read that book."

*-yō ni naru* ようになる  comes about so that the statement becomes true, e.g. *Konogoro Nihongo ga yomeru yō ni narimashita.* こ(此)の頃日本語が読めるようになりました. "Lately I have become able to read Japanese."

*-yō ni suru* ようにする  makes it so that the statement becomes true, e.g. *Heya o katazukete mina ga koko de asoberu yō ni shimashō.* 室を片付けて皆がここ(此処)で遊べるようにしましょう. "Let's clean up this room so that everybody can play here."

*-yori* より  than, e.g. *Sō suru yori kō suru hō ga ii desu.* そうするよりこうする方がいいです. "It is better to do this than that."

*-yori hoka [ni, wa] nai* より他ない  there is nothing else to do but ..., e.g. *Kyō wa jidōsha ga nai kara aruku yori hoka arimasen.* 今日は自動車がないから歩くより他ありません. "Since I don't have a car today, there is nothing else to do but walk."

*-yori hoka [ni] te ga nai* より他手がない  =*-yori hoka [wa] nai*

*-yori shikata ga nai* より仕方がない  =*-yori hoka [wa] nai*

*-yoshi [da]* 由  I am told that ..., e.g. *Raishū ni wa sore ga wakaru yoshi da.* 来週にはそれがわか(分)る由だ. "I am told that we'll find out next week."

*-yotei [da]* 予定  plan to, e.g. *Ashita kara gakkō e iku yotei da.* 明日から学校へ行く予定だ. "I plan to go to school starting tomorrow."

*-zo* ぞ  (sentence-ending particle) emphatic, e.g. *Kore wa muzukashii zo.* これは難しいぞ. "This is difficult, I tell you." Used by men.

## IV. Expressions which follow the *Fourth Base* 仮定形〈かていけい〉 of the verb.

*-ba* ば  see conditionals, pp. 6–12.

*-ba V₃ hodo* ば V₃ ほど  =*-ba V₃ dake* the more ... the more, e.g. *Takusan tabereba taberu hodo ōkiku narimasu.* 沢山食べれば食べるほど大きくなります. "The more you eat, the bigger you get."

*-ba ii n' desu ga* ばいいんですが  =V₃ *to ii n' desu ga* ... wish, e.g. *Ashita tomodachi ga kureba ii n' desu ga* ... 明日友達が来ればいいんですが... "I wish my friend would come tomorrow." For a more detailed explanation of the subjunctive, see pp. 33–34.

(interrogative word) *-ba ii no ka* ばいいのか  =(i.w.)+V*tara ii no ka* how (what, etc.) to do ..., e.g. *Dō shite kono kanji o shirabereba* *ii no ka wakarimasen.* どうしてこの漢字を調べればいいのかわか(分)りません. "I don't know how to look up this Chinese character."

*-ba ii no ni* ばいいのに wish, e.g. *Haha ga ireba ii no ni ...,* 母がいればいいのに... "I wish my mother were here." For a more detailed explanation of the subjunctive, see pp. 33-34.

*-ba koso* ばこそ =V₃ *kara koso* emphatic, e.g. *Anata o shinjireba koso ikasete agemashita.* あなたを信じればこそ行かせてあ(上)げました. "Precisely because I trusted you, I let you go."

## V. Expressions which follow the *Fifth Base* 命令形〈めいれいけい〉 of the verb.

*-to iu* と言う (indirect command) to tell someone to do something, e.g. *Otōto ni kore o shiro to iimashita.* 弟にこれをしろと言いました. "I told my younger brother to do this." *Sensei ni kono hon o yome to iwaremashita.* 先生にこの本を読めと言われました. "I was told by my teacher to read this book."

## VI. Expressions which follow the *Sixth Base* 推量形〈すいりょうけい〉 of the verb.

*-yō* よう (-ō) (お)う *-yō* with vowel-stem verb, *-ō* with consonant-stem verb.

Functions: 1. one's will 2. imperative, used by men "let's..." 3. probability, in case of copula

(interrogative word) *-yō (-ō) ga (to)* ようが =(i.w.)+*te (de) mo* no matter how (what, etc.), e.g. *Ika ni benkyō shiyō to, sonna muzukashii shiken ni wa ukaru hazu ga arimasen.* いか(如何)に勉強しようと，そんな難しい試験には受かるはず(筈)がありません. "No matter how hard he studies, he can't possibly pass that kind of difficult examination."

*-yō (-ō) ga (to) kamawanai* ようがかま(構)わない it does not matter if something happens, e.g. *Ano hito ga shinō to kamawanai.* あの人が死のうとかまわない, "It doesn't matter if she dies."

*-yō (-ō) ga (to) V_mai ga (to)* ようが V まいが whether... or not, e.g. *Ano hito ga ikō ga ikumai ga watakushi no shitta koto de wa nai.* あの人が行こうが行くまいが私の知ったことではない. "Whether he goes or not, I don't care (it's not my business)."

*-yō (-ō) ga (to)...yō (-ō) ga (to)* ようがようが even if...or..., e.g. *Ame ga furō ga yuki ga furō ga iku tsumori desu.* 雨が降ろうが雪

が降ろうが行くつも (積) りです. "Even if it rains or snows, I intend to go."

*-yō (-ō) ni mo* ようにも  even if you want to..., e.g.  *Nagusameyō ni mo nagusameru sube o shiranai.* 慰めようにも慰める術を知らない. "Even if I want to comfort her, I don't know how to."

*-yō (-ō) to omou (kangaeru)* ようと思う  I am thinking of doing..., e.g.  *Motto benkyō shiyō to omotte imasu.* もっと勉強しようと思っています. "I am thinking of studying more."

*-yō (-ō) to suru* ようとする

1. is about to do something (but not accomplishing it), e.g. *Dekakeyō to shite iru tokoro e tomodachi ga kimashita.* 出か(掛)けようとしているところへ友達が来ました. "My friend came just as I was about to go out."

2. trying (unsuccessfully) to do something, e.g. *Okiyō to shimashita ga amari nemukute okiraremasen deshita.* 起きようとしましたがあま (余) り眠くて起きられませんでした. "I tried to get up, but I was too sleepy and was unable to get up."

## VII. Expressions which follow the *Stems of the Adjectives* 形容詞〈けいようし〉.

Since Japanese adjectives are a form of verb, many of the suffixes which attach to the dictionary form of the verbs also attach to adjective dictionary forms as shown earlier. Therefore, some of the special suffixes which only attach to adjectives are given here.

The following suffixes attach to the stems of adjectives. To make the stem of an adjective, delete the last *i* from the dictionary form. e.g. *osoi* 遅い "to be late" is a dictionary form, while *oso* is a stem.

*-gari* がり  a person exceedingly sensitive to the quality described by the adjective, e.g. *samugari* 寒がり "a person sensitive to the cold," *kowagari* 怖がり "timid person, coward"

*-garu* がる

1. conjecture about the feelings or emotions of someone else other than the speaker, e.g. *Kodomo ga terebi o mite omoshirogatte imasu.* 子供がテレビを見て面白がっています. "A child is amused watching TV."

*-ge* げ  =*-sō* seeming condition of others, e.g. *Totemo ureshige ni hanashite imasu.* とても嬉しげに話しています. "He is talking

very happily (looking very happy)."

-*karō* かろう  =Adj₃ *darō* (tentative).  -*karō*-form is not as commonly used as Adj₃+*darō* (*deshō*).

(Interrogative word) -*karō ga* (*to*) かろうが  =(i.w.)+Adj_kute *mo* no matter how (what, etc.), e.g. *Donna ni takakarō ga kau tsumori desu.* どんなに高かろうが買うつもりです. "No matter how expensive it is, I intend to buy it."

-*kattara* かったら (conditional) if, e.g. *Takakattara kaimasen.* 高かったら買いません. "If it is expensive, I won't buy it."

-*ke* 気 makes an adjective into an abstract noun of the quality described by the adjective, e.g. *nemuke* 眠気 "sleepiness." *Hanashite iru uchi ni nemuke ga sashimashita.* 話している中に眠気がさしました. "While I was talking, I became sleepy." *Kaze o hiita no ka samuke ga shimasu.* 風邪をひいたのか寒気がします. "Probably because I caught cold, I feel chilly."

-*kereba* ければ (conditional) if, e.g. *Ikitakereba itte mo ii desu yo.* 行きたければ行ってもいいですよ. "You may go if you want."

-*ku* く

1. makes an adjective into an adverb, e.g. *Takaku narimashita.* 高くなりました. "It became expensive." "He became tall."

2. also makes a few adjectives into nouns, e.g. *Chikaku* 近く "neighborhood," *tōku* 遠く "distance," etc. For more *ku*-form, see pp. 88–89.

-*ku mo* Adj_ku *mo nai* くも Adj くもない  neither … nor, e.g. *Takaku mo hikuku mo arimasen.* 高くも低くもありません. "It is neither high nor low."

-*ku mo nashi* Adj_ku *mo nai* くもなし Adj くもない  =-*ku mo* Adj_ku *mo nai*

-*kunai* くない (negative), e.g. *Kitanakunai desu.* 汚くないです. "It is not dirty."

-*kute* くて  *te*-form of adjectives; the function of *kute*-form is similar to V_te

1. (conjunction) and, e.g. *Atarashikute ii uchi desu.* 新しくていい家です. "It is a new and nice house."

2. (cause) because …, e.g. *Furukute tsukaimono ni narimasen.* 古くて使いものになりません. "Because it is old, we can't use it. Use *kute*-form only when the resultant part is an

objective statement with no implication of one's will or desire. e.g. *Takakute kaemasen.* 高くて買えません. "Because it is expensive, I cannot buy it." If one's will or desire is implied, use *kara* (p. 64) or *no de* (p. 72). e.g. *Takai kara kaimasen.* 高いから買いません. "Because it is expensive, I am not going to buy it."

*-kute mo* くても =*-kuto mo* at Adj<sub>superlative</sub>, e.g. *sukunakute mo* 少くても "at least," *chiisakute mo* 小さくても "at the smallest," etc.

*-kute sumu* くて済む get by..., e.g. *Inaka ni sumu to yasukute sumimasu.* 田舎に住むと安くて済みます. "If we live in the country, we can get by cheaply."

*-kute tamaranai* くてたま(堪)らない is so...that it is unbearable, e.g. *Ano eiga ga mitakute tamarimasen.* あの映画が見たくてたまりません. "I really want to see that movie." "I want to see that movie so much that I can't stand it."

*-me* め attached to the stem of adjectives of quality or degree; it expresses the possession of this character, e.g. *Sukoshi hayame ni kite kudasai.* 少し早めに来て下さい. "Please come a little early."

*-sa* さ makes an adjective into an abstract noun, e.g. *atarashisa* 新しさ "newness."

*-sō da* そうだ, *sō na* そうな for attributive form; it appears, e.g. *Are wa takasō desu.* あれは高そうです. "That looks expensive." *Are wa oishisō na ringo desu.* あれはおい(美味)しそうなリンゴ(林檎)です. "That is a delicious-looking apple." Exception: When the stem is one syllable, insert *sa* between stem and *sō*, e.g. *nasasō* (na/sa/sō), *Nani mo nasasō desu.* 何もなさそうです. "It seems there is nothing." *yosasō* (yo/sa/sō), *yosasō na hito* よさそうな人 "man who seems nice."

*-sugi mo sezu* (*shinai shi*) Adj-stem (copular noun) *sugi mo shinai* す(過)ぎもせず Adj-stem す(過)ぎもしない neither...nor, e.g. *Nihon wa Ajia Tairiku kara tōsugi mo sezu* (*shinai shi*) *chikasugi mo shinai.* 日本はアジア大陸から遠すぎもせず近すぎもしない. "Japan is neither too far from nor too close to the Asian Continent."

*-sugiru* す(過)ぎる too..., e.g. *Ano uchi wa ōkisugimasu.* あの家は大きすぎます. "That house is too big."

*-sugiru kirai ga aru* す(過)ぎる嫌いがある there is a tendency to be too..., e.g. *Ano hito wa urusasugiru kirai ga arimasu.* あの人はうるさすぎる嫌いがあります. "He has a tendency to be too

noisy."

**-yagu** やぐ  become, e.g. *Ano hito wa konogoro hidoku wakayaide kimashita.*  あの人はこ(此)の頃ひどく若やいでできました.  "She is getting to look very young lately."

## VIII. Expressions which follow the *Copular Nouns* 形容名詞〈けいようめいし〉

**-garu** がる  See Adj-stem+*garu*, p. 83.

**-na** な  makes a copular noun into a modifier of another noun, e.g. *Kirei na hito* きれい(綺麗)な人 "a pretty person." For more about copular nouns, see pp. 152–53.  For more *na*, see pp. 117–18. *na* is often used after foreign adjectives, e.g. *Ano hito wa totemo chāmingu na hito desu.* あの人はとてもチャーミングな人です. "She is a very charming person."

**-ni** に  makes a copular noun into an adverb, e.g. *Genki ni narimashita.* 元気になりました. "I became well." *Kirei ni shite kudasai.* きれい(綺麗)にして下さい. "Please clean it (Please make it clean)."

**-sa** さ  makes a copular noun into an abstract noun, e.g. *Kireisa* きれい(綺麗)さ "quality of being pretty, or clean."

**-sō da** そうだ, **-sō na** そうな  for attributive form, it appears, e.g. *Ano hito wa totemo genki sō desu.* あの人はとても元気そうです. "He looks very healthy." *genki sō na hito* 元気そうな人 "a person who looks healthy."

**-sugi mo [sezu]** Copular noun (Adj-stem) *sugi mo shinai* す(過)ぎもせず Cop. n. す(過)ぎもしない  neither ... nor, e.g. *Jōzu sugi mo heta sugi mo shinai.* 上手すぎも下手すぎもしない. "He is neither too skillful nor too unskillful."

**-sugiru** す(過)ぎる  too..., e.g. *Ano hito wa otoko ni shite wa kirei sugimasu.* あの人は男にしてはきれい(綺麗)すぎます. "For a man he is too pretty."

**-sugiru kirai ga aru** す(過)ぎるきらい(嫌)がある  there is a tendency to be too..., e.g. *Jōzu sugiru kirai ga arimasu.* 上手すぎるきらいがあります. "He has a tendency to be too skillful."

**-zuki** 好き  person who likes..., e.g. *Ano hito wa totemo kireizuki desu.* あの人はとてもきれい(綺麗)好きです. "He is a person who likes to keep things very neat." *kireizuki na hito* きれい好きな人 "a tidy person"

# ADJECTIVES (VERBAL ADJECTIVES)
## 形容詞＜けいようし＞

As attributive adjectives, Japanese adjectives function like their English counterparts—that is, by preceding the nouns they modify. But as predicate adjectives they differ from English in that they function as verbs. For example, *akai* in the sentence *Kono hana wa akai.* この花は赤い. "This flower is red," means not just "red," but "is red." In the sentence, *Kono hana wa akai desu, desu* does not have a copulative verb function, but rather is used to make the ending level more polite (See Copulas, pp. 13-14). Because Japanese adjectives are thus a special class of verbs, they conjugate. The conjugation partially parallels that of ordinary verbs, but is much simpler. Dictionary forms of adjectives end in *-ai, -ii, -ui,* or *-oi,* but *never -ei.* (*Kirei* is not an adjective, but is a copular noun. It is, therefore, possible to say, *Kono hana wa kirei da,* see p. 14.)

The stems of adjectives are the form without the final *i.* The function of the adjective stems is very similar to the second base of the verb (See pp. 5-6). That is, the stem can be used to create compound words, such as *chikamichi* 近道 "shortcut," or *naga-gutsu* 長靴 "boots." Many suffixes are also attached to the stem. They are found in the Expressions which follow the Stems of Adjectives (pp. 83-86). The adjective stems of some colors become nouns. That is, *aka* from *akai* is the noun "red," and *ao* from *aoi* 青い is the noun "blue."

## CONJUGATION OF ADJECTIVES

### 1. takai 高い "(is) high"

|  | stem | base formative | suffix | arbitrary term for base |
|---|---|---|---|---|
| 1. | taka | ku* | -nai | Negative |
| 2. | taka | ku | -te, takakatta (contraction of takaku atta) | Continuative |
| 3. | taka | i | 1. —(desu, deshita, deshō) | Conclusive (Dictionary Form) |
|  |  |  | 2.  Noun | Attributive |
| 4. | taka | kere | -ba | Conditional |
| 5. | — |  | . |  |
| 6. | taka | karō (contraction of takaku arō) | | Tentative |

### 2. atarashii 新しい "(is) new"

| 1. | atarashi | ku | -nai | Negative |
|---|---|---|---|---|
| 2. | atarashi | ku | -te, atarashikatta | Continuative |
| 3. | atarashi | i | 1. —(desu, deshita, deshō) | Conclusive (Dictionary Form) |
|  |  |  | 2.  Noun | Attributive |
| 4. | atarashi | kere | -ba | Conditional |
| 5. | — |  |  |  |
| 6. | atarashi | karō |  | Tentative |

### 3. hikui 低い "(is) low"

| 1. | hiku | ku | -nai | Negative |
|---|---|---|---|---|
| 2. | hiku | ku | -te, hikukatta | Continuative |
| 3. | hiku | i | 1. —(desu, deshita, deshō) | Conclusive (Dictionary Form) |
|  |  |  | 2.  Noun | Attributive |
| 4. | hiku | kere | -ba | Conditional |
| 5. | — |  |  |  |
| 6. | hiku | karō |  | Tentative |

*Explanation of *ku*-form, see p. 89.

**4.** aoi 青い "(is) blue, green"

| 1. | ao | ku | -nai | Negative |
|---|---|---|---|---|
| 2. | ao | ku | -te, aokatta | Continuative |
| 3. | ao | i | 1. —(desu, deshita, deshō)<br>2.  Noun | Conclusive (Dictionary Form)<br>Attributive |
| 4. | ao | kere | -ba | Conditional |
| 5. | — | | | |
| 6. | ao | karō | | Tentative |

Note: Both *ii* and *yoi* "good" are used in the attributive form, but in all other conjugated forms, only *yoi* is used, i.e. *yoku, yokatta, yokereba, yokarō*, etc.

## KU-FORM OF ADJECTIVES  (See also p. 84)

*Ku*-form (identical in both 1st and 2nd base) of adjectives has an adverbial function.  It modifies verbs.  Some adjective *ku*-forms modify other adjectives and copular nouns plus *na* or *ni*.

  e.g.   Kono uchi wa *furuku* narimashita.   この家は古くなりました。
         "This house has become old."  (*furuku* modifies the verb *narimashita*)
         Kono uchi wa *sugoku* furui desu.   この家はすごく古いです。
         "This house is extremely old."  (*sugoku* modifies the adjective *furui*)
         *Sugoku* kirei na hito desu.   すごくきれい(綺麗)な人です。
         "She is an extremely pretty person."  (*sugoku* modifies the copular noun plus *na, kirei na*)
         *Kono kozutsumi wa hidoku ranbō ni toriatsukawareta rashii.*
         この小包はひどく乱暴に取扱かわれたらしい。  "This package seems to have been treated very roughly."  (*hidoku* modifies the copular noun plus *ni, ranbō ni*)

  For some adjectives, the *ku*-form has the function of a noun as well as an adverb.

  e.g.   Ano hito wa kono *chikaku* ni sunde imasu.   あの人はこの近くに住んでいます。  "He lives in this neighborhood."
         Daigaku wa eki kara *tōku* ni arimasu.   大学は駅から遠くにあります。  "The university is located far from the station."
         Ōku no hito wa sore o shirimasen.   多くの人はそれを知りま

せん. "Many people do not know it."

## KUTE-FORM OF ADJECTIVES

*Kute*-form is the *te*-form of adjectives. Like the verb *te*-form, it functions as the conjunction "and." (For more *kute*-form, see pp. 84-85)

## COMMON ADJECTIVAL TENSES

*takai* 高い "high, tall"

### Positive

| formality \ tense | present | perfective | tentative present perfective |
|---|---|---|---|
| polite | Takai desu | Takai deshita<br>Takakatta desu | Takai deshō<br>Takakatta deshō |
| informal | Takai | Takakatta | Takai darō<br>Takakatta darō |
| formal* | (O)takō gozaimasu | (Otakō)<br>gozaimashita | (O)takō gozaimashō<br><br>(O)takō gozai-<br>mashita deshō |

### Negative

| formality \ tense | present | perfective | tentative present perfective |
|---|---|---|---|
| polite | Takakunai desu<br>Takaku arimasen | Takakunai deshita<br>Takaku arimasen<br>deshita<br>Takaku nakatta<br>desu | Takakunai deshō<br>Takakunakatta<br>deshō |
| informal | Takakunai | Takakunakatta | Takakunai darō<br>Takakunakatta<br>darō |
| formal* | (O)takaku<br>gozaimasen | (O)takaku gozai-<br>masen deshita | (O)takaku gozai-<br>masen deshō<br>(O)takaku gozaima-<br>sen deshita deshō |

* Formal level of adjectives, see pp. 224-25.

## COMPARATIVE AND SUPERLATIVE DEGREES OF ADJECTIVES

The word hō is used to express comparatives (See pp. 62–63 for more details)

e.g.  *Kono jidōsha no hō ga (ano jidōsha yori motto) ōkii desu.*
この自動車の方が（あの自動車よりもっと）大きいです． "This car is bigger (than that car)."

The word *ichiban* is used to express superlatives.

e.g.  *Kono jidōsha ga (kono naka de) ichiban ōkii desu.* この自動 車が(この中で)一番大きいです． "This car is the biggest (among these)."

# NON-CONJUGATIVE ADJECTIVES 連体詞＜れんたいし＞

As stated in the previous chapter, Japanese adjectives are a special class of verbs and thus conjugate. They are, therefore, more appropriately called verbal adjectives. Japanese also has another kind of adjective which does not conjugate. The number of these non-conjugative adjectives is limited. Some of them correspond to English pronominal adjectives.

Following are some examples:

| *Kono*-type words | | | *Konna*-type words | | |
|---|---|---|---|---|---|
| kono | この | "this" | konna | こんな | "this kind of" |
| sono | その | "that" | sonna | そんな | "such" |
| ano | あの | "that" | anna | あんな | "that kind of" |
| dono | どの | "which" | donna | どんな | "what kind of" |

Differences of *ko, so, a,* and *do*

*Ko* indicates that the object referred to is close to the speaker.

*So* indicates that the object is close to the listener, or was previously referred to.

*A* indicates that the object is reasona ly distant from both.

Initial *do* often shows that the word is interrogative.

There are many more sets of words that start with *ko, so, a,* and *do* (See Pronouns, p. 192), but in each case the initial syllables carry the same basic meaning.

Besides the above types of words, there are several more non-conjugative adjectives.

Some of the very common ones are listed below:

| arayuru | あらゆる | "every" | naki | 亡き | "deceased" |
|---|---|---|---|---|---|
| aru | あ(或)る | "a certain" | saru | さる | "a certain" |
| kano | かの | "that" | | (more literary than *aru*) | |
| (more literary than *ano*) | | | taishita | たいした | "great" |
| kakaru | かかる | "this kind of" | tonda | とんだ | "outrageous" |
| | | "such" | | | "awful" |
| (more literary than *konna*) | | | | | |

Such words as *ōkina* 大きな "large," *chiisana* 小さな "small," *oka-shina* おかしな "funny," are also considered non-conjugative adjectives. They cannot be classified as copular nouns (pp. 152–53), even though they end with *na,* because *ōki, chiisa,* and *okashi* without *na* can neither be used as noun forms nor be followed by the copula *da (desu).*

# PARTICLES　助詞＜じょし＞

Japanese particles are non-conjugative words which attach to words, phrases, or clauses, and indicate the relationship of the preceding word(s) to the following word or to the rest of the sentence.

Some Japanese particles have functions similar to English equivalents.

e.g.　Yamada-san *no* bōshi　山田さんの帽子　"Mr. Yamada's hat."
*no* (possessive) is similar to English " 's."

Tanaka-san *to* Shimizu-san　田中さんと清水さん　"Mr. Tanaka *and* Mr. Shimizu." *to* (conjunction), "and," connects two nouns.

Other Japanese particles have functions similar to English prepositions, but differ in that the Japanese particles are post-positional, rather than pre-positional.

e.g.　Tokyo *e* ikimasu.　東京へ行きます.　"I go *to* Tokyo."
*e* (motion towards), "to," indicates the direction of a motion.
Tokyo *kara* kimashita.　東京から来ました.　"I came *from* Tokyo." *kara* (motion away from), "from."

Still others have a peculiar usage which is not found in English. These particles indicate the relationship between the preceding word(s) and the rest of the sentence.

e.g.　Watakushi *wa* gakusei desu.　私は学生です.　"I am a student."
*wa* (topical) indicates that the preceding word is the topic of the sentence.
Eiga *o* mimashita.　映画を見ました.　"I saw a movie."
*o* (accusatival) indicates that the preceding word is the direct object of the verb.

Most of the particles, however, are multi-functional. This section is intended to assist readers in becoming familiar with as many of these functions as possible, and also for use as a reference manual in reading.

In the following pages, corresponding English translations are suggested in the parentheses, while brief explanations, whenever needed, are given without parentheses. Also, the following abbreviations are used:

V*nai*—*nai*-form of the verb
V₂—2nd base of the verb
V₃—3rd base of the verb
V*ba*—*ba*-conditional of the verb
V*tentative*—tentative of the verb
V*ta*—*ta*-form of the verb
V*te*—*te*-form of the verb
Adj.—adjective
Cop. n.—copular noun

## ALPHABETICAL LIST OF PARTICLES AND THEIR FUNCTIONS

BAKARI ばかり　(*bakkari, bakashi,* and *bakkashi,* are more colloquial forms)

I. (only; merely; just)=*dake*

Noun+*bakari*　Jibun no *koto bakari* kangaete imasu.　自分の ことばかり考えています.　"He is thinking only about himself."

Verb+*bakari*

(V₃+*bakari*)　Benkyō *suru bakari* de hoka wa nani mo shimasen.　勉強するばかりで他は何もしません. "He only studies, and does nothing else."

(V*ta*+*bakari*)　*Kangaeta bakari* de mo zotto shimasu.　考 えたばかりでもぞっとします.　"I shudder at the mere thought of it."

Adj.+*bakari*　*Takai bakari* de yoku arimasen.　高いばかりで よくありません. "It's just expensive, not good."

Cop. n.+*na*+*bakari*　*Kirei na bakari* de yaku ni tachimasen. きれい(綺麗)なばかりで役に立ちません. "It's just pretty, not useful."

II. (always)

Noun+*bakari*　*Byōki bakari* shite imasu.　病気ばかりしてい ます. "He is always ill."

Verb+*bakari*

(V*te*+*bakari*)　*Byōki shite bakari* imasu.　病気してばかりい ます. "He is always ill."

(V₃+*to bakari omou*)　Kekkon *suru to bakari* omotte ima- shita.　結婚するとばかり思っていました.　"I always thought they were going to marry."

(V*ta*+*to bakari omou*)　Shinda *to bakari omotte* imashita.

死んだとばかり思っていました．　"I always thought he had died."

Adj.+*to bakari omou*　Ano uchi wa motto ōkii *to bakari omotte* imashita.　あの家はもっと大きいとばかり思っていました．　"I always thought that house was bigger."

III.　(about; approximately)

Number+*bakari Sanjū-nen bakari* mae ni Nihon ni ikimashita.　三十年ばかり前に日本に行きました．　"I went to Japan about thirty years ago."

*Gojū-en bakari* haraimashita.　五十円ばかり払いました．　"I paid about fifty yen."

IV.　(with only this little bit of...)—little sum, little quantity

*Kore*-type word+*bakari　Kore bakari* no okane de wa nani mo kaemasen.　こればかりのお金では何も買えません．　"With only this little bit of money, we can't buy anything."

*Sore bakari* de wa kodomo no yōfuku mo tsukuremasen.　そればかりでは子供の洋服も作れません．　"With only that little bit of material, we can hardly even make a dress for a child."

V.　(to the extent that...; virtually; practically; almost)=*kurai*

V₃+*bakari　Naku bakari* ni tanomimashita ga, kiite kuremasen deshita.　泣くばかりに頼みましたが，聞いてくれませんでした．　"She practically cried asking it of him, but he did not listen to her."

Kanashikute mune ga *sakeru bakari* deshita.　悲しくて胸が裂けるばかりでした．　"I was so sad, that my heart almost burst."

VI.　(be about to...)=*tokoro* (see p. 52 for the difference)

V₃+*bakari　Mō* hikkoshi *suru bakari* da kara uchi no naka ni wa nani mo arimasen.　もう引越しするばかりだから家の中には何もありません．　"Since we are about to move, there is nothing in the house."

VII.　(have just done)—action just completed=*tokoro*

V*ₜₐ*+*bakari　Ima* gohan o *tabeta bakari* desu.　今ごはん（御飯）を食べたばかりです．　"I have just eaten dinner."

VIII.　(just because...)

Verb+*bakari ni*

(V₃+*bakari ni*) Ano hito wa okane ga *aru bakari ni* itsu

mo hito ni damasaremasu.  あの人はお金があるばかりに
いつ(何時)も人にだまされます.  "Just because he has
money, he is always cheated by people."

(V*ta*+*bakari ni*)  Ip-pun *osokatta bakari ni* aemasen deshita.
一分遅かったばかりに会えませんでした.  "Just because I
was one minute late, I couldn't see him."

Adj.+*bakari ni*  Uchi ga *ōkii bakari ni* itsu mo okyaku ga
takusan arimasu.  家が大きいばかりにいつもお客が沢山あ
ります.  "Just because their house is big, they always
have many guests."

Cop. n.+*na*+*bakari ni*  *Binbō na bakari ni* itsu mo kurō
shimasu.  貧乏なばかりにいつも苦労します.  "Just be-
cause she is poor, she always has trouble."

IX.  (on the point of ...; just short of ...)
V*n**+*bakari ni*  *Nakan bakari ni* yorokonda.  泣かんばかりに
喜んだ.  "She was so happy that she was on the verge
of crying."

X.  (thinking that it is the best time to ...)—best chance
Noun+*to bakari* (*omotte* "thinking" is omitted after *bakari*)
Kono *toki to bakari* kanojo ni hanashikaketa.  この時
とばかり彼女に話しかけた.  "Thinking that this is the
time (the chance I had been waiting a long time for
had finally come), I talked to her."

Noun+*ka to bakari* (*omotte* is omitted after *bakari*)
*Ima ka to bakari* machikamaeta.  今かとばかり待ちかまえ
た.  "I waited, thinking that the chance would come
up at any minute."

XI.  (thinking that it was only ...)
Noun+*ka to bakari*  (*omotte* is omitted after *bakari*)
*Yume ka to bakari* yorokonda.  夢かとばかり喜んだ.
"Having thought that it was only a dream, I rejoiced
to find it was real."

XII.  (not only, but also ...)=*dake*
Verb+*bakari de wa naku*, ...*mo*
(V₃+*bakari de wa naku*, ...*mo*) Gakkō e itte *iru bakari
de wa naku*, nijū-jikan *mo* hataraite imasu.  学校へ

---

* *n* is a short form of *nai*. The effect of this expression is very similar
to the positive verb form, V₃+*bakari*, see BAKARI, V, p. 95.

行っているばかりではなく二十時間も働いています． "He not only goes to school, but also works as many as twenty hours."

(V*ₜₐ*+*bakari de wa naku, ... mo*) Nihon e *itta bakari de wa naku* Chūgoku e *mo* ikimashita． 日本へ行ったばかりではなく中国へも行きました． "He not only went to Japan, but also went to China."

## DAKE だけ（丈）

I.  (only)

Noun+*dake*

a.  *dake* in this usage is preceded by a noun and followed by both positive and negative verbs (cf. *shika*, pp. 132-33, *dake shika*, pp. 98-99).

b.  *dake* usually replaces *o, ga, wa*, except for special emphasis, in which case *dake* is used with them (See the following examples).

c.  *dake* never occurs with the particle *mo*.

d.  *dake* appears with other particles such as *ni, de, no, e, made, kara, to*, etc.

e.  *dake* either precedes or follows the other particles, except emphatic *o, ga, wa*, which *dake* always precedes.

e.g.  Yamamoto-san $\begin{Bmatrix} ni\ dake \\ dake\ ni \end{Bmatrix}$ misemashita． 山本さん $\begin{Bmatrix} にだけ \\ だけに \end{Bmatrix}$ 見せました． "I showed it only to Mr. Yamamoto."

Tokyo $\begin{Bmatrix} de\ dake \\ dake\ de \end{Bmatrix}$ mimashita． 東京 $\begin{Bmatrix} でだけ \\ だけで \end{Bmatrix}$ 見ました． "I saw it only in Tokyo."

Tanaka-san $\begin{Bmatrix} to\ dake \\ dake\ to \end{Bmatrix}$ hanashimashita． 田中さん $\begin{Bmatrix} とだけ \\ だけと \end{Bmatrix}$ 話しました． "I talked only to Mr. Tanaka."

Yamada-san *dake* [*ga*] kimashita． 山田さんだけ[が]来ました． "Only Mr. Yamada came."

Okashi *dake* [*o*] kaimashita． お菓子だけ[を]買いました． "I bought only a cake."

Sore *dake* [*wa*] kirai desu． それだけ[は]嫌いです．

"I dislike only that (... but I don't dislike other things).

II.  (as much as; as many as)

$V_3+dake$  *Moteru dake* motte itte kudasai.  持てるだけ持って行って下さい.  "Please take as many as you can carry."

$V_{tai}+dake$  *Tsukaitai\* dake* tsukaimashita.  使いたいだけ使いました.  "I used as much as I wanted to use."

III.  (just; only)=*bakari*

Verb+*dake*

($V_3$+dake)  *Taberu dake* de shigoto wa shimasen.  食べるだけで仕事はしません.  "He only eats, and doesn't work."

($V_{ta}$+*dake*)  Okane o *karita dake* de orei mo iwazu ni kaerimashita.  お金を借りただけでお礼も言わずに帰りました.  "He (just) borrowed the money and went home without even saying 'Thank you.'"

Adj.+*dake*  *Takai dake* de yoku arimasen.  高いだけでよくありません.  "It's just expensive, not good."

IV.  (the more ... the more)=*hodo*

$V_{ba}$  $V_3$+*dake*  (repetition of the same verb)  *Tabereba taberu dake* suki ni narimasu.  食べれば食べるだけ好きになります.  "The more I eat, the more I get to like it."

Nihongo wa benkyō *sureba suru dake* omoshiroku narimasu.  日本語は勉強すればするだけ面白くなります.  "The more I study Japanese, the more interesting it becomes."

## DAKE SHIKA  だけしか

(only; nothing but)

Noun+*dake shika*+negative verb

　　a.  *dake shika* is the same as *shika*, but more emphatic.

　　b.  *dake shika* is only followed by negative verbs.

　　c.  *dake shika* always replaces particles *o, ga, wa*.

---

\* When the final verb is in the perfective form ($V_{ta}$), the first part can be in the perfective form also, but it is more common to use the present-form ($V_3$).

**e.g.**  *Tsukaitai dake* tsukaimashita.  使いたいだけ使いました.  is more common than *Tsukaitakatta dake* tsukaimashita.  使いたかっただけ使いました.

**d.** *dake shika* appears with all the other particles, such as *ni, de, no, e, made, kara, to,* etc.

**f.** *dake shika* follows the above particles, or sometimes these particles can be placed between *dake* and *shika*.

    **e.g.** Ocha *dake shika* nomimasen. お茶だけしか飲みません. "He drinks nothing else but tea."

    Yamamoto-san $\begin{Bmatrix} ni\ dake\ shika \\ dake\ ni\ shika \end{Bmatrix}$ tegami o kaki-masen deshita. 山本さん $\begin{Bmatrix} にだけしか \\ だけにしか \end{Bmatrix}$ 手紙を書きませんでした. "I wrote a letter only to Mr. Yamamoto."

    Tokyo $\begin{Bmatrix} e\ dake\ shika \\ dake\ e\ shika \end{Bmatrix}$ ikimasen deshita. 東京 $\begin{Bmatrix} へだけ \\ だけしか \\ へしか \end{Bmatrix}$ 行きませんでした. "I went only to Tokyo."

Verb + *dake shika* + negative verb

(V₃ + *dake shika* + negative v.) Ano kodomo wa *taberu dake shika* nō ga *nai.* あの子供は食べるだけしか能がない. "That child has no other talent but eating."

(Vₜₐ + *dake shika* + negative v.) *Tsukatta dake shika* kaeshimasen deshita. 使っただけしか返しませんでした. "I returned only what I used."

## DANO だの

(and; or; and the like; and so forth; and what not)—often used in pairs.

Noun + *dano* + Noun + *dano*  Ano uchi ni wa *inu dano neko dano* ga imasu. あの家には犬だの猫だのがいます. "There are dogs, cats and more in that house."

*Ā*-type word + *dano* + kō-type word + *dano*  *Ā dano kō dano* to hontō ni urusai hito desu ne. ああだのこうだのと本当にうるさい人ですね. "He is always saying this and that, and is such a nuisance, isn't he?"

Verb + *dano* + Verb + *dano*

(V₃ + *dano* + V₃ + *dano*) Kore o *suru dano* are o *suru dano* to iinagara shimasen. これをするだのあれをするだのと言いながらしません. "Although he says he will do this and he will do that, he does not do it."

($V_{ta}+dano+V_{ta}+dano$) Asoko e *itta dano* koko e *itta dano* to itsu mo ibatte imasu. あそこへ行っただのここへ行っただのといつ(何時)もいばっています。 "He is always bragging that he has gone here and there."

Adj.+*dano*+Adj.+*dano*

($Adj_3+dano+Adj_3+dano$) Are mo *hoshii dano* kore mo *hoshii dano* to itte hontō ni yokubari desu. あれも欲しいだのこれも欲しいだのと言って本当に慾ばりです。 "He says he wants this and wants that, and is truly greedy."

($Adj_{ta}+dano+Adj_{ta}+dano$) Ā sureba *yokatta dano* kō sureba *yokatta dano* itsu mo kōkai bakari shite imasu. ああすればよかっただの こうすればよかっただの いつも後悔ばかりしています。 "She is always regretting that she did not do this or she did not do that."

## DE で

Some *de* are particles, while others are the second base as well as the *te*-form of the copula *da* (See p. 15). *De* as a particle has the meaning, "in the state of ..." With this meaning in mind, perhaps we can analyze some sentences as follows:

*Kore wa hon desu.* これは本です。 "This is a book."

   *desu*—short form of *de arimasu*

   Then: "This exists in the state of a book."

   Thus: "This is a book."

*Dōzo ogenki de (ite kudasai).* どうぞお(御)元気で. (*ite kudasai* is often omitted)

      "Please exist in the state of good health."

   Then: "Please stay in good health."

As shown below, one should choose an appropriate English equivalent in each case.

I.   Noun+*de* (occasionally Noun+other particle+*de*)

   1.  (by means of)—instrumental

      *Enpitsu de* kakimashita. 鉛筆で書きました。 "I wrote with a pencil."

      *Kami dake de* tsukurimasu. 紙だけで作ります。 "We make it only with paper."

      *Eigo de* hanashimasu. 英語で話します。 "We speak in English."

*Fune de* ikimasu. 船で行きます. "We go by boat."

*Rajio de* kikimashita. ラジオで聞きました. "We heard it on the radio."

2. (according to; by)

*Jikan de* haraimasu. 時間で払います. "We pay you by the hour."

3. (in exchange for; for)

*Sanbyaku-en de* kaimashita. 三百円で買いました. "We bought it for three hundred yen."

4. (at; in)

   a. location of action (cf. *ni*, location of existence)

     Kyō *toshokan de* benkyō shimashita. 今日図書館で勉強しました. "I studied at the library today."

     Kodomo ga *niwa de* asonde imasu. 子供が庭で遊んでいます. "Children are playing in the yard."

   b. time consumed for a certain action

     *Ichi-jikan* de ikemasu. 一時間で行けます. "We can get there in an hour."

     *Ikka-getsu de* dekimasu. 一ケ月で出来ます. "I can do it in a month."

5. (among; between; within; in)—limiting the condition

*Sekai de* ichiban ōkii desu. 世界で一番大きいです. "It is the biggest in the world."

Kyō *hitori de* ikimasu. 今日一人で行きます. "I will go alone today."

*San-nin de* kore o shimashita. 三人でこれをしました. "The three of us did this."

Kore to *sore* (*to*) *de* dochira ga suki desu ka? これとそれでどちらが好きですか. "Which do you like better, this or that?"

6. (at the age of)

*Nijus-sai de* shinimashita. 二十才で死にました. "He died at the age of twenty."

7. (with)

Ano hito wa *hadashi de* gakkō ni kimasu. あの人ははだしで学校に来ます. "He comes to school barefoot."

II. (so)

Beginning of a sentence: *De* dōshita n' desu ka? でどう

したんですか. "So, what did you do?"

DE may be considered either as the second base of the copula or as a particle.

(because)—causal

*Byōki* de nete imashita. 病気で寝ていました. "Because I was ill, I was in bed," or "I was ill, and was in bed."

Kono uchi wa *kirei de* hontō ni ii desu ne. この家はきれい(綺麗)で本当にいいですね. "This house is pretty, and it is very nice, isn't it?" or "Because this house is pretty, it is very nice, isn't it?"

Note: *de* meaning "because" is used only when the resultant clause is an objective statement. If one's will is implied, use *kara*.

e.g. Kono uchi wa *kirei de* ii desu ne. この家はきれいでいいですね. "Because this house is pretty, it is nice, isn't it?"
Kono uchi wa *ōkisugiru kara* kaimasen. この家は大きすぎるから買いません. "Because this house is too big, we are not going to buy it."

Kore de ii desu ka? これでいいですか "Is this OK?"

## DEMO でも

(...or something)

Noun+(particle)+*demo*

a. *demo* replaces the particles *o, ga, wa*.

b. *demo* appears with such particles as *ni, de, no, e, made, kara, to*, etc.

c. *demo* follows the above particles.

*Ocha demo* ip-pai ikaga desu ka? お茶でも一杯いかが(如何)ですか. "How would you like to have a cup of tea or something?"

*Inu ni demo* yarimashō. 犬にでもやりましょう. "Let's give it to the dogs or something."

$V_2$ *demo suru to* (*shitara*) Otto ni *shinare demo shitara* hontō ni taihen desu. 夫に死なれでもしたら本当に大変です. "It would be really awful if my husband should die or something like that."

## DO(MO) ど

(but, though, and yet)

Verb+*do*  Utedo(*mo*) tatakedo(*mo*) zenzen henji ga nakatta.

打てどたたけど全然返事がなかった．　"He knocked and knocked, but no one answered."

**E　へ**

(to)—motion towards

Noun+*e*　Watakushi wa *Nihon e* ikimasu. 私は日本へ行きます．"I'll go to Japan."

Kore wa *chichi e* no tegami desu. これは父への手紙です．"This is a letter to my father."

Note: *e* is often interchangeable with *ni*.

e.g.　Nihon $\begin{Bmatrix} e \\ ni \end{Bmatrix}$ ikimasu. 日本$\begin{Bmatrix} へ \\ に \end{Bmatrix}$行きます．　"I'll go to Japan."

(Strictly speaking, however, *ni* emphasizes arrival, while *e* emphasizes action of going.)

|  | Correct | Incorrect |
|---|---|---|
| e.g. | chichi *e* no tegami | chichi *ni* no tegami |
|  | 父への手紙 | 父にの手紙 |

"the letter to my father"

Note: *ni*+*no* is never possible.

**GA　が**

**I.** The word which precedes *ga* is the subject of the sentence (cf. *wa*)

Noun+*ga*

**1.** When the subject is emphasized in a sentence (or clause)

*Kono kata ga* Tanaka-san desu. この方が田中さんです．
"*This* is Mr. Tanaka (whom I told you about)."

Compare with:

*Kono kata wa* Tanaka-san desu. この方は田中さんです．
"This is Mr. Tanaka." (no implication)

*Watakushi ga* kakimashita. 私が書きました．"*I* wrote it."

**2.** When no contrast is involved.

Koko ni hon *ga* arimasu. ここに本があります．　"There is a book here." (no implication)

Compare with:

Koko ni *hon wa* arimasu ここに本はあります．"There is a book here (...but there is perhaps no notebook, or pencil, etc.)."

Soko ni Yamada-san *ga* imasu. そこに山田さんがいます．

"Mr. Yamada is there."　(no implication)

Soko ni Yamada-san *wa* imasu.　そこに山田さんはいます.
"Mr. Yamada is there (...but perhaps Mr. Shimizu is
not there)."

Note: In a positive sentence in which no contrasting element is involved, *ga* usually precedes the verbs *aru* and *iru*, instead of
*wa*.

3.　When an interrogative pronoun is the subject of the
sentence, it is always followed by *ga*, never by *wa*.
*Dare ga* kore o kakimashita ka.　誰がこれを書きました
か. "Who wrote this?"
*Dore ga* Yamamoto-san desu ka.　どれが山本さんですか.
"Which one is Mr. Yamamoto?"

4.　The subject of a relative clause takes *ga* (or *no*); it never
takes *wa*.
Watakushi *ga* (or *no*) kyonen katta jidōsha wa Toyota
desu.　私が去年買った自動車はトヨタです.　"The car
which I bought last year is a Toyota."
Anata *ga* (or *no*) yonda hon wa dare ga kakimashita ka.
あなたが読んだ本は誰が書きましたか.　"Who wrote the
book which you read (As for the book which you read,
who wrote it)?"

5.　The subject of a subordinate clause normally takes *ga*,
provided the subjects of the subordinate and principal
clauses are different.
Watakushi *ga* itta toki, ano hito wa mada nete imashita.
私が行った時あの人はまだ寝ていました.　"When I went
there, he was still asleep."

But:

Watakushi *wa* Nihon e iku toki, itsu mo hikōki de ikimasu. 私は日本へ行く時いつ(何時)も飛行機で行きます.
"When I go to Japan, I always go by airplane."

6.　The subject of a conditional clause normally takes *ga*,
provided the subjects of the subordinate and principal
clauses are different.
Anata *ga* byōki ni nattara, watakushi wa omimai ni
ikimasu.　あなたが病気になったら，私はお見舞に行きま

す。"If you become ill, I'll come and visit you."

　　　But:

Watakushi *wa* byōki ni nattara uchi ni imasu. 私は病
気になったら家にいます。"If I become sick, I'll stay
home (As for me, if I become sick, I'll stay home)."

　　　Or:

Byōki ni nattara, watakushi wa uchi ni imasu. 病気に
なったら，私は家にいます。"If I become sick, I'll stay
home."

Byōki ni nattara, uchi ni imasu. 病気になったら家にい
ます。"If I become sick, I'll stay home."

Note: The last sentence omits the subject completely. As long as
the subject is clear to both the speaker and the listener, this
type of sentence is most common among native speakers.

## II.　Conjunction

### 1.　(but)—adversative

Verb + *ga*

($V_3$ + *ga*) Toda-san wa koko ni *imasu ga*, Niki-san wa
imasen. 戸田さんはここにいますが，仁木さんはいませ
ん。"Miss Toda is here, but Miss Niki is not here."

($V_{ta}$ + *ga*) Watakushi wa *ikimashita ga*, Takahashi-san
wa ikimasen deshita. 私は行きましたが，高橋さんは
行きませんでした。"I went, but Mr. Takahashi did
not go."

Adj. + *ga*

(Adj$_3$ + ga) Kyō wa *isogahii* [*desu*] *ga*, ashita wa hima
desu. 今日は忙しいが，明日は暇です。 "I am busy
today, but I will be free tomorrow."

(Adj$_{ta}$ + ga) Ano uchi wa mae wa *shirokatta ga*, ima
wa aoi. あの家は前は白かったが，今は青い。 "That
house was white before, but it is blue now."

Note: Often the clause after *ga* is omitted.

　　e.g.　Watakushi mo ashita ikitai to omotte imasu ga...
　　　　　私も明日行きたいと思っていますが... "I too want to
　　　　　go tomorrow, but (...I don't know if I can)."

### 2.　(and)—no adversative implication

Verb + *ga*

($V_3$ + *ga*) Watakushi mo yoku *ikimasu ga*, ii tokoro

desu. 私もよく行きますが，いい所です. "I too go there often, and it is a nice place."

($V_{ta}+ga$) Watakushi mo yonde *mimashita ga*, totemo omoshiroi hon deshita. 私も読んでみ(見)ましたが，とても面白い本でした. "I read it too, and it was a very interesting book."

III. (whether ... or not ...)—*ga* after $V_{tentative}$ is interchangeable with *to*

$V_{tentative}$ *ga* ... $V_{tentative}$ *ga* ...(contrasting idea)
*Katō ga makeyō ga* kamawanai kara tomokaku ganbari-mashō. 勝とうが負けようが構わないからともかく頑張りましょう. "It doesn't matter if we win or lose. Let's do our best."

$Adj_{tentative}$ *ga* ... $Adj_{tentative}$ *ga* ... *Takakarō ga yasukarō ga* kau tsumori desu. 高かろうが安かろうが買うつもりです. "Whether it's expensive or inexpensive, I intend to buy it."

$V_{tentative}$ *ga* ... *mai ga* ... Ano hito ga *ikō ga ikumai ga* watakushi wa ikimasen. あの人が行こうが行くまいが私は行きません. "Whether he goes or not, I am not going."

Some verbs, adjectives, and copular nouns normally take the particle *ga* instead of *o* for a direct object marker, except those involving contrasting elements in which case *wa* replaces *ga*.

1. like, dislike
   Watakushi wa kore *ga suki* desu. 私はこれが好きです. "I like this (This is likeable to me)."

   Compare with:
   Watakushi wa kore *wa* suki desu. 私はこれは好きです. "I like this (...but I don't like that, etc.)."
   Watakushi wa kore *ga kirai* desu. 私はこれが嫌いです. "I dislike this (This is dislikeable to me)."

2. necessity
   Watakushi wa yoi jibiki *ga irimasu*. 私はよい字引がい(要)ります. "I need a good dictionary." cf. Watakushi wa yoi jibiki *wa* irimasu. 私はよい字引はいります. "I need a good dictionary (...but I don't need a bad one, etc.)."

Gaikokugo o yomu toki, jibiki *ga* hitsuyō desu. 外国語を読む時，字引が必要です. "When we read a foreign language, a dictionary is necessary."

3. potential

Nihongo *ga hanasemasu*. 日本語が話せます. "I can speak Japanese." cf. Nihongo *wa* hanasemasu. 日本語は話せます. "I speak Japanese (... but no other language, etc.)."

Nihongo *ga* wakarimasu. 日本語がわか(分)ります. "I understand Japanese."

> Note: *wakaru* 分る means "[something] is divisible," that is, "[something] is clear," hence one "understands [something]." Sometimes it can also be translated as "to know." cf. *shiru*, which means "to know a fact" or "to get acquainted with."
>
> e.g. Ashita iku ka dō ka mada *wakarimasen*. 明日行くかどうかまだわかりません. "I don't know (It is not clear to me) yet, if *I* will go tomorrow or not."
>
> Ashita iku ka dō ka *shirimasen*. 明日行くかどうか知りません. "I don't know (for a fact) if *he* will go tomorrow or not."
>
> Ano hito ga *wakarimasen*. あの人がわかりません. "I don't understand him; I have no understanding of him."
>
> cf. Ano hito o *shirimasen*. あの人を知りません. "I don't know him; I am not acquainted with him."

4. desiderative

Nihonshoku *ga tabetai* desu. 日本食が食べたいです. "I want to eat Japanese food." cf. Nihonshoku *wa* tabetai desu. 日本食は食べたいです. "I want to eat Japanese food (... but not Italian food, etc.)."

Motto okane *ga hoshii* desu. もっとお金が欲しいです. "I want more money." cf. Motto okane *wa* hoshii desu. もっとお金は欲しいです. "I want more money (... but I don't want any trouble which comes with money, etc.)."

> But: before *-tagaru* (the 3rd person desiderative), leave the particle *o*. Ano hito wa Nihon no kamera *o* kaitagatte imasu. あの人は日本のカメラを買いたがっています. "He wants to buy a Japanese camera."

5. fear

Obake *ga kowai* desu. お化けが怖いです. "I am afraid of monsters." cf. Obake *wa* kowai desu お化けは怖いです.

"I am afraid of monsters (...but I am not afraid of anything else, etc.)."

6.  envy

Ano hito *ga urayamashii* desu.  あの人が羨ましいです.  "I envy him."

But: Minna ga ano hito *o* urayamashigatte imasu.  皆があの人を羨ましがっています.  "Everyone is envious of him."

GIRI  ぎり  (see *kiri*)

GURAI ぐらい (see *kurai*)

HODO ほど(程)

I.  (to the extent of..., to the degree of...)—comparative

1.  Noun+*hodo*+positive verb (as...as)—This form is not used as often as Noun+*hodo*+negative verb (see 2, below).

Yamaguchi-san wa *Takada-san hodo takai* desu.  山口さんは高田さんほど高いです.  "Mr. Yamaguchi is as tall as Mr. Takada."

2.  Noun+*hodo*+negative verb (not so...as)

Kotoshi wa *kyonen hodo* samuku arimasen.  今年は去年ほど寒くありません.  "This year is not so cold as last year."

Noun+*hodo*+negative verb  (nothing is more...than)—This *hodo* is interchangeable with *kurai*.

*Nihongo hodo* muzukashii mono wa *arimasen*.  日本語ほど難しいものはありません.  "Nothing is more difficult than Japanese."

Verb+*hodo*+negative verb

Nihongo o hanasu no wa *yomu (no) hodo* muzukashiku nai desu.  日本語を話すのは読むほど難しくないです.  "To speak Japanese is not as difficult as to read it."

3.  Verb+*hodo da* (so...that)

Ano hito wa atama ga yokute mittsu no toki ni mō hon ga *yometa hodo* desu.  あの人は頭がよくて三つの時にもう本が読めたほどです.  "He is so bright that he could read a book when he was three (He is bright to the extent he could read a book when he was three)."

$V_{nai}+hodo$ (so...that...negative)

Ichi-gyō mo *yomenai hodo* nemui desu. 一行も読めな
いほど眠いです. "I am so sleepy that I can hardly
read a line."

II. (about)=*kurai*=*bakari*

Number+*hodo* Mada *mittsu hodo* nokotte imasu. まだ三
つほどのこっています. "There are still about three
left."

*Go-nin hodo* kite imashita. 五人ほど来ていました.
"About five people were there."

III. (the more...the more)=*dake*

$V_{ba}+V_3+hodo$ *Yomeba yomu hodo* omoshiroku narimasu.
読めば読むほど面白くなります. "The more I read, the
more interesting it becomes."

Nihongo o *hanaseba hanasu hodo* jōzu ni narimasu. 日
本語を話せば話すほど上手になります. "The more you
speak Japanese, the better you become."

# KA か

I. Sign of interrogative

    a. always placed at the end of the sentence.

    b. never placed after the copula *da*.

Verb+*ka* Ashita gakkō ni *ikimasu ka*. 明日学校に行きま
すか "Are you going to school tomorrow?"

Ashita *iku ka*. 明日行くか. "Are you going?" (not as
polite as the above; women should not use this
form)

Ano hito wa gakusei *desu ka*. あの人は学生ですか.
(never: Ano hito wa gakusei <u>*da*</u> ka.) "Is he a student?"

Ano hito wa gakusei *deshita ka*. あの人は学生でしたか.
"Was he a student?" Ano hito wa gakusei *datta ka*.
—permissable, but not as polite as the above.

II. Rhetorical question—emphatic, always at the end of a sentence.

$V_3+ka$ Sonna koto ga dekimasu ka. そんな事ができ(出来)
ますか. "I can't possibly do such a thing, can I?"

III. Uncertainty

$V_{tentative}+ka$ Sō *deshō ka*. そうでしょうか. "I wonder if

that's so." Iku *darō ka.* 行くだろうか. "I wonder if he is going."

Noun+*ka*  Byōki datta *no* [darō] *ka* yasete miemashita. 病気だったのか痩せて見えました. "I wonder if she has been sick; she looked skinny."

Verb+*ka*+*wakaranai* (*shiranai*)

(V₃+*ka*+*wakaranai*)—for the 1st person

Itsu kekkon *suru ka wakarimasen.* いつ(何時)結婚するかわか(分)りません. "I don't know when *I* am getting married."

(V₃+*ka*+*shiranai*)—for other than the 1st person

Kyonen doko ni *ita ka shirimasen.* 去年どこ(何処)にいたか知りません. "I don't know where *he* was last year."

IV.  (or)

    V₃+ka ... V₃+ka

    Anata ga iku n' *desu ka,* [soretomo] anata no oniisan ga iku n' *desu ka.* あなたが行くんですか, あなたのお兄さんが行くんですか. "Are you going, or is your brother going?"

V.  (either ... or)

    Noun+*ka*+Noun  Are wa *Shimizu-san ka Yamamoto-san* desu. あれは清水さんか山本さんです. "That is either Mr. Shimizu or Mr. Yamamoto."

    *Ani ka watakushi* ga ikimasu. 兄か私が行きます. "Either my older brother or I will go."

VI.  (whether ... or not)

    Noun+*ka dō ka*  Kare ga *gakusha ka dō ka* shirimasen. 彼が学者かどうか知りません. "I don't know whether he is a scholar or not."

    Noun+*ka*+Noun+*de nai ka*  Kare ga *gakusha ka gakusha de nai ka* shirimasen. 彼が学者か学者でないか知りません. "I don't know if he is a scholar or not."

    Kare ga *gakusha ka gakusha de nakatta ka* shirimasen. 彼が学者か学者でなかったか知りません. "I don't know if he was a scholar or not."

    Verb+*ka dō ka*

    (V₃+*ka dō ka*) *Iku ka dō ka* mada wakarimasen. 行くかどうかまだわか(分)りません. "I don't know whether we will go or not."

(V*ₜₐ*+*ka dō ka*)  *Itta ka dō ka* kiite kudasai.  行ったか
どうか聞いて下さい.   "Please ask him if he went or
not."

Verb+*ka* V*ₙₐᵢ ka*

(V₃+*ka* V*ₙₐᵢ ka*)  Ano eiga o *miru ka minai ka* kiite
mimashō.  あの映画を見るか見ないか聞いてみましょう.
"Let's ask him if he is going to see that movie or
not."

(V*ₜₐ*+*ka* V*ₙₐₖₐₜₜₐ ka*   Ano eiga o *mita ka minakatta ka*
kiite mimashita.   あの映画を見たか見なかったか聞いて
みました. "I asked him if he saw that movie or not."

VII.  (something to the effect)

Noun+*to ka*   Yamada-san *to ka* iu hito ga kimashita.  山
田さんとか言う人が来ました.  "A person called some-
thing like Mr. Yamada came."

Verb+*to ka kiku* (*iu*)

(V₃+*to ka kiku*)  Toda-san ga ashita *kuru to ka* kikimashita.   戸田さんが明日来るとか聞きました.   "I heard
something to the effect that Mr. Toda will come
tomorrow."

(V*ₜₐ*+*to ka kiku*)  Mō Nihon ni *itta to ka* kikimashita.
もう日本に行ったとか聞きました.   "I heard something
to the effect that he had gone to Japan already."

KA か  Colloquial form of *shika*

Go-nin *ka* konakatta.  五人か来なかった.  "Only five people came."

KARA から

I.  (from)

Noun+*kara*

1.  spatial    Watakushi wa *Nihon kara* kimashita.  私
は日本から来ました. "I came from Japan."

2.  temporal  *Kyō kara* koko de hatarakihajimemashita.
今日からここで働きはじめました.
"I started working here today."

II.  (after doing...)

V*ₜₑ*+*kara*  Gohan o *tabete kara* benkyō shimasu.  ごはん
(御飯)を食べてから勉強します.  "After eating

dinner, I am going to study."

III.  (since ..., because ...)

    Verb + *kara*

      ($V_3$ + *kara*)  Shigoto ga takusan *aru kara,* kyō wa iki-
      masen.  仕事が沢山あるから今日は行きません.  "Since
      I have lots of work to do, I won't go today."

      ($V_{ta}$ + *kara*)  Kinō ame ga *jutta kara,* ikimasen deshita.
      昨日雨が降ったから行きませんでした.          "Because it
      rained yesterday, I didn't go."

    Adj. + *kara*

      ($Adj_3$ + *kara*)  Kono uchi wa *ōkii kara* takai desu.  この
      家は大きいから高いです.    "Because this house is big,
      it is expensive."

      ($Adj_{ta}$ + *kara*)  Ano uchi wa *kitanakatta kara* kaimasen
      deshita.  あの家は汚かったから買いませんでした.
      "Because that house was dirty, we didn't buy it."

    $V_{nai}$ + *kara*

      ($V_{nai}$ + *kara*)  Nihongo ga *hanasenai kara* komarimasu.
      日本語が話せないから困ります.    "I am having trouble
      because I can't speak Japanese."

      ($V_{nakatta}$ + *kara*)  Kyonen *ikanakatta kara* kotoshi wa iki-
      masu.  去年行かなかったから今年は行きます.  "Because
      I didn't go last year, I'll go this year."

## KEREDO (MO)  けれど

    (but)—functions like the conjunction *ga,* but is more col-
loquial.

    Verb + *keredo(mo)*

      ($V_3$ + *keredo(mo)*)  Kyoto e wa *iku keredo* Osaka e wa
      ikimasen.  京都へは行くけれど大阪へは行きません.
      "I am going to Kyoto, but I won't go to Osaka."

      ($V_{ta}$ + *keredo(mo)*)  Yamada-san wa *kita keredo* Toda-san
      wa kimasen deshita.  山田さんは来たけれど戸田さんは
      来ませんでした.  "Mr. Yamada came, but Mr. Toda
      didn't come."

    Adj. + *keredo(mo)*

      ($Adj_3$ + *keredo*)  Kyō wa *samui keredo* ashita wa atata-
      kaku naru deshō.  今日は寒いけれど明日は暖くなるでし
      ょう.  "It is cold today, but perhaps tomorrow it will

become warm."

(Adj*ta*+*keredo*) Ano uchi wa *aokatta keredo* ima wa shiroi desu.　あの家は青かったけれど今は白いです.
"That house was blue, but now it is white."

## KIRI　きり

(only)

Number+*kiri* Ichinichi-jū *hitori kiri* de sugoshimashita.　一日中一人きりで過ごしました. "I spent the whole day all alone."

*Kore*-type word+*kiri*

1. quantity=*dake* Kore kiri desu. これきりです. "That's all."

2. time Sore kiri kimasen. それきり来ません. "He hasn't come since then."

## KOSO　こそ

I. emphatic

Noun+*koso* Anata koso ojōzu desu. あなたこそお上手です. "You are the one who is skillful."

Noun+particle+*koso* Tokyo ni koso sunde iru ga nani mo omoshiroi koto wa shimasen.　東京にこそ住んでいるが何も面白いことはしません. "I do live in Tokyo all right, but I do nothing particularly interesting."

II. (just because ...)

V*ba*+*koso* Okane ga *ireba koso* isshōkenmei hataraku n' desu.　お金がい(要)ればこそ一生懸命働くんです. "Just because I need money, I work hard."

## KURAI　くらい(位)　(*gurai* is more colloquial)

I. (to the extent that, so much so that, almost, even)—degree =*hodo*

Verb+*kurai*

(V₃+*kurai*) Onaka ga itaku *naru kurai* tabemashita.　お腹が痛くなるくらい食べました. "I ate so much that my stomach hurt (I ate to the extent that my stomach hurt)."

(V*ta*+*kurai*) Sonna hanashi mo *atta kurai* desu. そんな話もあったくらいです. "There was even such a story, too."

Adj₃+*kurai*   Mada jūgatsu na no ni mō *samui kurai* desu.
ま(未)だ十月なのにもう寒いくらいです. "Although it is
still October, it is almost cold."

*Nakitai kurai* deshita. 泣きたいくらいでした. "I felt like
crying." "I was on the verge of crying."

Noun+*kurai*   Ano hito kurai atama ga yokereba iikeredo
...あの人くらい頭がよければいいけれど... "It would be
nice if I were as bright as that person."

II.   (as much as, that much)

Noun+*kurai* [*wa*]   *Hiragana kurai* kakemasu. 平仮名く
らい書けます. "I can write as much as *hiragana* (...
but no more)."

*Kono*-type word+*kurai*   *Sono kurai* nara dekimasu. その
くらいならできます. "I can do that much."

*Kore*-type word+*kurai*   *Sore kurai* nara dekimasu. それ
くらいならできます. "I can do that much."

III.   (about)—approximate quantity, approximate number

Interrog. word+*kurai*   *Dono kurai* koko de matte imashita
ka.   どのくらいここで待っていましたか. "How long
have you been waiting here?"

*Dore kurai* benkyō shimashita ka. どれくらい勉強しまし
たか. "How long (How much) did you study?"

Number+*kurai*   *Mittsu kurai* tabemashita. 三つくらい食
べました. "I ate about three."

Mainichi *san-jikan kurai* benkyō shimasu. 毎日三時間く
らい勉強します. "I study about three hours a day."

# MADE まで

I.   (as far as)

Noun+*made*   Tokyo *made* ikimasu. 東京まで行きます.
"I will go as far as Tokyo."

*Sanjup-pēji made* yomimashita. 三十頁まで読みました.
"I read as far as Page 30."

II.   (until)

Noun of time+*made*   Ashita *made* koko ni imasu. 明日
までここにいます. "I will be here until tomorrow."

III.   (even)   a.   *made* is always followed by positive verbs (cf.
*sae*, which is used with both positive and nega-
tive verbs).

　　　b.　*made* in this usage replaces the particles *wa,
　　　　　ga, o.*
　　　c.　*made* generally follows other particles such as
　　　　　*ni, de, no, e, kara, to,* etc.
Noun+*made*　*Matsumoto-san made* kimashita.　松本さんま
　　　で来ました.　"Even Miss Matsumoto came."
Noun+particle+*made*　*Fujita-san ni made* misemashita.
　　　藤田さんにまで見せました.　"I even showed it to Mrs.
　　　Fujita."
*Inaka de made* utte imasu.　田舎でまで売っています.
　　　"They even sell it in the country."
V$_{te}$+*made*　Ano gakusei wa gakkō o *yasunde made* hon o
　　　yomimasu.　あの学生は学校を休んでまで本を読みます.
　　　"That student reads so much that he even skips
　　　school to do so."
Okane o *karite made* Nihon ni ikitai desu ka.　お金を
　　　借りてまで日本に行きたいですか.　"Do you want to go
　　　to Japan, even if you must borrow money?"

MO　も　a.　*mo* replaces the particles *wa, ga, o.*
　　　b.　*mo* is used with other particles such as *ni, de, no, e,
　　　　　made, kara, to,* etc.
　　　c.　when used with the above particles, *mo* follows
　　　　　these particles.

　I.　(also, too)
　　　Noun+*mo*　Anata *mo* mimashita ka.　あなたも見ましたか.
　　　"Did you see it, too?"

　II.　(as many as, as much as)
　　　Number+*mo*　Mittsu mo kaimashita.　三つも買いました.
　　　"I bought as many as three."
　　　Jū-nin mo kimashita.　十人も来ました.　"As many as ten
　　　people came."

　III.　(even)=*sae*
　　　Noun+*mo*+negative verb　*Aisatsu mo shinai* de itte
　　　shimaimashita.　あいさつ(挨拶)もしないで行ってしまい
　　　ました.　"He went away without even greeting me."

　IV.　(do not even do...)
　　　V$_2$+*mo shinai*—more emphatic than V$_{nai}$
　　　Byōki de mikka-kan gohan o *tabe mo shimasen.*　病気で

三日間ごはん（御飯）を食べもしません。 "He hasn't even eaten for three days because of his illness."

Watakushi no koto o *mi mo shimasen* deshita. 私の事を見もしませんでした。 "He didn't even look at me."

V. (both ... and)

Noun+*mo*+Noun+*mo*+positive verb *Hon mo zasshi mo koko ni arimasu.* 本も雑誌もここにあります。 "There are both books and magazines here."

V₂+*mo* [*shi*] V₂+*mo suru* Ano ko wa yoku *tabe mo nomi mo* shimasu. あの子はよく食べも飲みもします。 "That child both eats and drinks well."

VI. (neither... nor)

Noun+*mo*+Noun+*mo*+negative verb
*Hon mo zasshi mo* yomimasen. 本も雑誌も読みません。 "He reads neither books nor magazines."

V₂+*mo* [*sezu, shinai shi*] V₂+*mo shinai*
*Hataraki mo asobi mo shinai.* 働きも遊びもしない。 "He neither works nor plays."

VII. (whether ... or)

V*te*+*mo*+V*nakute*+*mo Itte mo ikanakute mo* ii desu. 行っても行かなくてもいいです。 "It is all right whether you go or not."

Adj*kute*+*mo*+Adj*nakute*+*mo*—If the second adjective is not a negative form, it is an adjective of contrast to the first.

*Yokute mo yokunakute mo* (*warukute mo*) kaimasu. 良くても良くなくても買います。 "Whether it's good or not good (bad), I'll buy it."

VIII. (even if)

V*te*+*mo* Kore o *tabete mo* ii desu ka. これを食べてもいいですか。 "Is it all right even if I eat this?" "May I eat this?"

Kyō *itte mo* ano hito wa uchi ni imasen yo. 今日行ってもあの人は家にいませんよ。 "Even if you go today, he won't be home."

IX. Double particles

Noun+particle+*mo Tokyo ni mo* ikimashita. 東京にも行きました。 "I went to Tokyo, too."

*Tanaka-san to mo* hanashimashita. 田中さんとも話しました. "I talked with Mrs. Tanaka, too."

## NA な
End of a sentence

1. (don't)—prohibition
   V₃+*na* (mostly used by men) *Okoru na!* 怒るな. "Don't get mad!"

2. (you know, you see, don't you think so?)
   Verb+*na* (mostly used by men)
   (V₃+*na*) Ano onna wa *kirei da na.* あの女はきれい (綺麗)だな. "That woman is pretty, isn't she?"
   (V*ₜₐ*+*na*) Yoku *yatta na.* よくやったな. "He did well, didn't he?"
   Adj.+*na*
   (Adj₃+*na*) Kono uchi wa *ōkii na.* この家は大きいな. "This house is big, isn't it?"
   (Adj*ₜₐ*+*na*) Tokyo wa *atsukatta na.* 東京は暑かったな. "Tokyo was hot, wasn't it?"

3. (I wonder)
   Verb+*ka na*
   (V₃+*ka na*) Ano hito wa *iku ka na.* あの人は行くかな. "I wonder if he would go."
   (V*ₜₐ*+*ka na*) Mō *kita ka na.* もう来たかな. "I wonder if he has come already."
   Interrog. word+*ka na* Are wa *dare ka na.* あれは誰かな. "I wonder who he is."
   *Kō*-type word+*ka na* Sō *ka na.* そうかな. "I wonder if it's so."

4. Imperative—vulgar speech only
   V₂+*na* Iki *na.* 行きな "Go!" Tabe *na.* 食べな "Eat!"

## NA な
This *na* is not a particle, but the attributive form of the copula *da*. It comes from the classical copula form *nari*.

Cop. n.+*na* (attributive phrase)
Ano hito wa *kirei na* hito desu. あの人はきれい(綺麗)な人です. "She is a pretty person."
Koko ni wa *suki na* hito ga takusan imasu. ここには好きな人

が沢山います. "There are many people whom I like here."
Foreign lang. adj.+*na*  (attributive phrase)
Ano *hansamu na* hito wa dare desu ka. あのハンサムな人は誰
ですか. "Who is that handsome man?"

## NĀ  なあ

I. Exclamation  (used by men)
  Verb+nā
    (V₃+nā)  Yoku ame ga *furu nā*.  よく雨が降るなあ.
    "How hard this rain pours!"
    (V*ₜₐ*+nā)  Yoku sonna koto ga *ieta nā*.  よくそんなこと
    が言えたなあ. "How could he have said such a thing!"
  Adj.+nā
    (Adj₃+nā)  *Kitanai nā*.  汚いなあ. "How dirty!"
    (Adj*ₜₐ*+nā)  Ano ko wa *kawaikatta nā*.  あの子は可愛い
    かったなあ. "How cute that child was!"

II. Wish
  V*ᵦₐ*+*ii nā*  Ano hito ga kyō kureba *ii nā*.  あの人が今日
  来ればいいなあ. "I wish he would come today."
  V₃+*to ii nā*  Ano hito ga kyō kuru to ii nā.  あの人が今
  日来るといいなあ. "I wish he would come today."

III. Informal salutation
  Beginning of a sentence (used by men)
    *Nā* kimi, sō darō.  なあ君, そうだろう. "Say you, isn't
    it so?"

## NADO  など

  (such things as, for example, and the like, something like)
  Noun+*nado*
    a. *nado* usually replaces *wa*, *ga*, *o*, except for emphasis.
    b. *nado* appears with other particles such as *ni*, *de*,
       *no*, *e*, *made*, *kara*, *to*, etc.
    c. *nado* precedes the above particles.

  Uchi de wa *inu nado* katte imasu. 家では犬など飼って
  います. "At our house we raise such animals as dogs."
  *Haha nado* sonna koto o itte imashita. 母などそんなこ
  とを言っていました. "Mother, for example, said such
  a thing."
  *Tokyo nado* e ikimashita. 東京などへ行きました.  "We

went to such places as Tokyo."

Watakushi wa *neko nado* [ga] suki desu.  私は猫など好きです.  "I like such things as cats."

Verb+*nado*

(V₃+*nado*)  Rainen Nihon ni *iku nado* to itte imashita. 来年日本に行くなどと言っていました.  "He said something to the effect that he was going to Japan next year."

(V*ta*+*nado*)  Kinō ichinichi-jū benkyō shita nado to itte imashita. 昨日一日中勉強したなどと言っていました. "He said something to the effect that he studied all day yesterday."

Adj.+*nado*

(Adj₃+*nado*)  Ikitakunai *nado* to iwanai de kudasai.  行きたくないなどと言わないで下さい.  "Please don't say such things as not wanting to go."

(Adj*ta*+*nado*)  *Tsumaranakatta nado* to itte imashita. つまらなかったなどと言っていました. "He said something to the effect that it was uninteresting."

## NAGARA  ながら

I. Simultaneous action of one subject

1.  (while)

V₂+*nagara*  Rajio o *kikinagara* benkyō shimasu. ラジオを聞きながら勉強します.  "While listening to the radio, he studies."

Note: If two different subjects are involved, the expression V₃+*aida* should be used.

e.g.  Kare ga hon o yonde *iru aida*, watakushi wa tegami o kakimashita. 彼が本を読んでいる間, 私は手紙を書きました. "While he was reading a book, I wrote a letter."

2.  (although)

V₂+*nagara*  Shitte *inagara* oshiete kuremasen. 知っていながら教えてくれません.  "Although he knows it, he won't tell me."

Note: If two different subjects are involved, the expression V₃ *no ni* should be used.

e.g.  Kare ga shitte *iru no ni*, kanojo wa shirimasen.

彼が知っているのに彼女は知りません. "Although
he knows it, she doesn't know it."

Noun+*nagara* *Jibun nagara* iya ni narimashita.
自分ながらいやになりました. "Although it is
about myself, I became fed up." "I hate
myself."

*Fuyu nagara*, koko wa minami na no de, tenki
sae yokereba atatakai. 冬ながらここは南なの
で天気さえよければ暖い.  "Although it is
winter, this place, because it is located in the
south, is warm when the weather is good."

II. (all)

Number+*nagara* Kodomo wa *go-nin nagara* mina deki ga
ii desu. 子供は五人ながら皆出来がいいです. "All five
children are doing well (academically)."

III. Before and now

Some nouns of time+*nagara* *Mukashi nagara* no oshaberi
desu. 昔ながらのおしゃべりです. "She is just as talkative as she was before."

V₂+*nagara* *Umare nagara* no geijutsuka desu. 生れなが
らの芸術家です. "He is a born artist."

## NARI なり

I. (whether...or, either...or)—*nari* can be used alone, but
more often it is used in duplication.

V₃+*nari*+V₃+*nari* *Iku nari yameru nari* hayaku okime-
nasai. 行くなりやめるなり早くお決めなさい. "Whether
you go or not, decide quickly."

Noun+*nari*+Noun+*nari*  *Matsuda-san nari Yamada-san
nari* ni kikinasai.  松田さんなり山田さんなりに聞きなさ
い. "Ask Miss Matsuda or Miss Yamada."

II. (as soon as)

V₃+*nari* Asa *okiru nari* uchi o demashita. 朝起きるなり
家を出ました. "As soon as I got up, I left home."

III. Conditions unchanged=*mama de*

V_{ta}+*nari de* Uchi o kitanaku *shita nari de* dete kimashita.
家を汚くしたなりで出て来ました. "I left home, leaving
it as dirty as it was.

**IV.** (no matter what [how, etc.])

Interrog. word+*nari to*　*Nan nari* to kaite misete kudasai. 何なりと書いて見せて下さい.　"Please write anything and show it to me." "No matter what it is, just write and show it to me."

## NE ね

I. (n'est-ce pas?)—seeks confirmation of the statement.

End of a sentence

Kyō wa ii otenki desu *ne.* 今日はいいお天気ですね. "It's a beautiful day today, isn't it?"

II. Shows speaker's familiarity to listener.

Between clauses or at end of sentence

Mō kaerō ne. もう帰ろうね. "Let's go home, OK?"

Koko wa *ne*, kō shiyō *ne.* ここはね, こうしようね. "Let's do (it) this way here, OK?"

## NI に

**I.** Noun+*ni*

1. (in, at)—location of existence (cf. *de*, location of action)

Shimizu-san wa ima heya no *naka ni* imasu. 清水さんは今部屋の中にいます. "Miss Shimizu is in the room now."

Matsumoto-san wa ima *Tokyo ni* sunde imasu. 松本さんは今東京に住んでいます.　"Mr. Matsumoto is living in Tokyo now."

2. Point of arrival

*Tokyo ni* tsukimashita. 東京に着きました. "We arrived in Tokyo."

3. (at)—designates time

*Ichi-ji ni* kimasu. 一時に来ます.　"He will come at one o'clock."

Note: When *goro* is used, either take *ni* out, or place *ni* after *goro*. e.g. Ichi-ji *goro* kimasu. 一時頃来ます. or Ichiji *goro ni* kimasu. 一時頃に来ます. "He will come around one o'clock."

4. (per)

*Ichi-jikan ni* san-doru haratte kuremasu. 一時間に三ドル(弗)払ってくれます. "They pay us three dollars per hour."

5. (in, into)—entering motion
   *Heya ni* hairimasu. 部屋に入ります. "I go into the room."

6. (into)—change of situation, status
   *Sensei ni* narimashita. 先生になりました. "He became a teacher."
   Kono ki o *hako ni* shimasu. この木を箱にします. "I will make this wood into a box."

7. (against)
   *Chichi ni* hantai shimashita. 父に反対しました. "I opposed my father."
   Watakushi ga iku *no ni*, ano hito wa ikimasen. 私が行くのにあの人は行きません. "In spite of the fact that I am going, he is not going."

8. (to)—indirect object
   *Yamamoto-san ni* hon o agemashita. 山本さんに本を上げました. "I gave Mrs. Yamamoto a book."
   Sensei ga *watakushi ni* hon o kudasaimashita. 先生が私に本を下さいました. "The teacher gave me a book."
   Note: Usually an indirect object precedes a direct object.

9. (as)=*to shite*—purpose
   Ano hon o *kyōkasho ni* tsukatte imasu. あの本を教科書に使っています. "We use that book as a text-book."

10. (and)=*to*—connects two nouns
    *Yamada-san ni Tanaka-san ni Matsumoto-san* o erandara dō deshō ka. 山田さんに田中さんに松本さんを選んだらどうでしょうか. "What would you think if we chose Mrs. Yamada, Mrs. Tanaka, and Mrs. Matsumoto?"

11. a. agent of passive verb (by)—the one who actually performs the action of the passive verb
    *Haha ni* shikararemashita. 母に叱られました.
    "I was scolded by my mother."

    b. agent of causative verb—agent who is caused to perform the action of the causative verb
    *Imōto ni* yomasemashita. 妹に読ませました. "I

made my sister read."

**c.** agent of causative-passive verb (by)—agent who forces the subject to perform the action of the causative-passive verb

*Sensei ni* muzukashii *kanji* o kakaseraremashita. 先生に難しい漢字を書かせられました．　"I was made to write difficult Chinese characters by my teacher."

**d.** with the verb, *itadaku (morau)*—one who is giving; the one who receives is the subject; this *ni* is interchangeable with *kara*.

*Ane ni (kara)* hon o moraimashita. 姉に本をもら(貰)いました．　"I received a book from my elder sister."

with V*te*+*itadaku (morau)*—one who performs the act of V*te*; the one who receives the act of V*te* is the subject.

*Sensei ni* tegami o kaite itadakimashita. 先生に手紙を書いていただきました．"My teacher was nice enough to write a letter for me."　(I asked her to do it first.)

Note: For the particle used with the other directional verbs, *ageru (yaru)*, *kudasaru (kureru)*, see 8 of the particle *ni*, p. 122, for the indirect object.

**e.** with V$_{\text{causative-}te}$+*ageru (yaru)*, *kudasaru (kureru)* —the one who is permitted to perform the action of V*te*

Watakushi wa *Hanako ni* eigo no benkyō o tsuzukesasete yarimashita.　私は花子に英語の勉強を続けさせてやりました．"I allowed Hanako to continue her study of English."

Sensei ga *watakushi ni* sono hon o yomasete kudasaimashita.　先生が私にその本を読ませて下さいました．"The teacher allowed me to read that book."

**f.** with V$_{\text{causative-}te}$+*itadaku (morau)*—the one who permits the subject to perform the action of V*te*

Watakushi wa *haha ni* suki na yōfuku o erabasete moraimashita.　私は母に好きな洋服を選ば

せてもら(貰)いました.  "I was permitted by my mother to select the dress I like."

II.  V₂+*ni*+motion verb (in order to ...)—purpose
Nihonshoku o *tabe ni* Nihon no ryōriya ni *ikimashita*.
日本食を食べに日本の料理屋に行きました.  "I went to a Japanese restaurant in order to eat Japanese food."

III.  *o*V₂+*ni naru*—makes an honorific verb
Mō ocha o *onomi ni narimashita* ka.  もうお茶をお飲みになりましたか.  "Have you drunk tea already?"

IV.  V₂+*ni*+Verb—emphasis, duplication of the same verb
*Hashiri ni hashirimashita* ga oitsukimasen deshita.  走りに走りましたが追いつきませんでした.  "I ran and ran, but I couldn't catch up."

V.  V₃+*ni*+V_negative-potential—duplication of the same verb (cannot do even if we want to)
*Iu ni iwarenu* ii keshiki desu.  言うに言われぬいい景色です.  "It is an indescribably good view."  "It is a good view which we cannot describe even if we want to."

**Verbs and adjectives which should be remembered with the particle *ni*.**

NI AU に会う   meet, e.g.  Kyō Tanaka-san *ni aimashita*.  今日田中さんに会いました.  "I met Mr. Tanaka today," or "I saw Mr. Tanaka today."

Note: *ni au* is used for meeting a new friend or seeing an old acquaintance.  In Japanese the verb *miru* is not used in this context.  *Miru* means "to look at" and takes a direct object particle *o miru*.
e.g.  Tanaka-san *ni aimashita*.  "I saw Mr. Tanaka."—actually exchanged greetings with Mr. Tanaka.  cf. Tanaka-san *o mimashita*.  田中さんを見ました.  "I saw Mr. Tanaka."—The subject saw Mr. Tanaka, but Mr. Tanaka did not see him.

NI (=*kara*) CHIKAI に近い   be close to, e.g.  Watakushi no uchi wa gakkō *ni chikai* desu. 私の家は学校に近いです.  "My house is near the school."

NI HANSURU に反する   be against, oppose, e.g.  Oya no iken *ni hanshite* kanojo to kekkon shimashita.  親の意見に反して彼女と結婚しました.  "Opposing my parents' opinion, I married her."

NI HANTAI SURU に反対する   =*ni hansuru*

NI (to) HITOSHII に等しい  be equal to, e.g.  Nihon no menseki wa Kariforunia-shū no menseki *ni hitoshii.*  日本の面積はカリフォルニア州の面積に等しい.  "The size of Japan is equal to the size of California."

NI KAGIRU に限る  is the best (literally, limited to), e.g.  Nihon-shoku nara ano ryōriya *ni kagirimasu.*  日本食ならあの料理屋に限ります.  "If it's Japanese food (you mean), that restaurant is the best."

NI KAKARU にかかる  start, e.g.  Shigoto *ni kakarimashō.*  仕事にかかりましょう.  "Let's start our work."

NI KAKERU にかける  hang, e.g.  Uwagi o kugi *ni kakemashita.*  上着を釘にかけました.  "I hung my jacket on a nail."

NI KANSURU に関する  concerning (attributive) e.g.  Nihon *ni kansuru* hon o kaimashita.  日本に関する本を買いました.  "I bought a book concerning Japan."  cf. *ni kanshite* (adverbial) Nihon *ni kanshite* benkyō shite imasu.  日本に関して勉強しています.  "We are studying about Japan."

NI KATSU に勝つ  win, e.g.  Oregon Daigaku ga Washinton Daigaku *ni kachimashita.*  オレゴン大学がワシントン大学に勝ちました.  "The University of Oregon won over the University of Washington."

NI KIKU に聞く  ask someone, e.g.  Yamada-san *ni kiitara* oshiete kuremashita.  山田さんに聞いたら教えてくれました.  "When I asked Mr. Yamada, he taught (told) me."

NI KIMERU に決める  decide on, e.g.  Kore *ni kimemashō* ka.  これに決めましょうか.  "Shall we decide on this?"

NI KURUSHIMU に苦しむ  be puzzled at, e.g.  Rikai *ni kuru-shimimasu.*  理解に苦しみます.  "I find it hard to understand."  cf. *Byōki de kurushinde* imasu.  病気で苦しんでいます.  "He is suffering from illness."

NI MAKASERU に任せる  entrust, e.g.  Jimu o subete musuko *ni makasemashita.*  事務をすべ(総)て息子に任せました.  "I entrusted my business entirely to my son."

NI MAKERU に負ける  lose, e.g.  Ano hito *ni makete* shimaimashita.  あの人に負けてしまいました.  "I lost to him."

NI NARU

1. become, e.g.  Sensei *ni narimashita.*  先生になりました.

"He became a teacher."

2. be (=*ni ataru*), e.g. Ano hito wa watakushi no itoko *ni narimasu.* あの人は私のいとこになります. "He is my cousin."

NI (*to*) NIRU に似る resemble, e.g. Yoshio-san wa otō-san *ni nite imasu.* 良雄さんはお父さんに似ています. "Yoshio resembles his father."

NI NORU に乗る get into a vehicle, ride in a vehicle, e.g. Kinō densha *ni notte* Shibuya made ikimashita. 昨日電車に乗って渋谷まで行きました. "Yesterday I went to Shibuya by train."

NI ODOROKU に驚く be surprised at, e.g. Tori no naku koe *ni odorokasaremashita.* 鳥の鳴く声に驚かされました. "I was surprised at the song of the birds."

NI (*to*) ONAJI に同じ same as—perhaps *to* is more common, but sometimes *ni* is used, e.g. Kodomo o omou no wa watakushi mo anata *ni onaji* desu. 子供を思うのは私もあなたに同じです. "I think of my children just as you think of yours."

NI OYOBU に及ぶ reach, amount to, match, e.g. Hiyō ga jūman-en *ni oyonda.* 費用が十万円に及んだ. "The expenses amounted to ¥100,000." Sainō no ten de kare *ni wa oyobanai.* 才能の点で彼には及ばない. "I can't match him in talent."

NI TOMONAU に伴う keep step with, e.g. Shūnyū *ni tomonawanai* zeitaku na seikatsu o shite wa ikemasen. 収入に伴わない贅沢な生活をしてはいけません. "Don't lead a life of luxury out of proportion to your income."

NI TSUKAERU に仕える serve someone, e.g. Watakushi wa moto yūmei na kazoku *ni tsukaemashita.* 私はもと有名な華族に仕えました. "I served a famous nobleman of old."

NI TSUZUKU に続く

1. follow, e.g. Chichi no shi ga haha no shi *ni tsuzukimashita.* 父の死が母の死に続きました. "Father's death followed mother's death."

2. be connected to, e.g. Kono michi wa daigaku no seimon *ni tsuzuite imasu.* この道は大学の正門に続いています. "This road leads to the front gate of the university."

NI YORU によ(因, 依)る depend on, e.g. Ashita iku ka ikanai ka wa tenki *ni yorimasu.* 明日行くか行かないかは天気によります. "Whether we go tomorrow or not will depend on the weather."

## NO の

I.  a. (of, 's)—possessive (or the noun before *no* modifies the noun after *no*)

Noun+*no*  *Watakushi no* uchi wa Tokyo ni arimasu. 私の 家は東京にあります. "My house is in Tokyo."

*Yamamoto-san no* heya no rajio wa ōkii desu.  山本 さんの室のラジオは大きいです.  "The radio in Mr. Yamamoto's room is big."

Note: The final noun can be omitted, if it is clear to both speaker and listener.

    e.g. Are wa *Tamura-san no* desu. あれは田村さんのです. "That is Mr. Tamura's."

b. The noun before *no* modifies the noun after *no*, e.g. Kono *hon no hyōshi no iro.* この本の表紙の色. "the color of the cover of this book."

Note: In Japanese *no* may be used many times in one sentence.

    e.g.  watakushi *no* uchi *no* daidokoro *no* todana *no* naka *no* chawan 私の家の台所の戸棚の中の茶わん(碗). "the bowl inside the cupboard of the kitchen of our house" Though this is a bit exaggerated, it is not uncommon to see *no* used many times in one sentence. In this usage normal Japanese order is from large to small, or general to specific; thus, *watakushi no uchi* is bigger than *daidokoro*, *daidokoro* is bigger than *todana*, etc.

II.  Apposition

Noun+*no*+Noun  *Ano kata* wa *isha no* Tanaka-san de, *kono kata* wa *sensei no* Tanaka-san desu. あの方は 医者の田中さんで, この方は先生の田中さんです. "That is Mr. Tanaka, who is a doctor, and this is Mr. Ta- naka, who is a teacher."

III.  The noun which precedes *no* is the subject of the relative clause. (This *no* is interchangeable with the particle *ga*.)

Noun+*no*+Verb+Noun  *Watakushi no* (*ga*) *katta nōto* wa ōkii desu. 私の買ったノートは大きいです. "The note- book which I bought is big."

*Watakushi no* (*ga*) *itte ita gakkō* wa yama no ue ni arimashita.  私の行っていた学校は山の上にありました. "The school I went to was on the top of the hill."

IV.  Double particles—*no* always follows the other particle, the noun plus some particle before *no* modifies the noun after *no*

Noun+particle+*no*  Kore ga *chichi e no* tegami desu. こ れが父への手紙です. "This is the letter to my father." Sore wa *Tokyo kara no* kisha desu. それは東京からの汽

車です. "That is the train from Tokyo."

**V.** Nominalizing verbs

$V_3+no=V_3+koto$  Asobu no ga suki desu. 遊ぶのが好きです. "I like to play."

**VI.** As a noun—In some cases this *no* is contracted to *n'*.

Verb+*no*

1. fact   Watakushi wa *iku n'* desu. 私は行くんです.
   "I'll go." "It is a fact that I'll go."
   Kyō *tsukareta no* de uchi ni imashita. 今日疲れたので家にいました. "Because (the fact being that) I was tired, I was at home today."

2. thing  Koko ni *aru no* ga watakushi no hon desu. ここにあるのが私の本です. "The one which is here is my book."

3. time   Kono mae Nihon e *itta no* wa san-nen mae deshita. この前日本へ行ったのは三年前でした. "The last time I went to Japan was three years ago."

4. person  Asoko ni suwatte *iru no* ga Tanaka-san desu. あそこに坐っているのが田中さんです. "The one who is sitting there is Miss Tanaka."

Note: As shown in the above examples, 2, 3, and 4, in a sentence ending with the copula (*desu, da, deshita,* etc.), the noun which directly precedes the copula tells what the subject *no* represents.

e.g. Ichiban sei no takai *no* ga Matsuda-san desu. 一番背の高いのが松田さんです. "The tallest person is Mr. Matsuda." (Matsuda-san is a person, so *no* refers to a person, too.)

Nihon ni itta *no* wa sakura ga saite ita toki deshita. 日本に行ったのは桜が咲いていた時でした. "When we went to Japan it was the time when the cherry blossoms were blooming." (*Toki* is a time, so *no* refers to a time also.)

Cop. n.+*na*+*no*

one   *Kirei na no* ga suki desu. きれい(綺麗)なのが好きです. "I like pretty ones."

Adj.+*no*

one    *Ōkii no* o kudasai. 大きいのを下さい.   "Please
give me a big one."

VII.   Sentence-ending—colloquial, used more often by women
1.   interrogative—takes the place of *ka*
Ashita iku *no*. 明日行くの.   "Are you going tomorrow?"
2.   softens the tone
Ee, ashita iku *no*. ええ. 明日行くの.   "Yes, I'll go
tomorrow."

VIII.  (whether ... or)
Verb+*no*+V*nai no to* [*itte*]  *Iku no ikanai no to* nakanaka
kesshin  shimasen.   行くの行かないのと中々決心しませ
ん.  "Saying that he will go, and then that he won't
go, he does not easily make up his mind."

NOMI のみ=*dake, bakari.* (only, merely)
Noun+*nomi*  Sonna shigoto o nashiuru no wa *kare nomi* da.   そ
んな仕事をなし得るのは彼のみだ.   "He is the only one
who can do such work."

O を
Noun+*o*

I.  The preceding noun is the direct object of the verb, except
when contrast is involved, in which case this *o* is replaced
by *wa*.
Sono *hon o* yomimashita. その本を読みました. "I read that
book." cf. Sono hon *wa* yomimashita. その本は読みま
した. "I read that book (...but I didn't read this book)."
*Shigoto o* shimasu. 仕事をします. "We'll do our work."
cf. Shigoto *wa* shimasu. 仕事はします. "We'll do the
work (...but we won't do anything else, etc.)."

Direct object of a passive sentence
Okane o *dorobō ni* toraremashita. お金を泥棒にとられまし
た. "My money was stolen by a thief."

Direct object of a causative sentence (used particularly when
the verb is intransitive)
*Takeo o* tsukai ni ikasemashita. 武雄を使いに行かせました.
"I made Takeo go on an errand."

Direct object of a causative-passive sentence

Nigai *kusuri o* nomasaremashita.  苦い薬を飲まされました.
"I was made to take bitter medicine."

II. Route of motion
Hikōki ga sora *o* tobimasu.  飛行機が空を飛びます.  "The
airplane flies through the air."
Michi *o* arukimasu.  道を歩きます.  "I walk along the
street."

III. Point of departure
*Uchi o* demasu.  家を出ます.  "I leave home."
*Heya o* demasu.  部屋を出ます.  "I go out of the room."
Kyonen *gakkō o* sotsugyō shimashita.  去年学校を卒業し
ました.  "I graduated from school last year."

## Some verbs which should be remembered with the particle *o*

O DERU を出る  start, leave, e.g.  Uchi *o demasu.* 家を出ます.
"I am leaving home."

O GAMAN SURU を我慢する  bear, suppress, e.g.  Kurushii no
*o gaman shimashita.*  苦しいのを我慢しました.  "I suppressed my
pain."

O KIKU を聞く  hear something, e.g.  Kinō sono nyūsu *o kikimashita.*  昨日そのニュースを聞きました.  "I heard that news
yesterday."

O MATSU を待つ  wait for, e.g.  Suda-san *o matte* imasu.  須田
さんを待っています.  "I am waiting for Mr. Suda."

O SOTSUGYŌ SURU を卒業する  graduate from, e.g.  Daigaku
*o sotsugyō shimashita.*  大学を卒業しました.  "I graduated from
the university."

O SURU をする  See the verb *suru*, pp. 10–11.

O TASUKERU を助ける  help someone, e.g.  Kyō kawaisō na
rōjin *o tasukete* agemashita.  今日可哀そうな老人を助けて上げま
した.  "I helped a pitiful old man today."

O TATSU を発(立)つ  leave, start, e.g.  Kinō Tokyo no hikōjō *o
tatte* Amerika ni kimashita.  昨日東京の飛行場を発ってアメリカ
に来ました.  "I left Tokyo Airport yesterday and came to
America."

O WARAU を笑う  laugh at, e.g.  Hito no koto *o waratte* wa
ikemasen.  人の事を笑ってはいけません.  "You must not laugh
at others."

O WATARU を渡る  cross over, e.g. Igirisu Kaikyō *o watari-mashita*. イギリス海峡を渡りました. "I crossed over the English Channel."

SA さ

I. sentence-ending or phrase-ending particle—slight emphasis, sometimes a slightly boastful feeling.

Noun+*sa*   Kore ga *hon sa*. これが本さ. "This is the book (... which I told you about)."

Verb+*sa*

(V₃+*sa*)   Ashita *iku sa*. 明日行くさ. "I'll go tomorrow (... naturally)."

(V*ta*+*sa*)   Kinō *itta sa*. 昨日行ったさ  "I went yesterday (... of course)."

Adj.+*sa*

(Adj₃+*sa*)   *Ōkii sa*. 大きいさ. "It's big (... you should see it yourself)."

(Adj*ta*+*sa*)   *Takakatta sa*. 高かったさ. "It was expensive (... of course)."

Cop. n.+*sa*  *Daisuki sa*. 大好きさ. "I just love it."

II. makes an adjective or a copular noun into an abstract noun.

Adj*stem*+*sa*   *ōkisa* 大きさ "bigness, size."

Cop. n.+*sa*  *shizukasa* 静かさ "quietness."

SAE さえ

a. *sae* always replaces the particles *ga, wa, o.*

b. *sae* appears with all the other particles such as *ni, de, no, e, made, kara, to,* etc.

c. *sae* always follows the above particles.

d. *sae* is sometimes used with *mo*; when used with it, *sae* precedes *mo,* and is more emphatic than *sae* alone.

e. *sae* is used with both positive verbs and negative verbs.

I. (even)

Noun+*sae*   Ugoku *koto sae* dekimasen. 動くことさえでき(出来)ません. "I can't even move."

*Yamaguchi-san ni sae* misemashita. 山口さんにさえ見せました. "I showed it even to Miss Yamaguchi."

Senji-chū tabemono ga nakute niwa no *kusa sae mo* tabeta sō desu. 戦時中食物がなくて庭の草さえも食べた

そうです. "I understand that during the war, because there wasn't enough food, people ate even the grass in the yard."

II. (only if)

Noun+*sae*+V$_{ba}$  Ano hito wa *osake sae nomeba* manzoku shite imasu. あの人はお酒さえ飲めば満足しています. "He is satisfied only if he drinks *sake*."

V$_2$+*sae sureba*  Ano hito wa osake o *nomi sae sureba* manzoku shite imasu. あの人はお酒を飲みさえすれば満足しています. "He is satisfied only if he drinks *sake*."

V$_{te}$+*sae ireba*  Ano hito wa osake o *nonde sae ireba* manzoku shite imasu. あの人はお酒を飲んでさえいれば満足しています. "He is satisfied only if he drinks *sake*."

SHI し (V$_2$ of *suru*) V$_2$ has a conjunctive function, see pp. 5-6.

(and, not only...but also)—connects two clauses (cf. *to* which connects two nouns)

V$_3$+*shi*

(V$_3$+*shi*)  Ano hito wa e mo *kaku shi*, uta mo utaimasu. あの人は絵もかくし歌も歌います. "He paints as well as sings."

(V$_{ta}$+*shi*)  Uchi mo *katta shi*, jidōsha mo kaimashita. 家も買ったし自動車も買いました. "He bought not only a house, but also a car."

Adj.+*shi*

(Adj$_3$+*shi*)  Ano uchi wa ōkii shi kirei desu. あの家は大きいしきれい(綺麗)です. "That house is big and pretty."

(Adj$_{ta}$+*shi*)  Kare wa *yasashikatta shi*, omoiyari mo atta. 彼は優しかったし, 思いやりもあった. "He was not only gentle, but was also thoughtful."

SHIKA しか (cf. *dake*)

a. *shika* always replaces *o, ga, wa*.
b. *shika* never occurs with the particle *mo*.
c. *shika* appears with all other particles such as *ni, de, no, e, made, kara, to*, etc.
d. *shika* always follows the above particles.

**e.** *shika* is always used with negative verbs.

(only, nothing but)=*dake shika*

Noun+particle+*shika*+negative verb

*Ocha shika nomimasen.* お茶しか飲みません. "I drink nothing but tea."

*Zasshi shika yomimasen.* 雑誌しか読みません. "He reads nothing but magazines."

*Tokyo ni shika ikimasen* deshita. 東京にしか行きません でした. "I went only to Tokyo."

*Tokyo de shika* mimasen deshita. 東京でしか見ませんで した. "I saw it only in Tokyo."

*Miura-san to shika hanashimasen.* 三浦さんとしか話し ません. "I'll talk only to Mr. Miura."

## SURA すら (=sae)

(even)—emphatic

Noun+*sura* Sonna *koto sura* shimasu. そんな事すらしま す. "He even does that sort of thing."

Sonna *koto sura shimasen.* そんな事すらしません. "He doesn't even do that sort of thing."

## TARI たり —Contrary to the way most particles are used, this particle never follows a noun. See pp. 53-54.

**I.** (sometimes do this, sometimes do that)—action in alternation (duplication of the same verb)

$V_{tari}$+$V_{tari}$ (*suru*) Itsumo *tattari suwattari* ochitsukanai hito desu ne. いつ(何時)も立ったり坐ったり落着かない 人ですね. "He is a restless person, always standing up and sitting down, isn't he?"

$Adj_{tari}$+$Adj_{tari}$ (*suru*) *Samukattari atatakakattari shimasu.* 寒かったり暖かかったりします. "Sometimes it is cold, and sometimes it is warm."

**II.** (do such things as)—representative action

$V_{tari}$ *suru* Natsu yama ni *ittari shimasu.* 夏山に行ったり します. "During the summer we do such things as go to the mountains."

Note: *tari* is often followed by the verb *suru*, which itself has no specific meaning.

## TE て

In traditional grammar, *te* is considered a particle, but it is better thought of as a verb ending (see pp. 16-18, 54-59).

## TO と

I. (and)—connects only nouns and pronouns, never connects clauses

Noun+*to*+Noun *Pen to enpitsu* ga arimasu. ペンと鉛筆があります. "There are pens and pencils."

*Dore to dore* ga anata no desu ka. どれとどれがあなたのですか. "Which ones are yours (which one and which one are yours)?"

II. (together with)=*to issho ni*

Noun+*to* *Suzuki-san to* ikimasu. 鈴木さんと行きます. "I'll go with Mr. Suzuki."

III. Comparative

Noun+*to*+Noun+*to* *Kono hon to sono hon to* dochira ga ōkii desu ka. この本とその本とどちらが大きいですか. "Which one is bigger, this book or that book?"

IV. Quotative—use before such words as *iu, kiku, omou,* etc.

Verb+*to iu* (kiku, etc.) Yamada-san ga ashita *kuru to iimashita.* 山田さんが明日来ると言いました. "Miss Yamada said that she would come tomorrow."

Noun+*to iu* (*kiku,* etc.) Ano kata ga *byōki* [da] *to kikimashita.* あの方が病気と聞きました. "I heard he is ill."

V. (if, when)—conditional (see pp. 29-30 for more details)

$V_3$+*to* Natsu Nihon ni *iku to* totemo atsui desu. 夏日本に行くととても暑いです. "If you go to Japan during the summer, it is very hot."

$Adj_3$+*to* *Atsui to* umi ni ikimasu. 暑いと海に行きます. "When it's hot, we go to the beach."

VI. (is about to do something)

$V_{tentative}$+*to*+*suru* *Dekakeyō to shite* iru tokoro e tomodachi ga kimashita. 出かけようとしている所へ友達が来ました. "My friend came just as I was about to go out."

VII. (trying [unsuccessfully] to do something)

$V_{tentative}$+*to*+*suru* *Okiyō to shimashita* ga, okiraremasen deshita. 起きようとしましたが起きられませんでした. "I tried to get up, but I couldn't."

VIII. (whether... or, even if)

$V_{tentative}+to+V_{tentative}+to$

Yuki ga *furō to* arare ga *furō to* iku tsumori desu. 雪が降ろうと霰が降ろうと行くつもりです. "I intend to go even if it snows or hails."

$V_{tentative}+to+V_{mai}+to$ (*mai* is a negative tentative form, see pp. 39–40, 68)

Kare ga *ikō to ikumai to* kamaimasen. 彼が行こうと行くまいと構いません. "I don't care whether he goes or not."

IX. (in the manner of)—adverbial

*Atto* odorokimashita. あっと驚きました. "I was taken aback." (Oh! was I surprised!)

*Nikotto* waraimashita. にこっと笑いました. "He smiled."

**Verbs, adjectives, copular nouns which should be remembered with *to*.**

TO CHIGAU と違う be different from, e.g. Watakushi no iken wa anata no *to chigaimasu.* 私の意見はあなたのと違います. "My opinion is different from yours."

TO HITOSHII と等しい =*ni hitoshii* be equal to, see p. 125.

TO NARU となる =*ni naru* *to naru* is more literary, see pp. 125–26.

TO ONAJI と同じ same as, e.g. Anata no *to onaji* yōfuku o kaimashita. あなたのと同じ洋服を買いました. "I bought the same dress as yours."

TOKA とか

(and, or, such as)—used in duplication

Noun+*toka*+Noun+*toka* Hon *toka* zasshi *toka* takusan kaimashita. 本とか雑誌とか沢山買いました. "I bought lots of things, such as books and magazines."

TOMO とも

I. (either... or, between)

Noun+*tomo*+Noun+*tomo* *Yama tomo umi tomo* miwake ga tsukimasen. 山とも海とも見分けがつきません. "We can't distinguish between the mountains and the ocean."

II. (of course)—emphatic

End of a sentence  Kinō benkyō shimashita ka. Shimashita *tomo.* 昨日勉強しましたか. しましたとも. "Did you study yesterday?" "Of course I did."

III. (at + Adj<sub>superlative</sub>)

Adj*ku* + *tomo*  *Sukunaku tomo* kyō wa kore dake shinakereba narimasen. 少くとも今日はこれ丈しなければなりません. "At least I have to do this much today."

*Osoku tomo* go-ji made ni wa kite kudasai. 遅くとも五時までには来て下さい. "Please come by five at the latest."

IV. Of his status

Noun + *tomo*  Daigaku no *sensei tomo* arō hito ga sonna koto o itta n' desu ka. 大学の先生ともあろう人がそんなことを言ったんですか. "Did a person who is a university professor say such a thing?"

V. Uncertain number

Number + *tomo*  *Nanbyaku-nin tomo* kazoerarenai hodo hito ga ōzei ita. 何百人とも数えられないほど(程)人が大勢いた. "There were several hundred people there—so many that I could hardly count them."

VI. (all)

Number + *tomo*  *San-nin tomo* kyō wa kesseki deshita. 三人とも今日は欠席でした. "All three of them were absent today."

VII. (no matter...) emphatic

Noun + *tomo*  *Zehi tomo* goissho shitai desu. 是非とも御一緒したいです. "No matter what happens, I want to accompany you."

Interrog. word + *tomo* (= *te mo*)  *Donna* ni isogashiku *tomo* suru koto wa shinakereba naranai. どんなに忙しくともする事はしなければならない. "No matter how busy we are, we have to do what should be done."

VIII. (even though not...) = *te mo*

V*naku* + *tomo*  *Konaku tomo* yoi desu yo. 来なくともよいですよ. "You don't have to come, you know."

## WA は

I. Topic—The word which precedes *wa* is the topic of the sentence.

  a. *wa* isolates the noun which precedes it from other words.

  b. *wa* in this sense functions similarly to the English expression, "as for."

    1. The word which precedes *wa* can be treated as a subject.

      Watakushi *wa* gakusei desu.  私は学生です。 "I am a student."

      Kore *wa* hon desu.  これは本です。 "This is a book."

Note: In this sentence structure with the copula at the end, the word preceding *wa* is neither emphasized nor contrasted with any other element. (cf. *ga*, pp. 103–105).

    2. Contrasting element

      a. Single particle *wa*

        Watakushi *wa* gakusei desu ga, anata *wa* sensei desu.  私は学生ですが、あなたは先生です。 "I am a student, but you are a teacher."

        Kono hon *wa* yomimashita ga, ano hon *wa* yomimasen deshita.  この本は読みましたが、あの本は読みませんでした。 "I read this book, but I didn't read that book."

Note: In the second sentence, both *wa* replace the direct object marker, *o*.

      b. Double particles

        Tokyo ni *wa* ikimashita ga, Osaka ni *wa* ikimasen deshita.  東京には行きましたが、大阪には行きませんでした。 "I went to Tokyo, but I didn't go to Osaka."

        Hikōki ni *wa* norimashita ga, densha ni *wa* norimasen deshita.  飛行機には乗りましたが、電車には乗りませんでした。 "I rode in the airplane, but I didn't ride in the trolley."

Note: The second clause is often omitted. That is, the contrasting element is often implicit.

Kono hon *wa* yomimashita. この本は読みました; "I read this book (...but I didn't read some other book, etc.)."
In the case of double particles, *wa* always signifies a contrasting element.

Tokyo *ni* ikimashita. 東京に行きました. "I went to Tokyo." cf. Tokyo *ni wa* ikimashita. 東京には行きました. "I went to Tokyo (...but I didn't go to some other place, etc.)."

Ashita *kara* shigoto o shimasu. 明日から仕事をします. "I'll work from tomorrow." cf. Ashita *kara wa* shigoto o shimasu. 明日からは仕事をします. "I'll work from tomorrow (...but perhaps not from today, etc.)."

Frequently *wa* is used with negative verbs. Here too, the negative idea is in contrast to the positive idea.

II. (as far as...is concerned, it is all right, but...)
Noun+*wa*+Noun *da  Hon wa hon desu* ga, amari ii hon de wa arimasen. 本は本ですがあま(余)りいい本ではありません. "It's a book all right, but it is not a good book."

V₃+*ni* (=*koto*) *wa*+Verb *Yomu ni wa yomimashita* ga amari omoshiroku arimasen deshita. 読むには読みましたがあま(余)り面白くありませんでした. "I read it all right, but it wasn't too interesting."

III. Emphasis
V₂+*wa suru  Nomi wa shimashita* ga, *tabe wa shimasen* deshita. 飲みはしましたが食べはしませんでした. "I did drink, but I didn't eat."

WA わ Colloquial sentence-ending particle for women
Verb+*wa*  Ashita kore *suru wa*. 明日これするわ. "I'll do this tomorrow."

YA や
I. (such things as, and so forth)—inexhaustive conjunction
Noun+*ya*+Noun *Tsukue ya isu* ga arimasu. 机や椅子があります. "There are such things as desks and chairs."

II. (as soon as)
V₃+*ya*+(*ina ya*) *Tsuku ya* (*ina ya*) sugu kare ni denwa o kakemashita. 着くやす(直)ぐ彼に電話をかけました.

"As soon as I arrived, I telephoned him."

III.  End of a sentence
Person's name+*ya*  *Tomoko ya*  友子や  "Tomoko." (addressing Tomoko)
V<sub>tentative</sub>+*ya*  *Mō tsumaranai kenka wa yameyō ya.*  もう
つまらないけんか(喧嘩)はやめようや.  "Let's quit our
trivial fighting." (tone of light urging) Used by men.

## YARA やら

I.  Sign of uncertainty=*ka*
Interrog. word+*yara*  *Nani yara* kaite imasu.  何やら書い
ています.  "He is writing something."
*Nan' no koto yara* zenzen wakarimasen deshita.  何のこ
とやら全然わか(分)りませんでした.  "I didn't understand
at all what that was about."

II.  Conjunction=*ya*
Noun+*yara*+Noun+*yara*  *Are yara kore yara* suru koto
ga takusan arimasu.  あれやらこれやらすることが沢山あ
ります.  "What with this and that, we have so many
things to do."

## YO よ

End of a sentence
Verb+*yo*  *Mado ga aite imasu yo.*  窓があ(開)いていますよ.
"The window is open, you know."—giving information to others, mild emphasis.
*Ashita iku yo.* (used by men)  明日行くよ.  "I'll go
tomorrow."
*Ashita iku wa yo.* (used by women—*wa* is inserted
between the verb and *yo*)  明日行くわよ.  "I'll go
tomorrow."
Noun+*yo* (addressing) *Yama yo.*  山よ. "You, mountain."
Used mainly in poetry or literary writing.

## YORI より

I.  (than)
Noun+*yori*  Kono hito wa ano *hito yori* sei ga takai desu.
この人はあの人より背が高いです.  "This man is taller
than that man."

II.  (from)—more literary than *kara*
    Noun+*yori*    *Tarō yori*—commonly used at the end of a
    letter.  太郎より.

III.  (more)
    *yori*+Adj.   Kono hō ga *yori takai* desu.  この方がより高い
    です.  "This is more expensive."

## ZE ぜ

(you know)
    End of a sentence   Kyō *iku ze*.  (used by men)  今日行く
    ぜ.  "I'll go today, you know."

## ZO そ

Emphasis
    End of a sentence   Muzukashii *zo*.  (used by men)  難し
    いぞ.  "It's difficult."

# INTERROGATIVE WORDS　疑問詞＜ぎもんし＞
# PLUS PARTICLES　助詞＜じょし＞

The following interrogative words are sometimes followed by the particles *ka* and *mo,* and the resulting combination produces entirely new meanings. These interrogative words also may be followed by the verb or adjective *te*-form plus *mo* (V*te* mo, Adj*kute mo*), or by *de mo* (copular *te*-form + *mo*), again producing a new meaning.

### List of Interrogative Words

| | |
|---|---|
| *dare* 誰 | who |
| *dochira* どちら | which of the two—more polite than *dotchi* |
| *doko* どこ (何処) | where |
| *donata* どなた | who—more polite than *dare* |
| *donna* + noun どんな | what kind of (noun) |
| *donna ni* どんなに | to what extent |
| *dono* + noun どの | which (noun) among many (three or more) |
| *dō* どう | how |
| *dore* どれ | which among many (three or more) |
| *dotchi* どっち | which of the two |
| *iku* + counter 幾(人) = *nan'* + counter | how many (noun) |
| *ikura* いく(幾)ら | how much |
| *ikutsu* いく(幾)つ | how many |
| *itsu* いつ(何時) | when |
| *nan'* + counter 何(人) = *iku* + counter | how many (noun) |
| *naniᵢ* = *nan* 何 | how many (noun) (n' is used before the consonants b, p, d, t, n, r, z) |
| *naze* なぜ(何故) | why |

### Interrogative word + *ka*　"some..."

*dare ka* 誰か　someone, e.g. Kyō *dare ka* kimashita.　今日誰か来ました.　"Someone came today."

*dochira ka* どちらか　either one, e.g. *Dochira ka* [o] otori ni natte kudasai.　どちらかおとりになって下さい.　"Please choose either one of the two."

*doko ka* どこ(何処)か　somewhere, e.g. Haha wa kyō *doko ka* e ikimashita.　母は今日どこかへ行きました.　"My mother went somewhere today."

*donata ka* どなたか someone, e.g. *Donata ka* irasshaimashita.
どなたかいらっしゃいました. "Someone came."

*donna*+noun+*ka* (non-existent, except for case 1, pp. 147-48)

*donna ni ka* どんなにか how very much, e.g. Okā-sama mo *donna
ni ka* oyorokobi deshō. お母様もどんなにかお喜びでしょう.
"How happy your mother must be!"

*dono*+noun+*ka* (non-existent, except for case 1, pp. 147-48)

*dō ka*=*dō ni ka* どうか somehow, e.g. Dō ka nareba ii desu ga
... どうかなればいいですが... "It would be nice if it works
out somehow, but..."

*dore ka* どれか one of many, e.g. *Dore ka* kudasai. どれか下さ
い. "Give me one."

*dotchi ka* どっちか either one, e.g. *Dotchi ka* [o] erande kudasai. どっちか選んで下さい. "Please choose one of the two."

*iku*+counter+ka 幾―か several, e.g. *Iku-nin ka* kimashita. 幾
人か来ました. "Several people came."

*ikura ka* いく(幾)らか some amount, e.g. *Ikura ka* hanasemasu.
いくらか話せます. "I can speak a little (some)."

*ikutsu ka* いく(幾)つか some quantity, some number, e.g. *Ikutsu
ka* kaimashita. いくつか買いました. "I bought some."

*itsu ka* いつ(何時)か some time, e.g. *Itsu ka* Nihon ni ikitai to
omotte imasu. いつか日本に行きたいと思っています. "I am
thinking that I would like to go to Japan some day."

*nan'*+counter+*ka* 何―か several, e.g. *Nan-nin ka* iku to omoimasu. 何人か行くと思います. "I think several people will go."

*nani ka* 何か something, e.g. *Nani ka* tabetai desu. 何か食べた
いです. "I want to eat something."

*naze ka* なぜ(何故)か somehow, e.g. *Naze ka* kono uchi wa
amari suki de wa arimasen. なぜかこの家はあま(余)り好きでは
ありません. "Somehow I don't like this house very much."

> Note: When other particles are used, they always follow *ka*, and
> never come between the interrogative word and *ka*.
>
>      e.g. *Dare ka ni* agemashita ka. 誰かに上げましたか. "Did
> you give it to someone?"

## Interrogative word+mo

An interrogative word+*mo* has two separate meanings depending
on whether it is followed by a negative verb or a positive verb.

### I. *Interrog. word+mo+positive verb* "every..." (inclusive)

     *dare mo* 誰も everyone, e.g. *Sonna koto wa dare mo ga*

*shitte iru.* そんな事は誰もが知っている. "Everyone knows such a thing."

*dochira mo* どちらも  both, e.g. *Dochira mo ii desu.* どちらもいいです. "Both are good."

*doko mo* どこ(何処)も  everywhere, e.g. *Doko mo konde imashita.* どこも混んでいました. "It was crowded everywhere (Everywhere was crowded)."

*donata mo* どなたも  everyone, e.g. *Donata mo eigo ga ojōzu desu.* どなたも英語がお上手です. "Everyone speaks English well."

*donna*+noun+*mo* どんな―も  every kind of, e.g. *Donna hito mo imasu.* どんな人もいます. "Every kind of person is here."

*donna ni mo*  (non-existent)

*dono*+noun+*mo* どの―も  every, e.g. *Dono hon mo muzukashisugimasu.* どの本も難しす(過)ぎます. "Every book is too difficult."

*dō mo*  (non-existent, except for case 2, p. 148)

*dore mo* どれも  every one of them, e.g. *Dore mo omoshiroi desu.* どれも面白いです. "Every one of them is interesting."

*dotchi mo* どっちも  both, e.g. *Dotchi mo kirei desu.* どっちもきれい(綺麗)です. "Both of them are pretty."

*iku*+counter+*mo* 幾―も  any number, several, e.g. *Iku-nin mo kimashita.* 幾人も来ました. "Several people came."

*ikura mo* いく(幾)らも  any amount, many, e.g. Mada *ikura mo nokotte imasu.* ま(未)だいくらものこっています. "There are still any number (many) of them left."

*ikutsu mo* いく(幾)つも  any number, several, e.g. *Ikutsu mo kaimashita.* いくつも買いました. "I bought several."

*itsu mo* いつ(何時)も  always, e.g. *Itsu mo uchi ni imasu.* いつも家にいます. "I am always home."

*nan'*+counter+*mo* 何―も  any number, e.g. *Nan-satsu mo kaimashita.* 何冊も買いました. "I bought several books."

*nani mo*  (non-existent, except for case 3, p. 148)

*naze mo*  (non-existent)

Note: When other particles are used, they always go between the interrogative word and *mo*.

e.g. *Dochira ni mo* kyōmi ga *arimasu.* どちらにも興味があり
ます. "I am interested in both." *Dono hon ni mo* kaite *arimasu.* どの本にも書いてあります. "It is written in
every book."

## II. *Interrogative word + mo + negative verb* "no . . ." (exclusive)

*dare mo* 誰も  nobody, e.g. *Dare mo kimasen* deshita.
誰も来ませんでした. "Nobody came."

*dochira mo* どちらも  neither, e.g. *Dochira mo* yoku *arimasen.* どちらもよくありません.  "Neither of them is
good."

*doko mo* どこ(何処)も  nowhere, e.g. *Doko ni mo ikimasen.* どこにも行きません. "I won't go anywhere."

*donata mo* どなたも  nobody, e.g. *Donata mo irasshaima-
sen* desita. どなたもいらっしゃいませんでした.  "Nobody
came."

*donna + noun + mo* どんな—も  no kind of, e.g. *Donna hon
mo* yaku ni *tachimasen.* どんな本も役に立ちません. "No
kind of book is useful."

*donna ni mo*  (non-existent)

*dono + noun + mo* どの—も  no, e.g. *Dono hon mo omoshiroku arimasen.* どの本も面白くありません.  "None of
the books is interesting."

*dō mo* どうも  not at all, somehow, e.g. *Dō mo yoku arimasen.* どうもよくありません. "It is not good at all," or
"Somehow it isn't good."

*dore mo* どれも  none, e.g. *Dore mo yasuku arimasen.*
どれも安くありません. "None is cheap."

*dotchi mo* どっちも  neither, e.g. *Dotchi mo chiisaku arimasen.* どっちも小さくありません.  "Neither of them is
small."

*iku + counter + mo* 幾—も  not many, e.g. *Amari iku-nin
mo kimasen deshita.* 余り幾人も来ませんでした. "Not too
many people came."

*ikura mo* いく(幾)らも  not much, e.g. *Ikura mo nokotte
imasen.* いくらも残っていません. "Not much is left."

*ikutsu mo* いく(幾)つも  not many, e.g. *Mō ikutsu mo
arimasen.* もういくつもありません. "Not many are left
any more."

*itsu mo* いつ(何時)も  never, e.g. *Itsu mo ikemasen.* いつ
も行けません. "I can never go."

*nan'*+counter+*mo* 何一も not many, e.g. *Nan-mai mo
kakimasen* deshita. 何枚も書きませんでした. "I didn't
write many pages (sheets)."

*nani*+*mo* 何も nothing, e.g. *Nani mo arimasen.* 何もあ
りません. "There is nothing."

*naze mo* (non-existent)

> Note: When other particles are used, they always go between the
> interrogative word and *mo*.
>> e.g. *Doko ni mo* ikimasen. どこ (何処) にも行きません. "I
>> won't go anywhere." *Dare ni mo misemasen* deshita.
>> 誰にも見せませんでした. "I didn't show it to anyone."

## *Interrogative word*+*V*$_{te}$ *mo* "no matter who (what, etc.)"

*De mo* is used in the same manner as *V*$_{te}$ *mo*, but it follows an
interrogative word directly. *De* is the *te*-form of the copula *da*.
Therefore, an interrogative word+*de mo* means "no matter who
(what, etc.) it is." Thus it is often translated into English as
"anyone," "anything," etc. This expression is used mainly with positive verbs. See 6, p. 149

*dare*...*V*$_{te}$ *mo* 誰...Vても no matter who, e.g. *Dare ga kite mo*
odorokimasen. 誰が来ても驚きません. "No matter who comes,
I won't be surprised." *Dare de mo* hairemasu. 誰でも入れます.
"Anyone (no matter who he is) can enter."

*dochira*...*V*$_{te}$ *mo* どちら...Vても no matter which, e.g. *Dochira
o erande mo* ii desu. どちらを選んでもいいです. "No matter
which one you choose, it will be all right." *Dochira de mo*
kamaimasen. どちらでも構いません. "It doesn't matter with
either one."

*doko*...*V*$_{te}$ *mo* どこ(何処)... Vても no matter where, e.g. *Doko
e itte mo* atsui desu. どこへ行っても暑いです. "No matter where
we go, it is hot." *Doko de de mo* utte imasu. どこででも売っ
ています. "It is sold anywhere."

*donata*...*V*$_{te}$ *mo* どなた...Vても no matter who, e.g. *Donata
ga irasshatte mo* ano kata wa aitakunai to osshaimasu. どなた
がいらっしゃってもあの方は会いたくないとおっしゃいます. "No
matter who comes, he says that he doesn't want to see him."
*Donata ni de mo* omise shimasu. どなたにでもお見せします.
"I'll show it to anyone."

*donna*+noun...*V*$_{te}$ *mo* どんなN... Vても no matter what kind
of, e.g. *Donna hon o katte mo* yomanai deshō. どんな本を買っ

ても読まないでしょう. "No matter what kind of book we buy, he probably won't read it." *Donna hon de mo* yomimasu. どんな本でも読みます. "He will read any kind of book."

*donna de mo* どんなでも no matter how, e.g. *Donna de mo* kamawanai kara shite kudasai. どんなでも構わないからして下さい. "No matter how you do it, it's all right; please do it."

*donna ni ... V_{te} mo* どんなに... V ても no matter how much, e.g. *Donna ni hataraite mo* mada binbō desu. どんなに働いてもまだ貧乏です. "No matter how hard I work, I am still poor." Okane ga takusan mōkaru nara *donna ni de mo* hatarakimasu. お金が沢山儲かるならどんなにでも働きます. "If I can earn so much money, I'll work a lot (no matter how much work I have to do, I'll do it)."

*dono+noun ... V_{te} mo* どのN... V ても no matter which, e.g. *Dono hon o yonde mo* tsumarimasen. どの本を読んでもつまりません. "No matter which book I read, I become bored." *Dono hon de mo* ii kara misete kudasai. どの本でもいいから見せて下さい. "Any book is all right; please show it to me."

*dō V_{te} mo* どう V ても no matter how, e.g. *Dō mite mo* ano hito wa chotto okashii desu. どう見てもあの人は一寸おかしいです. "No matter how I look at him, he is a little odd." *Dō de mo* kamaimasen. どうでも構いません. "No matter how it is, it doesn't matter."

*dore ... V_{te} mo* どれ... V ても no matter which one, e.g. *Dore o mite mo* yoku arimasen. どれを見てもよくありません. "No matter which one I see, none is good." *Dore de mo* kekkō desu. どれでも結構です. "Any one of them is fine."

*dotchi ... V_{te} mo* どっち... V ても no matter which, e.g. *Dotchi o tabete mo* oishikunai deshō. どっちを食べてもおいしくないでしょう. "No matter which one I eat, it probably won't be tasty." *Dotchi ni de mo* hairemasu. どっちにでも入れます. "You can enter either one."

*iku+counter ... V_{te} mo* 幾―V ても no matter how many, e.g. *Iku-nin ite mo* tarimasen. 幾人いても足りません. " No matter how many people are here, it's not enough." *Iku-nin ni de mo* agemasu. 幾人にでも上げます. "I'll give it to any number of people."

*ikura ... V_{te} mo* いく(幾)ら... V ても no matter how much, e.g. *Ikura nonde mo* mada nodo ga kawaite imasu. いくら飲んでもまだ喉が渇いています. "No matter how much I drink, I am still

thirsty." *Ikura de mo* tsukatte kudasai. いくらでも使って下さ
い. "Please use any amount."

*ikutsu*...V*te* *mo* いく(幾)つ...Vても no matter how many, no
matter how old, e.g. *Ikutsu ni natte mo* mada kodomo no yō
desu. いくつになってもまだ子供のようです. "No matter how old
he gets, he is still like a child." *Ikutsu de mo* katte agemasu.
いくつでも買って上げます. "I'll buy you any number of them
(no matter how many)."

*itsu* V*te* *mo* いつ(何時)Vても no matter when, e.g. *Itsu itte mo*
uchi ni imasu. いつ行っても家にいます. "No matter when I go,
he is home." *Itsu de mo* ii desu. いつでもいいです. "Any time
is fine."

*nan'*+counter+V*te* *mo* 何—Vても no matter how many, e.g.
*Nan-nin kite mo* kamaimasen. 何人来ても構いません. "No matter how many people come, it doesn't matter." *Nan-nin de mo*
ii desu. 何人でもいいです. "Any number of people will be all
right."

*nani*...V*te* *mo* 何...Vても no matter what, e.g. *Nani o tabete
mo* oishiku arimasen. 何を食べてもおいしくありません. "No
matter what I eat, it doesn't taste good." *Nan' de mo* dekimasu.
何でもでき(出来)ます. "He can do anything."

*naze de mo* なぜ(何故)でも no matter why (see 4, pp. 148-49)
*Naze de mo* ikemasen. なぜでも行けません. "No matter why, I
can't go."

> Note: In the case of interrogative word+*de mo*, when other particles
> are used, they always go between the interrogative word and
> *de mo*.
>
> e.g. *Doko e de mo* ikimasu. どこ(何処)へでも行きます. "I'll go
> anywhere."

## Convenient Things to Remember Concerning Some Forms of Interrogative Word+Particle.

1. When an interrogative word+*ka* is followed by the verbs
   *shiru* or *wakaru*, this combination does not have the special
   meanings listed on pp. 141–42.

   e.g. *Dare ka* kimashita. 誰か来ました. "Someone came."
   *Dare* [da] *ka*\* shirimasen. 誰か知りません. "I don't
   know who." The copula *da* is often omitted.
   *Doko ka* e ikimashita. どこ(何処)かへ行きました.

---

\*This *ka* shows uncertainty.

"He went somewhere."

*Doko* [da] *ka\** shitte imasu ka.　どこか知っていますか.

"Do you know where?"

2. *Dō+mo* has become the adverbial word *dōmo* meaning "very much," "quite," "somehow," etc., when it is used with a positive verb.

   e.g.　Dōmo arigatō gozaimasu.　どうも有難うございます.

   "Thank you very much."　Dōmo Nihongo wa muzu-kashii desu.　どうも日本語は難しいです. "Japanese is really difficult (no matter how hard I work)."

3. There is no expression *nani mo* meaning "everything." The expression *nan' de mo* is close to "everything," although strictly speaking it means "anything."

   e.g.　*Nan' de mo* tabemasu.　何でも食べます. "He eats anything (everything)."

   Note: The adverbial word *nanimo* used with negative verbs is used as an emphatic expression.

   e.g.　Yori ni mo yotte *nanimo* kyō konakute mo yokatta no ni...　よりにもよって何も今日来なくてもよかったのに... "Of all the days of the year, he had to come today (he didn't have to come today)!"

4. There is no expression *naze*...V*te* mo, but there is the expression *naze de mo* meaning "no matter why (no matter what the reason)," which is followed by both positive and negative verbs.

   e.g.　*Naze de mo* ikitakatta n' desu.　なぜ(何故)でも行きたかったんです. "No matter what the reason, I wanted to go."

   *Naze de mo* ikitakunakatta n' desu.　なぜでも行きたくなかったんです. "No matter what the reason, I didn't want to go."

   Note: These sentences can be considered as the answers to such questions as:

   e.g.　Naze ikitakatta n' desu ka.　なぜ行きたかったんですか. "Why did you want to go?"　Naze ikitakunakatta n' desu ka. なぜ行きたくなかったんですか. "Why didn't you want to go?"

---

\*This *ka* shows uncertainty.

The one who answers does not want to give information as to why he does or doesn't do the action.  Depending on the tone, it may even sound belligerent.

5. Confusion arises over the use of an interrogative word+*mo* or an interrogative word+*de mo*.
   a. followed by a positive verb
      Interrogative word+*mo*+positive verb "every..."
      Interrogative word+*de mo*+positive verb "any..."
      e.g. *Dore mo* ii desu.  どれもいいです.  "Everything is good."
           *Dore de mo* ii desu.  どれでもいいです.  "Any one is all right."
   b. followed by a negative verb
      Interrogative word+*mo*+negative verb "no..." (followed by only a very few verbs, see 6)
      e.g. *Nani mo* arimasen.  何もありません.  "There is nothing."
           *Nan' de mo* arimasen.  何でもありません.  "It's nothing."
           *Nani mo* kamaimasen.  何も構いません.  "He doesn't care about anything."
           *Nan' de mo* kamaimasen.  何でも構いません.  "It doesn't matter what it is."

6. Interrogative word+*de mo*+negative verb
   An interrogative word+*de mo* is followed only by a very few verbs in a negative form such as *nai* or *kamawanai*.
   e.g. *Dare de mo nai.*  誰でもない.  "It's nobody."
        *Dotchi de mo kamawanai.*  どっちでも構わない.  "It doesn't matter which one," etc.

7. The expression *ikura de mo nai* is not too common, but sometimes it is used in the sense that "the amount is not too much."
   e.g. *Ikura de mo arimasen* ga, orei no shirushi ni totte kudasai.  いく(幾)らでもありませんが, お礼のしるしにとって下さい.  "It (the amount) is not much, but please take it as a token of my thanks."

# NOUNS 名詞〈めいし〉

I. Characteristics of Japanese Nouns (Though pronouns are a class of nouns, for convenience they are treated under a separate heading in this book [pp. 191–92]).

  1. Generally no distinction between singular and plural
     Exceptions:
       a. Occasionally a suffix is attached to nouns or pronouns to form plurals (e.g. *watakushi* 私 "I," *watakushi-tachi* 私たち(達) "we," *kodomo* 子供 "child," *kodomo-tachi* 子供たち "children"), see noun suffixes for plural forms, pp. 179–82
       b. Repetition of the same word makes the plural of certain nouns (*hito* 人 "person," *hitobito* 人々 "people," *shima* 島 "island," *shimajima* 島々 "islands." See p. 154, 3b

  2. No gender (no feminine, masculine, neuter)

  3. No case (Particles which follow nouns decide the case in Japanese, see Particles, pp. 93–140.)

II. Various Forms of Japanese Nouns

  1. Noun usage similar to English usage
       a. Common nouns 普通名詞〈ふつうめいし〉
          Concrete nouns 具体名詞〈ぐたいめいし〉 (*hon* 本 "book," *hana* 花 "flower")
          Abstract nouns 抽象名詞〈ちゅうしょうめいし〉 (*jiyū* 自由 "liberty")
       b. Proper nouns 固有名詞〈こゆうめいし〉 (*Tokyo* 東京 "Tokyo," *Tanaka-san* 田中さん "Mr. Tanaka")

  2. Nouns used as adverbs without changing in form
       a. Numerals 数詞〈すうし〉
          Cardinal numbers 基数〈きすう〉 (*mittsu* 三つ or *san* 三 "three")
          e.g. Koko ni *mittsu* no ringo ga arimasu. (noun)
               ここに三つのリンゴ(林檎)があります.
               "There are three apples here."
               Ringo o *mittsu* kudasai. (adverb) リンゴを

三つ下さい．"Please give me three apples."

Ordinal numbers 序数〈じょすう〉(*ichiban* 一番 "first")

e.g.  Ano gakusei wa kono kurasu de *ichiban* desu. (noun) あの学生はこのクラスで一番 です．"He is the top in this class."

Kore ga *ichiban* ōkii desu. (adverb) これが 一番大きいです．"This is the largest."

b. Nouns of quantity

(*takusan* 沢山 "many," *sukoshi* 少し "a little," *zenbu* 全部 "all," *mina* 皆 or *minna* 皆 "all," *ōzei* 大勢 "many [people]")

e.g.  *Takusan* no okashi o tabemashita. (noun) 沢山のお菓子を食べました．"I ate lots of cakes."

Okashi o *takusan* kaimashita. (adverb) お菓 子を沢山買いました．"We bought many cakes."

c. Some abstract nouns

(*jijitsu* 事実 "truth" or "in fact," zettai 絶対 "absoluteness" or "absolutely," *wariai* 割合 "rate" or "relatively")

e.g.  Sore wa *jijitsu* desu. (noun) それは事実です． "That is a fact."

*Jijitsu* sonna koto wa shiranakatta. (adverb) 事実そんな事は知らなかった．"In fact I didn't know such a thing."

d. Nouns of generalized time

(*kyō* 今日 "today," *konshū* 今週 "this week")

e.g.  *Kyō* no gogo ikimasu. (noun) 今日の午後行 きます．"I am going this afternoon."

*Kyō* ikimasu. (adverb) 今日行きます． "I am going today."

3.  Nouns which are modified not by adjectives but by adverbs or non-conjugative adjectives

a. Nouns of directions

(*higashi* 東 "east," *nishi* 西 "west")

e.g.  Hokkaido wa Nihon no *mottomo kita* ni aru. 北海道は日本の最も北にある．"Hokkaido is situated furthest north in Japan."

*Sonna minami* ni aru n' desuka. そんな南

にあるんですか．"Is it situated that far south?"

4. Nouns which can be used as adjectives as well as adverbs.
  a. *onaji* 同じ "same," "anyway" (traditional grammar categorizes this word as adjective, but in modern Japanese it is easier to treat it as noun. The only adjectival inflection still used is the *ku*-form, *onajiku*, meaning "similarly," "equally."
    e.g. Kore to sore wa *onaji* desu. (noun) これとそれは同じです．"This and that are the same."
    *Onaji* hito de wa arimasen. (adjective) 同じ人ではありません．"It's not the same person."
    *Onaji* iku ni (to) shite mo, kyō wa hontō wa ikitaku nai n' desu. (adverb) 同じ行くにしても今日は本当は行きたくないんです．"I'll go all the same, but I don't really want to go today."

5. Nouns which are unique to Japanese
  a. Copular nouns (adjectival nouns)
    (*kirei* [*na*] きれい(綺麗)な "pretty," or "clean," *shizuka* [*na*] 静かな "quiet")

  Characteristics of copular nouns
    1. Not used as an independent word in a sentence, but always followed by a copular (*da, desu,* etc. or *na* before nouns).
    2. Never becomes the subject or the direct object in a sentence.
    3. Modified by adverbs, not by adjectival words.

    Note: These words are often not translatable as nouns. Together with a copula, they have an adjectival meaning. Since it is difficult for non-natives to distinguish between regular nouns and copular nouns, they should memorize all the copular nouns together with *na*. In order to determine if a noun is regular or copular, Japanese-English dictionaries should be consulted, since most of them list copular nouns with *na*.
      e.g. Kore wa *kirei* desu. これはきれいです．"This is pretty."

Kore wa *kirei na* hana desu. これはきれ
いな花です. "This is a pretty flower."
*kirei de* ōkii heya きれいで大きい部屋
"a pretty and big room"

## COMMON COPULAR NOUNS

| | |
|---|---|
| atataka na 暖かな | warm |
| aware na 哀れな | pitiful |
| benri na 便利な | convenient |
| gōjō na 強情な | stubborn |
| hade na 派手な | showy |
| heibon na 平凡な | commonplace |
| idai na 偉大な | great |
| igai na 意外な | unexpected |
| ijiwaru na 意地悪な | mean |
| ijō na 異常な | abnormal |
| iya na いや(厭)な | distasteful |
| kantan na 簡単な | simple |
| kasuka na かすかな | faint |
| kirai na 嫌いな | distasteful |
| kiraku na 気楽な | carefree |
| kirei na きれい(綺麗)な | pretty |
| kōka na 高価な | expensive |
| mottomo na もっと(尤)もな | reasonable |
| onwa na 温和な | mild |
| reisei na 冷静な | cool |
| shizuka na 静かな | quiet |
| suki na 好きな | favorite |
| tabō na 多忙な | busy |
| tsūkai na 痛快な | thrilling |
| teinei na 丁寧な | polite |
| yōi na 容易な | easy |
| yukai na 愉快な | pleasant |
| zeitaku na 贅沢な | extravagant |

(ōkina, chiisana, okashina, see p. 92)

b. Pseudo-noun (Noun in form) 形式名詞＜けいしきめいし＞
(*mama* まま "as it is," *tame* ため(為) "for the sake
of," *tōri* 通り "just as")

This is a group of nouns which are never used
independently. They are always used with a modifier (see Noun modifiers, pp. 189–90).

e.g. Uchi o deta *mama*, mada kaette kimasen. 家
を出たまま，まだ帰って来ません． "He left
home, and as of now he still has not come
home." (*mama* means "as it is," *status quo*.)

III. Derivation of Noun Forms

1. True nouns
   (*tsukue* 机 "desk," *ki* 木 "tree," *hon* 本 "book")

2. Nouns derived from other parts of speech
   a. V₂ (*kaeri* 帰り "return," *kangae* 考え "thought,"
      *nozomi* 望み "hope")
   b. Adj$_{ku}$ (*chikaku* 近く "neighborhood") See pp. 84, 89
      for *ku*-form.
   c. Adj$_{stem}$ (adjective of colors) *aka* 赤 "red," *shiro* 白
      "white"
   d. Particle (*no* の "fact," "one")

3. Compound nouns
   a. Noun+Noun (*yonaka* 夜中 "middle of the night,"
      *asahi* 朝日 "morning sun")
   b. Repetition of two nouns (used as plurals) (*hitobito*
      人々 "people," *hibi* 日々 "days") The initial sound
      of the second noun often becomes voiced.
   c. Noun+V₂ (*enpitsukezuri* 鉛筆削り "pencil sharp-
      ener")
   d. V₂+V₂ (*yomikaki* 読書き "reading and writing,"
      *tabesugi* 食過ぎ "overeating")
   e. V₂+Noun (*kaimono* 買物 "shopping," *tabemono* 食物
      "food," *keshigomu* 消しゴム "eraser")
   f. Adj$_{stem}$+Noun (*chikamichi* 近道 "short cut," *ureshi-
      namida* 嬉し涙 "tears of joy")
   g. Noun+Adj$_{stem}$ (*kimijika* 気短か "short temper,"
      *Ashibaya* 足早 "quick walker")
   h. Adj$_{stem}$+V₂ (*takatobi* 高飛び "high jump," *tōmawari*
      遠回り "detour")
   i. Adj$_{stem}$+Adj$_{stem}$ (*tōasa* 遠浅 "shoal")
   j. Adj$_{stem}$+suffix *sa* (*utsukushisa* 美しさ "beauty")
      Adj$_{stem}$+suffix *ke* (*samuke* 寒け "chill")
      Cop. n.+suffix *sei* (*hitsuyōsei* 必要性 "necessity")
   k. Adverb+Noun (*mataitoko* またいとこ "second cous-
      in," *tadagoto* 只事 "ordinary matter")

    1.  Noun+V$_2$+Noun (*hitosashiyubi* 人差指 "index finger")

4.  Abbreviated nouns
    (*kokuren* 国連 from *kokusairengō* 国際連合 "the United
    Nations," kōkō 高校 from kōtōgakkō 高等学校 "high
    school"

5.  Japanized Western words
    (*arubaito* アルバイト "part-time job," from German *Arbeit*;
    *dansu* ダンス "dance," from English dance)
    There are literally thousands of foreign words used
in this manner, but pronunciations, and sometimes
meanings, are Japanized, and it is often difficult to
tell from what words they actually originate. These
words come from such foreign languages as English,
German, French, Russian, Portuguese, and others.
Moreover, some of these words are often shortened in
Japanese, so that they are even more difficult to recognize. For example, *suto* means "strike," *hansuto*
means "hunger strike," *demo* means "demonstration,"
and so forth. No list of all these words is possible;
moreover, new words are continually being added. Fortunately, however, they are written in *katakana*, so that
readers are made aware that they have foreign origins.

# NOUN-FOLLOWING WORDS AND EXPRESSIONS

BAKARI DE WA NAKU...MO ばかりではなく...も not only...
but also, e.g. *Jidōsha bakari de wa naku uchi mo kaimashita.*
自動車ばかりではなく家も買いました. "They bought not only a car,
but also a house."

BAKARI KA...MO ばかりか...も not only... but also, e.g. *Ano
hito wa Furansugo bakari ka Doitsugo mo hanashimasu.* あの人
はフランス語ばかりかドイツ語も話します. "He not only speaks
French, but he also speaks German."

BAMU ばむ be slightly in some condition, e.g. *Ase bande kimashita.* 汗ばんで来ました. "I am getting slightly sweaty."

BIRU びる apparent state of, e.g. *Ano ko wa otona bite imasu.*
あの子は大人びています. "That child looks like a grown-up."

BURI ぶり lapse of time, e.g. *San-nen buri de aimashita.* 三年ぶ
りで会いました. "I saw him after a lapse of three years."

BURU ぶる pretend to be, pose as, assume airs, e.g. *Ano hito wa
tensai butte ite okashii desu.* あの人は天才ぶっていておかしいです.
"It's funny because he pretends to be a genius." *Itsu mo jōhin
butte imasu.* 何時も上品ぶっています. "She always assumes airs
of gentility."

DAKARA TO ITTE だからと言って just because, e.g. *Kodomo
dakara to itte baka ni dekinai.* 子供だからと言って馬鹿にでき(出来)
ない. "Just because he is a child, we can't belittle him."

DAKE ATTE だけ(丈)あって =*dake ni*

DAKE NI だけ(丈)に as expected of, e.g. *Kanemochi dake ni yoku
okane o tsukaimasu.* 金持だけによくお金を使います. "As expected
of a rich person, he spends a lot of money." *Onna dake ni yoku
ki ga tsukimasu.* 女だけによく気が付きます. "As expected from
a woman, she is thoughtful."

DARAKE だらけ full of, e.g. *Kono sakubun wa machigai darake
desu.* この作品は間違いだらけです. "This composition is full of
mistakes."

DATERA NI だてらに =*to iu no ni* in spite of the fact that...
e.g. *Onna datera ni yoku yarimasu.* 女だてらによくやります. "In
spite of the fact that she is a woman, she does well."

DATTA だった　=*de atta*　was, e.g. *Chiisana machi datta ga ima wa ōkina tokai ni natta.* 小さな町だったが今は大きな都会になった. "It was a small town, but now it has become a big city."

DATTE だって = *de atte mo*　even if, e.g. *Okanemochi datte muda na koto o shite wa ikemasen.* お金持だって無駄なことをしてはいけません. "Even if a person is rich, he should not be wasteful."

DE ARU である　=*naru*=*taru*

DE ARU BAKARI DE [WA] NAKU...MO であるばかりでなく...も　not only...but also, e.g. *Ano hito wa bijin de aru bakari de naku, atama mo ii desu.* あの人は美人であるばかりでなく，頭もいいです. "Not only is she attractive, but she is also smart."

DE ARU KOTO であること　=*taru koto*

DE ARU TO WA であるとは　=*to wa*

DE ATTA であった　=*datta*

DE ATTE MO であっても　even though, e.g. *Yononaka ni wa kanemochi de atte mo kechi na hito ga takusan imasu.* 世の中には金持であってもけちな人が沢山います. "In this world there are many who are stingy, even though they are rich."

DE MANIAU で間に合う　suffice, e.g. *Kore de maniaimasu ka.* これで間に合いますか. "Will this do?"

DE MANIAWASERU で間に合わせる　manage with, serve the purpose, e.g. *Sen-en de maniawaseru tsumori desu.* 千円で間に合わせるつも(積)りです. "I intend to manage with one thousand yen."

DE MANIAWASU で間に合わす　=*de maniawaseru*

DE MO でも

1. even, e.g. *Konna mono de mo ii desu ka.* こんなものでもいいですか. "Is even this kind of thing all right?"

2. whether...or (used in pairs) e.g. *Otoko de mo onna de mo kamawanai kara hitori tetsudai ga hoshii desu.* 男でも女でも構わないから一人手伝いが欲しいです. "I don't care if it's a man or a woman; I want to have a helper."

DE MO NAI でもない　not even, e.g. *Kanemochi de mo nai no ni, itsu mo ōkii jidōsha o kaimasu.* 金持でもないのにいつ(何時)も大きい自動車を買います. "Although he is not even rich, he always buys big cars."

DE MO NAI...DE MO NAI でもない...でもない　it isn't...it isn't, e.g. *Are de mo nai kore de mo nai to hontō ni urusai hito desu.*

あれでもないこれでもないと本当にうるさい人です. "He is a person who says 'this isn't it, that isn't it,' and is so particular."

DE MO NAN' DE MO でも何でも　everything, including..., e.g. *Ano hito wa kanji de mo nan' de mo shitte imasu.* あの人は漢字でも何でも知っています. "He knows everything, including Chinese characters."

DE MO NAN' DE MO NAI でも何でもない　nothing of that sort, e.g. *Ano hito wa yūmei de mo nan' de mo nai no ni, itsu mo ibatte imasu.* あの人は有名でも何でもないのに, 何時も威張っています. "He is not famous or anything like that, but he is always putting on airs."

DE WA では

1. if=*de areba, nara* e.g. *Sūgaku de wa kare wa dare ni mo makenai.* 数学では彼は誰にも負けない. "In (If it is) mathematics, he is equal to anyone."

2. according to, e.g. *Ano hito no iu tokoro de wa amari ii eiga de wa nai yō desu.* あの人の言うところではあま(余)りいい映画ではないようです. "According to what he says, it isn't that good of a movie."

3. used in comparison, e.g. *Kore to sore [to] de wa dochira ga ōkii desu ka.* これとそれではどちらが大きいですか. "Which is bigger, this or that (Between this one and that one, which is bigger)?"

DE WA ARU GA ではあるが (the following clause is often a negative concept) *Ano kyōju wa gakusha de wa aru ga, yoi sensei de wa nai.* あの教授は学者ではあるが, よい先生ではない. "That professor is a good scholar but not a good teacher."

DE WA NAI ではない is not (negative of *de aru, da*) e.g. *Are wa Yamamoto-san de wa arimasen.* あれは山本さんではありません. "That isn't Mr. Yamamoto."

DOKORO DE WA NAI どころではない =*dokoro no hanashi de wa nai* far from... (emphatic) e.g. *Hirune dokoro de wa arimasen deshita.* 昼寝どころではありませんでした. "I certainly did not have time to take a nap (far from taking a nap)."

DOKORO KA どころか far from...but..., rather, on the contrary, e.g. *Hima dokoro ka isogashikute taberu hima mo arimasen deshita.* 暇どころか忙しくて食べる暇もありませんでした. "Far from having free time, I was busy and I didn't even have time to eat."

GA ATTE NO KOTO があってのこと  because of, e.g.  *Anna koto o shita no mo mina zurui kangae ga atte no koto da.*  あんなことをしたのも皆ずるい考えがあってのことだ.  "Because of his sly thinking, he did all that."

GAKARI DE がかりで  combined, e.g.  *Go-nin gakari de mochiageyō to shimashita ga mochiageraremasen deshita.*  五人がかりで持ち上げようとしましたが持ち上げられませんでした.  "With all five people's strength combined they tried to lift it, but they could not do it."

GAKARU がかる  tinged with, e.g.  *Sora ga haiiro gakatte kimashita.*  空が灰色がかって来ました.  "The sky is becoming tinged with grey."

GAMASHII がましい  looks like, sounds like, smacks of, e.g.  *Ano hito wa itsu mo iken gamashii koto o iimasu.*  あの人はいつ(何時)も意見がましいことを言います.  "He always says something which sounds like admonition."  *Hontō no musume na no ni taihen tanin gamashiku furumaimasu.*  本当の娘なのに大変他人がましく振舞います.  "Although she is their real daughter, she behaves like a stranger."

GATERA [NI] がてら  while, at the same time, e.g.  *Sanpo gatera Yamada-san no uchi ni itta.*  散歩がてら山田さんの家に行った.  "While taking a walk I went to Mr. Yamada's house."

GE 気  seeming condition of others, e.g.  *Ano hito no okonai wa otonage ga nai.*  あの人の行いは大人気がない.  "That man's behavior is childish (unbecoming of a grown-up person)."

GORO 頃  approximate time, e.g.  *Ima ichi-ji goro desu.*  今一時頃です.  "It's about one o'clock."  *Kotoshi no haru goro kara byōki desu.*  今年の春頃から病気です.  "She has been sick since about springtime this year."

GOTO ごと  =*gurumi* and all, together with, inclusive, e.g.  *Hatake goto omae ni yarō.*  畑ごとお前にやろう.  "I'll give you the field and all (my property including the field)."

GOTO NI ごと(毎)に  every, e.g.  *Nichiyōbi goto ni ane no uchi ni ikimasu.*  日曜日ごとに姉の家に行きます.  "I go to my sister's house every Sunday."  *Hi goto ni atatakaku narimasu.*  日ごとに暖かくなります.  "It gets warmer every day." (cf. *oki ni*, p. 170)

Note: Difference between *mainichi* and *hi goto ni*: *Mainichi gakkō ni ikimasu.* 毎日学校に行きます. "I go to school every day." *Hi goto ni samuku narimasu.* 日ごとに寒くなります. "Every day it gets colder."—resultant part indicates progressive increase or decrease.

GURAI ぐらい(位)　=*hodo*=*kurai* e.g. *Kare gurai atama ga yokereba ii nā.* 彼ぐらい頭がよければいいなあ. "I wish I were as smart as he is!"

GURUMI ぐるみ　=*goto* altogether, including, e.g. *Ōkina sakana o honegurumi tabemashita.* 大きな魚を骨ぐるみ食べました. "He ate a big fish, bones and all."

IGAI NI 以外に　except, outside of, e.g. *Ano hito igai ni tomodachi ga imasen.* あの人以外に友達がいません. "I have no other friend but him." *Gekkyū igai ni mo shūnyū ga arimasu.* 月給以外にも収入があります. "I have income besides my salary."

IGO 以後　after, e.g. *Raishū no Nichiyō igo wa uchi ni imasu.* 来週の日曜以後は家にいます. "I'll be home after next Sunday." *Sore igo ano hito ni atte imasen.* それ以後あの人に会っていません. "I haven't seen him since then."

IJŌ 以上　more than, beyond, further, e.g. *Kinō wa go-jikan ijō benkyō shimashita.* 昨日は五時間以上勉強しました. "I studied more than five hours yesterday." *Sore ijō no koto wa shirimasen.* それ以上の事は知りません. "I know nothing beyond that." *mittsu ijō* 三つ以上 "three or more"

IKA 以下　less than, below, e.g. *Sen-en ika nara kaimasu.* 千円以下なら買います. "I'll buy it if it is less than one thousand yen." *Kotoshi no deki wa heinen ika desu.* 今年の出来は平年以下です. "This year's crop is below the average year."

IKŌ 以降　on and after, e.g. *Gogatsu ikō kono shigoto o shite imasu.* 五月以降この仕事をしています. "We have been doing this work since May."

IZEN 以前　before, ago, e.g. *Goroku-nen izen ni ichi-do ikimashita.* 五六年以前に一度行きました. "I went there five or six years ago."

JIMIRU じみる　acquire a characteristic which did not exist before (*jimiru* comes from the verb *shimiru*, meaning "soak into, penetrate into," e.g. *Nagai aida inaka ni ita no de inaka jimite shimaimashita.* 長い間田舎にいたので田舎じみてしまいました. "Since I have lived in the country for a long time, I have become rustic."

JŌ 上　from the standpoint of, e.g. *Kono machi wa rekishijō jūyō na machi de aru.* この町は歴史上重要な町である. "This city is important from the historical standpoint."

KANA かな I wonder if that is, e.g. *Are wa Konno-san ka na.* あれは今野さんかな. "I wonder if that is Miss Konno."

KA SHIRA [N] かしら I wonder if (used more by women), *Kore ka shira.* これかしら. "I wonder if this is it."

KA TO BAKARI [OMOU] かとばかり

1.  thinking that it is the best time to..., e.g. *Ima ka to bakari omotte machikamaeta.* 今かとばかり思って待ち構えた. "I waited, thinking that the chance would come at any minute."

2.  thinking that was only, e.g. *Yume ka to bakari yorokonda.* 夢かとばかり喜んだ. "Thinking that it was only a dream, I rejoiced to find it was real."

KARA SHITE からして at a mere glance (sound, taste, etc.) of..., e.g. *Fukusō kara shite sude ni okashii.* 服装からして既におかしい. "From a mere glance at his clothing, I already think he is weird."

KE 気 essence, quality, e.g. *Watakushi wa aburake no nai assari shita mono ga suki desu.* 私は油気のないあっさりしたものが好きです. "I like greaseless, simple food."

KORO 頃 =*goro*

KUSAI 臭い smell of, e.g. *Kono hen wa sakanakusai desu ne.* この辺は魚臭いですね. "There is a fishy smell around here, isn't there?"

MADE NI までに by, e.g. *Kyō no ban go-ji made ni kite kudasai.* 今日の晩五時までに来て下さい. "Please come by five o'clock this evening."

MEKASU めかす intentionally shows himself to be of the quality of the preceding noun, e.g. *Ano hito wa itsu mo bijin mekashite imasu.* あの人は何時も美人めかしています. "She is always trying to make herself a beauty."

MEKU めく have the appearance of, show signs of, e.g. *Kare wa ima o toki meku jitsugyōka desu.* 彼は今を時めく実業家です. "He is a businessman who prospers now." *Dandan haru meite kimashita.* 段々春めいてきました. "Signs of spring show more and more."

MI 味 flavor, essence, e.g. *Ano hito wa ninjōmi ga aru kara suki desu.* あの人は人情味があるから好きです. "I like him, because he has a warm, human touch."

MO ARŌ NI もあろうに unexpected occurrence, e.g. *Hito mo arō ni kyō Tomita-san ni aimashita.* 人もあろうに今日富田さんに会いました. "Of all the people in the world, I met Mr. Tomita today."

MO SOKOSOKO NI もそこそこに hurriedly, e.g. *Asahan mo sokosoko ni uchi o deta.* 朝飯もそこそこに家を出た. "Hurriedly eating breakfast, I left home."

MUKI 向き suitable for, e.g. *Kono resutoran no tabemono wa mannin muki da.* このレストランの食物は万人向きだ. "The food of this restaurant suits all tastes (suitable for ten thousand people)."

NA NO なの sentence-ending phrase for women, more familiar than *desu no. Hanako-san ga ichiban no nakayoshi na no.* 花子さんが一番の仲良しなの. "Hanako is my best friend."

NA NO (N') DA なのだ it is the fact that it is; slightly emphatic ending. *na no da* usually does not have to be translated. *Isu na no desu.* 椅子なのです. "It is a chair."

NA NO DE なので because it is (was), e.g. *Ame na no de uchi ni imashita.* 雨なので家にいました. "Because it was raining, I was home."

NA NO NI なのに although it is (was), in spite of the fact that it is (was), e.g. *Ii otenki na no ni uchi ni imashita.* いいお天気なのに家にいました. "Although the weather was beautiful, I stayed home."

NAMI 並 ordinary, e.g. *Ano gakusei wa sūgaku wa jū-nin nami desu.* あの学生は数学は十人並です. "He is an average student in mathematics (same level as ten other students)."

NAMI IJŌ 並以上 more than average, e.g. *Ano hito wa nami ijō no sainō o motte imasu.* あの人は並以上の才能を持っています. "He has talents above the average."

NAMI NI 並に as, e.g. *Kazoku nami ni toriatsukatte kudasai.* 家族並に取扱って下さい. "Please treat me as a member of your family."

NAMI NO 並の common, ordinary, e.g. *Kodomo ni wa seken nami no seikatsu o sasete yaritai to omoimasu.* 子供には世間並の生活をさせてやりたいと思います. "I want to let my children lead a normal life in this world."

NARA DE WA ならでは　without, none but, except=*de nakute wa*,
e.g. *Sonna koto wa ano hito nara de wa dekimasen.* そんなこと
はあの人ならではでき(出来)ません. "None but he can do such a
thing." *Ano hito nara de wa yo mo hi mo akemasen.* あの人な
らでは夜も日も明けません. "Without him, I can't live."

NARA TOMOKAKU ならと(兎)もかく(角)　it would be excusable
if it were..., but..., e.g. *Kodomo nara tomokaku ōkina otona
ga sonna koto o shitara okashii desu yo.* 子供ならともかく大きな
大人がそんな事をしたらおかしいですよ. "It would be excusable if a
child were to do it, but if an adult does such a thing, it would
be funny."

NARA TONIKAKU ならと(兎)にかく(角)　=*nara tomokaku*

NARI NI なりに　in the capacity of, e.g. *Otona nara otona nari ni
furumainasai.* 大人なら大人なりに振舞いなさい. "If you are an
adult, behave like an adult." *Chichi wa chichi nari ni haha wa
haha nari ni jibun no iken o motte imasu.* 父は父なりに母は母な
りに自分の意見を持っています. "Father has his own opinion and
mother has her own, each in his and her respective capacity."

NARU なる　=*de aru*=*taru*, e.g. *Watakushi wa jibun no haha naru
hito o shirimasen deshita.* 私は自分の母なる人を知りませんでした.
"I didn't know the person who was my own mother." Literary
expression.

NASHI DE なしで　without, e.g. *Norikae nashi de ikaremasu.* 乗
換えなしで行かれます. "You can go without transferring."

NASHI DE WA なしでは　without, followed by a negative idea,
e.g. *Gohan nashi de wa shokuji o tabeta ki ga shimasen.* ごはん
(御飯)なしでは食事を食べた気がしません. "Without rice I don't feel
that I ate a meal."

NASHI NO なしの　without, e.g. *Nihon no Kurisumasu wa Kirisuto
nashi no Kurisumasu desu.* 日本のクリスマスはキリストなしのクリ
スマスです. "Japanese Christmas is a Christmas without Christ."

NI CHIGAINAI に違いない　=*ni sōi nai* there is no doubt of, e.g.
*Ano hito wa Amerika-jin ni chigainai.* あの人はアメリカ人に違い
ない. "There is no doubt that he is an American."

NI DATTE にだって　=*ni de mo* even to, even at, e.g. *Konna
chiisana machi ni datte ii omise ga takusan arimasu yo.* こんな小

さな町にだっていいお店が沢山ありますよ．  "There are many good stores even in such a small town, you know."

**NI DE MO** にでも  =*ni datte*

**NI HIREI SHITE** に比例して  in proportion to, e.g. *Uchi no ōkisa ni hirei shite zei mo takaku narimasu.* 家の大きさに比例して税も高くなります．  "In proportion to the size of the house, the tax becomes higher, too."

**NI HOKA NARANAI** に他ならない  no other than, nothing but, e.g. *Daigaku wa gakusei no benkyō suru tokoro ni hoka naranai.* 大学は学生の勉強する所に他ならない．  "A university is nothing but a place for students to study."

**NI ITARU MADE** に至るまで  until, e.g. *Kare wa shi ni itaru made shujin ni* tsukaeta. 彼は死に至るまで主人に仕えた．  "He served his master until he died."

**NI ITATTE [WA]** に至って  reaching, e.g. *Koko ni itatte wa iu beki kotoba mo nai.* ここに至っては言うべき言葉もない．  "Reaching this stage, I don't even have a word to say."

**NI IWASEREBA** に言わせれば  according to, e.g. *Yamada-san ni iwasereba chikagoro no Tokyo wa totemo suminikui tokoro da sō desu.* 山田さんに言わせれば近頃の東京はとても住みにく（難）い所だそうです．  "According to Mr. Yamada, Tokyo has been a very difficult place to live recently."

**NI KAGITTE** に限って  particularly, one out of all of the things, e.g. *Ano hito ni kagitte sonna koto wa shinai to omoimasu.* あの人に限ってそんな事はしないと思います．  "He is the last man in the world to do a thing like that."

**NI KAKETE** にかけて  extending over, e.g. *Kyonen no natsu kara aki ni kakete byōki deshita.* 去年の夏から秋にかけて病気でした．  "I was ill last year from summer to autumn."

**NI KAKETE WA** にかけては  as far as...is concerned, e.g. *Gogaku ni kakete wa ano hito wa tensai desu.* 語学にかけてはあの人は天才です．  "As far as language learning is concerned, he is a genius."

**NI KANSEZU** に関せず  regardless, e.g. *Seibetsu ni kansezu sainō de saiyō shimasu.* 性別に関せず才能で採用します．  "Regardless of their sex we'll hire by their ability."

**NI KANSHITE** に関して  =*ni tsuite* concerning, e.g. *Nihon ni* *kanshite kyō gakkō de iroiro na koto o naraimashita.* 日本に関して今日学校でいろいろ(色々)な事を習いました. "We learned lots of things about Japan today at school."

NI KANSURU KAGIRI に関する限り as far as... is concerned, e.g. *Nihon bungaku ni kansuru kagiri kare no chishiki wa taishita mono da.* 日本文学に関する限り彼の知識は大したものだ. "As far as Japanese literature is concerned, his knowledge is profound."

NI KAWATTE に代って in place of, e.g. *Kyō Yoshida-san ni kawatte kimashita.* 今日吉田さんに代って来ました. "I came here in place of Miss Yoshida today."

NI KI GA TSUKU に気がつ(付)く notice, e.g. *Heya no sumi ni iru Toshiko-san ni ki ga tsukimashita.* 部屋の隅にいる俊子さんに気がつきました. "I noticed Toshiko, who was in the corner of the room."

NI KI O TSUKERU に気をつ(付)ける pay attention to, e.g. *Kono tsugi wa motto yoku kore ni ki o tsukete kudasai.* この次はもっとよくこれに気をつけて下さい. "Please pay more attention to this next time."

NI KOSHITA KOTO WA NAI にこしたことはない nothing can be better than, e.g. *Sore ni koshita koto wa arimasen.* それにこしたことはありません. "Nothing could be better than that."

NI MENJITE に免じて in consideration for, e.g. *Toshi ni menjite yurushite agemasu.* 年に免じて許して上げます. "I'll forgive you, considering your age."

Note: The age can be taken as either too old or too young.

NI MIERU に見える it looks as if it were, e.g. *Koko kara wa hito ni miemasu.* ここからは人に見えます. "It looks like a person from here."

NI MO HODO GA ARU にもほど(程)がある goes beyond the limit, e.g. *Ano hito no yokubari ni mo hodo ga arimasu.* あの人の欲ばりにもほどがあります. "His greediness knows no limit."

NI MO KAKAWARAZU にもかかわ(拘)らず in spite of, e.g. *Samui tenki ni mo kakawarazu ōzei no hito ga kimashita.* 寒い天気にもかかわらず大勢の人が来ました. "In spite of the cold weather, many people came."

NI NOZONDE に臨んで in the presence of..., at the time of..., e.g. *Kono ki ni nozonde hitotsu itte okitai koto ga aru.* この機に

臨んで一つ言っておきたい事がある．"At this opportunity I have one thing I want to tell you."

NI OKERU にお(於)ける　=*de* in, e.g. *Sekai ni okeru mottomo kyōryoku na kuni wa Beikoku to Soren de aru.* 世界における最も強力な国は米国とソ連である．"The strongest countries in the world are the United States and the Soviet Union."

NI ŌJITE に応じて　in response to, e.g. *Hitsuyō ni ōjite doko e de mo ikimasu.* 必要に応じてどこ(何処)へでも行きます．"In response to necessity, I'll go anywhere."

NI OYOBI に及び　=*ni itatte* reaching, e.g. *Koto koko ni oyobi watakushi wa ketsui shita.* ことここに及び私は決意した．"The situation having reached this stage, I made up my mind."

NI SAISHITE に際して　when, at the time of..., e.g. *Kiki ni saishite awatezu furumau koto wa taisetsu de aru.* 危機に際してあわてず振舞うことは大切である．"It is important to behave without haste at a time of crisis."

NI SEYO にせよ　=*ni shiro*

NI SESSHITE に接して　be in receipt of, e.g. *Kono shirase ni sesshite sugu ie o demashita.* この知ら(報)せに接して直ぐ家を出ました．"Receiving this news, I left home immediately."

NI SHICHA にしちゃ　colloquial for *ni shite wa*

NI SHIRO Noun NI SHIRO にしろ Noun にしろ　whether... or, e.g. *Hon ni shiro zasshi ni shiro dochira ka ni kimenasai.* 本にしろ雑誌にしろどちらかに決めなさい．"Whether a book or a magazine, decide on one."

NI (TO) SHITA TOKORO DE にしたところで　=*ni shite mo* even, e.g. *Kono hon ni shita tokoro de amari yoku arimasen.* この本にしたところであま(余)りよくありません．"Even this book isn't very good."

NI SHITAGATTE に従って　following, e.g. *Chichi no chūkoku ni shitagatte kono daigaku ni haitta.* 父の忠告に従ってこの大学に入った．"Following my father's advice, I entered this university."

NI SHITE MO にしても　=*ni shita tokoro de* even, e.g. *Sore ni shite mo anmari desu.* それにしてもあんまりです．"Even so, that's too much (Even in such circumstances, his behavior was too much)."

NI (TO) SHITE WA にしては　for, e.g. *Amerika-jin ni shite wa*

*sei ga hikui desu.* アメリカ人にしては背が低いです. "For an American he is short."

**NI SŌI NAI** に相違ない =*ni chigainai* it must be, e.g. *Are ga Shimizu-san ni sōi arimasen.* あれが清水さんに相違ありません. "That must be Mr. Shimizu (There is no doubt of his being Mr. Shimizu)."

**NI SOTTE** に沿って along, e.g. *Sono hōshin ni sotte susumimashō.* その方針に沿って進みましょう. "Let's proceed along this line."

**NI SUGINAI** にす(過)ぎない nothing but, no more than, e.g. *Kodomo no itta koto ni sugimasen.* 子供の言ったことにすぎません. "It's no more than what a child said."

**NI TAISHITE** に対して

1. concerning, e.g. *Ano mondai ni taishite donna iken o motte imasu ka.* あの問題に対してどんな意見を持っていますか. "What kind of opinion do you have concerning that problem?"

2. as opposed to, e.g. *Ani ga namakemono de aru no ni taishite otōto wa kinben desu.* 兄が怠け者であるのに対して弟は勤勉です. "While the older brother is lazy, the younger brother is diligent."

**NI TOMONAI** に伴い in keeping with, e.g. *Kagaku no shinpo ni tomonai wareware no seikatsu ga raku ni natta.* 科学の進歩に伴い我々の生活が楽になった. "With the advancement of science, our life has become easy."

**NI TOMONATTE** に伴って =*ni tomonai*

**NI TOTTE** にとって from the standpoint of, for, e.g. *Watakushi ni totte kore wa taihen daiji na koto na no desu.* 私にとってこれは大変大事な事なのです. "This is a very important thing for me."

**NI TSUITE** について concerning, e.g. *Nihon ni tsuite benkyō shimashita.* 日本について勉強しました. "I studied about Japan."

**NI TSURETE** につれて in accordance with, in proportion to, e.g. *Ongaku ni tsurete odotte kudasai.* 音楽につれて踊って下さい. "Please dance with the music."

**NI WA** には for, e.g. *Amerika-jin ni wa mezurashii desu.* アメリカ人には珍しいです. "It (this quality) is rare for an American."

**NI YOREBA** によれば according to, e.g. *Shinbun ni yoreba ashita ame ga furu sō desu.* 新聞によれば明日雨が降るそうです. "According to the newspaper, (I hear) it will rain tomorrow (If we depend on the newspaper...)."

NI YORI により　from, e.g. *Kesa no shinbun ni yori sore o shirimashita.* 今朝の新聞によりそれを知りました。 "We found it out from this morning's newspaper."

NI YORU TO によると　=*ni yoreba* according to, e.g. *Shimizu-san no hanashi ni yoru to Toda-san no otō-san wa totemo okane-mochi da sō desu.* 清水さんの話によると戸田さんのお父さんはとてもお金持だそうです。 "According to Mr. Shimizu, Toda's father is very wealthy."

NI YOTTE によって

1. by, =*de* e.g. *Kono hōhō ni yotte shimashita.* この方法によってしました。 "I did it by this method."

2. depending on, e.g. *Hi ni yotte chigaimasu.* 日によって違います。 "Depending on the day, it is different."

NO AMARI NI のあま(余)りに　because of the intensity of, e.g. *Kanashisa no amari ni hitoban-jū nakidōshimashita.* 悲しさのあまりに一晩中泣き通しました。 "Because of the intensity of grief, I cried all through the night."

NO HAZU DA のはず(筈)だ　is supposed to, is expected to, e.g. *Gozonji no hazu desu.* 御存じのはずです。 "He must know it."

NO HŌ の方　comparison, e.g. *Kono uchi no hō ga ōkii desu.* この家の方が大きいです。 "This house is bigger."

NO IU の言う　so-called, e.g. *Are ga kimi no iu bijin ka.* あれが君のいう美人か。 "Is she what you would call beautiful?"

NO KAWARI NI のかわりに　instead of, replacing something, e.g. *Yamamoto-sensei no kawari ni Shimoda-sensei ga oshiete kudasai-mashita.* 山本先生のかわりに下田先生が教えて下さいました。 "Mr. Shimoda taught us today instead of Mr. Yamamoto."

NO KIRAI GA ARU のきら(嫌)いがある　have a tendency to be, e.g. *Ano hito wa oshaberi no kirai ga arimasu.* あの人はおしゃべりのきらいがある。 "She has a tendency to be a talkative person."

NO KOTO のこと　about, e.g. *Ano hito no koto o kangaete ima-shita.* あの人のことを考えていました。 "I was thinking about him."

NO KOTO DAKARA のことだから　knowing how one is, e.g. *Yamada-san no koto dakara, mata osoku kuru deshō.* 山田さんの

ことだから，又遅く来るでしょう。"Knowing Mr. Yamada (I suspect that) he will come late again."

NO KOTO TO IEBA のことと言えば speaking of, e.g. *Matsudasan no koto to ieba raigetsu Amerika ni iku sō desu yo.* 松田さんのことと言えば来月アメリカに行くそうですよ。"Speaking of Mr. Matsuda, I understand that he will go to America next month."

NO SEI DE のせいで because of, e.g. *Toshi no sei de konogoro wa sugu tsukaremasu.* 年のせいでこの頃はす(直)ぐ疲れます。"Because of my age, I get tired easily nowadays."

NO SEI KA のせいか Perhaps because of, e.g. *Kaze no sei ka atama ga itakute komatte imasu.* 風邪のせいか頭が痛くて困っています。"Perhaps because of a cold, I am suffering from a bad headache."

NO TAME NI のため(為)に

1. because of, e.g. *Byōki no tame ni gakkō o yasumimashita.* 病気のために学校を休みました。"Because of illness, I didn't go to school."

2. for the sake of, e.g. *Kodomo no tame ni tsukurimashita.* 子供のために作りました。"I made it for the children."

NO TŌRI の通り according to, e.g. *Haha no kotoba no tōri ni shimashita.* 母の言葉の通りにしました。"I did just as my mother said."

NO TSUIDE NI のついでに while doing..., e.g. *Kaimono no tsuide ni tomodachi no tokoro e yoru koto ni shimashita.* 買物のついでに友達の所へよることにしました。"I decided to drop in at my friend's house on my way to (back from) the stores."

NO UE DE の上で

1. in, on, e.g. *Chizu no ue de wa sō natte imasu.* 地図の上ではそうなっています。"It appears that way on the map."

2. upon doing, e.g. *Kenkyū no ue de oshiraseshimasu.* 研究の上でお知らせします。"Upon doing research we shall let you know."

NO UE NI の上に in addition to, e.g. *Kaze no ue ni ōame made futte imasu.* 風の上に大雨まで降っています。"In addition to being windy, it is pouring, too."

NO YŌ DA のようだ appears, e.g. *Ano hito wa kodomo no yō da.* あの人は子供のようだ。"He is like a child." (cf. *rashii*, p. 171)

NO YŌ NA のような (attributive of *no yō da*), e.g. *Kodomo no yō na hito desu.* 子供のような人です. "He is (a man) like a child."

NO YŌ NI のように (adverbial of *no yō da*), e.g. *Kodomo no yō ni yorokobimashita.* 子供のように喜びました. "He rejoiced like a child."

NOMI DE [WA] NAKU...MO のみでなく...も not only...but also, e.g. *Kare wa tanin nomi de naku kazoku no mono ni mo amari shinsetsu de wa nai.* 彼は他人のみでなく家族の者にもあま(余)り親切ではない. "Not only is he not kind to strangers, but he is also not kind to his own family either."

NOMI NARAZU のみならず =*nomi de [wa] naku*

O HAJIME [TO SHITE] を初め beginning with, e.g. *Saeki-san o hajime taihen ōzei no hito ga kite imashita.* 佐伯さんを初め大変大勢の人が来ていました. "So many people were there, starting with Mrs. Saeki."

O MOTO NI SHITE を基にして based on, e.g. *Hiragana wa kanji o moto ni shite tsukuraremashita.* 平仮名は漢字を基にして作られました. "Hiragana were made on the basis of Chinese characters."

O MOTTE を以て with, e.g. *Hankōshin o motte oya ni tachimukatta.* 反抗心を以て親にたちむかった. "He confronted his parents with antagonism."

O NEGATTE YAMANAI を願ってやまない desire sincerely (do not stop hoping), e.g. *Anata-gata no seikō o negatte yamimasen.* あなた方の成功を願ってやみません. "I sincerely wish for your success."

O TŌSHITE を通して through, e.g. *Yokoyama-san o tōshite Minami-san ni aimashita.* 横山さんを通して南さんに会いました. "I met Mr. Minami through Mr. Yokoyama."

OKI NI おきに at intervals of, e.g. *Is-shūkan oki ni shiken ga arimasu.* 一週間おきに試験があります. "We have exams every other week." *Gakkai wa futa-tsuki oki ni hirakaremasu.* 学会は二月おきに開かれます. "The academic conference is held every third month."

Note: When the figure gets above three, there is often some confusion in the use of this *oki*, depending on the users.

e.g. *Itsu-ka oki ni kite kudasai.* 五日おきに来て下さい. Theoretically, "Please come every six days (five days between)." But it is more common to interpret, "Please come every five days." In this case, *oki ni* is used in the same way as *goto ni*, p. 159.

**-PPOI** っぽい showing a trait of character, -ish, e.g. *Ano hito wa sukoshi kodomoppoi hito desu.* あの人は少し子供っぽい人です. "He is a little childish."

**RASHII** らしい like, has all the characteristics of, e.g. *Otoko rashii hito desu.* 男らしい人です. "He is a manly man." "He is a man who has all the characteristics of a man." (cf. *no yō na* "like," *Otoko no yō na hito desu.* 男のような人です. "She is a woman who is like a man." See p. 170.

**SHIDAI** 次第

1. depending on, e.g. *Kotoshi Nihon ni iku ka ikanai ka wa okane shidai desu.* 今年日本に行くか行かないかはお金次第です. "Whether I'll go to Japan or not this year depends upon the money."

2. as soon as, e.g. *Tōchaku shidai denwa o kakemasu.* 到着次第電話をかけます. "I'll telephone you as soon as I arrive."

**TARU** たる ＝*de aru*＝*naru*, e.g. *Watakushi wa watakushi no chichi taru hito ga donna hito de atta ka shiranakatta.* 私は私の父たる人がどんな人であったか知らなかった. "I didn't know what kind of a person my father was." literary expression.

**TARU KOTO** たること ＝*de aru koto*, e.g. *Gakusha taru koto ni shūchi o kanjita.* 学者たることに羞恥を感じた. "I was ashamed of the fact that I was a scholar."

**TARU NI MO KAKAWARAZU** たるにもかかわ(拘)らず in spite of the fact that (he) is, e.g. *Kare wa gakusha taru ni mo kakawarazu, hidoku hanashibeta da.* 彼は学者たるにもかかわらず, ひどく話し下手だ. "Although he is a scholar, he is a very poor speaker."

**TARU NI SUGINAI** たるにす(過)ぎない be no more than, e.g. *Are wa kodomo taru ni suginai* あれは子供たるにすぎない. "He is no more than a child."

**TE** て ＝*to iu no wa*

**TEKI** 的 -ic, -cal, e.g. *Iroiro na rekishiteki jinbutsu o kenkyū suru no wa omoshiroi.* 色々な歴史的人物を研究するのは面白い. "It is interesting to study various historical characters."

Note: *rekishiteki* is more literary than *rekishiteki na* (both attributive) *rekishiteki* jinbutsu 歴史的人物 "historical character"

*rekishiteki na* dekigoto 歴史的な出来事 "historical event"
*rekishiteki ni* (adverbial) 歴史的に "historically"
Exception: *hikakuteki* is used adverbially without *ni*
e.g. hikaku*teki* ōkii 比較的大きい "comparatively big"

TO BAKARI OMOU とばかり思う   always think that, e.g. *Sasaki-san to bakari omotte itara Nomura-san deshita.* 佐々木さんとばかり思っていたら野村さんでした. "I always thought that it was Mr. Sasaki, but it turned out to be Mr. Nomura."

TO CHIGATTE と違って   unlike, different from, e.g. *Watakushi to chigatte otōto wa taihen benkyōka desu.* 私と違って弟は大変勉強家です. "Unlike me, my younger brother studies very hard."

TO IEBA と言えば   speaking of, e.g. *Tanaka-san to ieba, chikagoro chittomo aimasen.*   田中さんと言えば近頃ちっとも会いません. "Speaking of Miss Tanaka, I haven't seen her at all lately."

TO IU と言う   which is called, who is called, referred to as, e.g. *Yamada-san to iu hito o shitte imasu ka?* 山田さんと言う人を知っていますか. "Do you know a person called Mrs. Yamada?"

TO IU HODO NO と言うほど(程)の   what you can call, e.g. *Kessaku to iu hodo no mono de wa arimasen ga, omise shimashō.* 傑作と言うほどの物ではありませんがお見せしましょう. "It isn't what you would call a masterpiece, but please look at it."

TO IU NO WA と言うのは   =*te* one which is called, e.g. *Amerika to iu no wa ōkii kuni desu ne.* アメリカというのは大きい国ですね. "America (The country called America) is a big country, isn't it?"

TO IU YŌ NA と言うような   such things as, e.g. *Nihon eiga to iu yō na mono wa mita koto ga arimasen.* 日本映画と言うようなものは見たことがありません. "I have never seen such things as Japanese movies."

TO KA IU とか言う   something like, something to the effect, e.g. *Kyō Sasaki-san to ka iu hito ga kimashita.* 今日佐々木さんとか言う人が来ました. "Today a person called something like Mr. Sasaki came."

TO [WA] KAGIRANAI と限らない   is not necessarily, e.g. *Eigo ga yoku hanaseru hito ga mina Eikoku-jin to wa kagiranai.* 英語がよく話せる人が皆英国人とは限らない. "All those who can speak English fluently are not necessarily English people."

TO (NI) MIERU と見える   it looks as if, e.g. *Asoko wa shizuka na tokoro to miemasu.* あそこは静かな所と見えます. "That looks like a quiet place."

TO (NI) NATTE となって  as, e.g.  *Ano hito wa machi no chūshin to natte yoku hatarakimasu.*  あの人は町の中心となってよく働きます. "He works hard as (by becoming) a central figure in the city."

TO SHITE として  in the capacity of, e.g.  *Kono kotoba o daiji na mono to shite oboete oite kudasai.*  この言葉を大事なものとして覚えておいて下さい. "Please remember this word as a precious thing."

TO SHITE MO としても  =*totemo*

TO SHITE NO としての  as, e.g.  *Hahaoya to shite no sekinin ga arimasu.*  母親としての責任があります. "I have a responsibility as a mother."

TO SHITE WA としては  for, e.g.  *Amerika de umareta hito to shite wa eigo ga heta desu.*  アメリカで生れた人としては英語が下手です. "For a person who was born in the United States, his English is poor."

TO TOMO NI と共に  with, e.g.  *Watakushi no chichi wa toshi to tomo ni yasashiku narimashita.*  私の父は年と共に優しくなりました. "My father became gentle with age."

TO WA とは  =*de aru to wa*  shows surprise, following the topic, e.g.  *Sonna koto to wa yume ni mo shirimasen deshita.*  そんな事とは夢にも知りませんでした. "I wouldn't even have dreamed such a thing!"

TOTEMO とても  =*to shite mo*  even, e.g.  *Watakushi totemo itsu made mo konna shigoto wa shite itaku arimasen.*  私とてもいつ(何時)までもこんな仕事はしていたくありません. "Even I myself do not want to do this kind of work forever."

WA MOCHIRON [NO KOTO] は勿論  not only..., but..., e.g. *Machi wa mochiron mukaigawa no yama mo miemasu.*  町は勿論向い側の山も見えます. "Not only can we see the city, but we can also see the mountains on the other side."

WA OROKA [NA KOTO] はおろか  to say nothing of, much less, e.g.  *Hanasu koto wa oroka, ai mo shimasen deshita.*  話すことはおろか, 会いもしませんでした. "I did not even see him, much less talk with him."

WA TOMOKAKU はと(兎)もかく(角)  setting aside, not to mention, to say nothing of, e.g.  *Jōdan wa tomokaku kore kara dō shite iku tsumori desu ka.*  冗談はともかくこれからどうして行くつ

も（積）りですか．"All jokes aside, what do you intend to do from now on?"

WA TONIKAKU はと（兎）にかく（角）　=*wa tomokaku*

YORI HOKA [NI] NAI より他ない　is the only one, there isn't any other, e.g. *Daitōryō nara kare yori hoka ni nai.* 大統領なら彼より他にない． "If it's a president, there isn't any other one but him."

YORI MO よりも　than (comparison), e.g. *Ano hito no hō ga watakushi yori mo toshiue desu.* あの人の方が私よりも年上です． "She is older than I."

ZEN 然　have an air of, e.g. *Ano hito wa totemo gakusha zen to shite imasu.* あの人はとても学者然としています． "He has a scholarly air."

ZUKU DE ずくで　by means of, e.g. *Chikara zuku de sono shoku o emashita.* 力ずくでその職を得ました． "He obtained the job by force."

ZUTSU ずつ　a certain amount or quantity at a time, e.g. *Nisannin zutsu kimashita.* 二三人ずつ来ました． "They came by twos and threes."

# COMMON NOUN-PREFIXES 接頭語＜せっとうご＞

| Prefix | Kanji | Meaning | Example | Kanji | Meaning |
|--------|-------|---------|---------|-------|---------|
| *bō-* | 某 | a certain | *bōjitsu* | 某日 | a certain day |
| *bō-* | 亡 | deceased | *bōfu* | 亡父 | deceased father |
| *chō-* | 超 | super | *chōjin* | 超人 | superman |
| *dai-* | 第 | No. | *daiichi* | 第一 | No. 1 |
| *dai(tai)-* | 大 | great | *daisakka* | 大作家 | prominent writer |
| *dō-* | 同 | the same | *dōnin* | 同人 | same person |
| *fu-* | 不 | dis-, un- | *futei* | 不定 | uncertainty |
| *fuku-* | 副 | vice-, assistant, sub- | *fukudai-tōryō* | 副大統領 | vice-president |
| | | | *fukuiinkai* | 副委員会 | subcommittee |
| *fuku-* | 複 | double compound | *fukusha* | 複写 | duplication |
| | | | *fukubun* | 複文 | compound sentence |
| *fuku-* | 復 | re- | *fukki* | 復帰 | reversion |
| *gi-* | 義 | in-law artificial | *gibo* | 義母 | mother-in-law |
| | | | *gisoku* | 義足 | artificial leg |
| *giji-* | 疑似 | pseudo- | *giji-shūkyō* | 疑似宗教 | pseudo-religion |
| *hai* | 排 | anti- (exclude) | *hainichi* | 排日 | · anti-Japanese |
| *han-* | 反 | anti- (oppose) | *hanbei* | 反米 | anti-American |
| *han-* | 汎 | Pan- | *Han-Tai-heiyō Kaigi* | 汎太平洋会議 | Pan-Pacific Conference |
| *han-* | 半 | half, semi- | *han-byōnin* | 半病人 | person not quite well |
| *hi* | 被 | receiving, be subjected to | *hisen-ryōkoku* | 被占領国 | occupied country |

| Prefix | Kanji | Meaning | Example | Kanji | Meaning |
|--------|-------|---------|---------|-------|---------|
| *hi-* | 非 | non-, un- | *hibunmei-koku* | 非文明国 | uncivilized country |
| *hira-* | 平 | common | *hirashain* | 平社員 | mere clerk |
| *hon-* | 本 | this, the same | *honnin* | 本人 | the person himself |
| *iku-* | 幾 | several, some | *ikunichi* | 幾日 | several days |
| *ima-* | 今 | modern | *imadoki* | 今時 | present age |
| *ji-* | 次 | next | *jinan* | 次男 | the second son |
| *ji-* | 地 | of the place | *jizake* | 地酒 | *sake* of the place |
| *jō-* | 定 | regular | *jōtokui* | 定得意 | regular customer |
| *jun-* | 準 | semi-, quasi- | *jun-kesshō* | 準決勝 | semi-final |
| *ki-* | 貴 | your | *kikō* | 貴校 | your school |
| *ko-* | 小 | small, petty | *koyaku-nin* | 小役人 | petty official |
| *ko-* | 故 | the late | *ko Miki-shi* | 故三木氏 | the late Mr. Miki |
| *kon-* | 今 | this time | *konshū* | 今週 | this week |
| *kō-* | 好 | good, favorable | *kō-jinbutsu* | 好人物 | good-natured man |
| *kyū-* | 旧 | former, ex- | *kyū-gunjin* | 旧軍人 | ex-soldier |
| *ma-* | 真 | mid-, right | *manatsu* | 真夏 | midsummer |
|  |  |  | *mashita* | 真下 | right below |
|  |  |  | *mas-shōjiki* | 真正直 | plain honesty |
| *mai-* | 毎 | every | *mainichi* | 毎日 | every day |
| *mame-* | 豆 | miniature | *mame-ningyō* | 豆人形 | miniature doll |
| *man-* | 満 | full | *mangetsu* | 満月 | full moon |
| *me-* | 女 | female (human) | *megami* | 女神 | goddess |
|  | 牝(雌) | female (animal) | *meushi* | 牝(雌)牛 | cow |
| *mei-* | 名 | noted | *meimon* | 名門 | noted family |
| *mu-* | 無 | non-, -less | *mujō* | 無情 | heartless |

| Prefix | Kanji | Meaning | Example | Kanji | Meaning |
|--------|-------|---------|---------|-------|---------|
| *nii-* | 新 | new | *niizuma* | 新妻 | new wife |
| *oni-* | 鬼 | tough | *onikenji* | 鬼検事 | relentless prosecutor |
| *rai-* | 来 | next, coming | *rainen* | 来年 | next year |
| *sai-* | 最 | the most | *saidai* | 最大 | the biggest |
| *sai-* | 再 | re- | *saiken* | 再建 | reconstruction |
| *sei-* | 正 | regular | *seikaiin* | 正会員 | regular member |
| *sen-* | 先 | last | *sengetsu* | 先月 | last month |
| *shita-* | 下 | under, lower | *shitabaki* | 下履 | footwear |
| | | rough | *shitagaki* | 下書 | rough copy |
| | | sub- | *shitauke* | 下請け | sub-contract |
| *sho-* | 諸 | many, several | *shokoku* | 諸国 | several countries |
| *shō-* | 正 | genuine | *shōkin* | 正金 | hard cash |
| | | just | *shō ni-ji* | 正二時 | exactly two o'clock |
| *sō* | 総 | entire | *sōin* | 総員 | the whole membership |
| *sora-* | 空 | feigned, pretended | *soramimi* | 空耳 | feigned deafness |
| *sū-* | 数 | several | *sūjitsu* | 数日 | several days |
| *ta-* | 多 | many | *tahōmen* | 多方面 | many sides |
| *ta-* | 他 | strange | *tanin* | 他人 | strangers |
| *tai-* | 大 | big, prominent | *taishi* | 大使 | ambassador |
| *tai-* | 対 | toward, against | *taibei seisaku* | 対米政策 | policy towards America |
| *takaku-* | 多角 | many-sided, multiple | *takaku keiei* | 多角経営 | multiple enterprise |
| *tan-* | 単 | single | *tandoku* | 単独 | singleness, separateness |
| *tō-* | 当 | the said | *tōnin* | 当人 | the said person |
| *toko-* | 常 | ever | *tokonatsu* | 常夏 | eternal summer |

| Prefix | Kanji | Meaning | Example | Kanji | Meaning |
|--------|-------|---------|---------|-------|---------|
| *usu-* | 薄 | light | *usugi* | 薄着 | thin clothing |
|        |    |       | *usucha[iro]* | 薄茶 | light brown |
| *uwa-* | 上 | upper, upward | *uwagi* | 上着 | upper garment |
|        |    | outward | *uwabe* | 上辺 | outward appearance |
| *yō-* | 洋 | Western | *yōfuku* | 洋服 | Western clothes |
| *zai-* | 在 | situated in | *Zaibei Nihon Taishikan* | 在米日本大使館 | Japanese Embassy in the United States |
| *zen-* | 前 | ex-, former | *zen-daitōryō* | 前大統領 | ex-president |
| *zen-* | 全 | whole | *zen-kokumin* | 全国民 | the whole nation |

# COMMON NOUN-SUFFIXES 接尾語＜せつびご＞

| Suffix | Kanji | Meaning | Example | Kanji | Meaning |
|--------|-------|---------|---------|-------|---------|
| -amari =yo | 余り | over | jū-nen amari | 十年余り | over ten years |
| -ban | 番 | ordinal | ichi-ban | 一番 | No. 1 |
| -banme | 番目 | ordinal | ichi-banme | 一番目 | the first |
| -chaku | 着 | arriving at | Tokyo chaku (ressha) | 東京着 | (train) arriving at Tokyo |
| -chū | 中 | during, in the midst of | kyūka-chu | 休暇中 | during the vacation |
| -dai | 大 | size | jitsubutsu-dai | 実物大 | life size |
| -dai | 台 | level | ichiman-en dai | 一万円台 | level of ¥10,000 |
| -dai | 代 | period, age | senkyūhyaku hachijūnen-dai | 1980年代 | 1980s |
| -dan | 壇 | circle | bundan | 文壇 | literary circle |
| -domo | 共 | humble form of plural | watakushi-domo | 私共 | we |
| -dō | 堂 | shop name | Fūgestsu-dō | 風月堂 | Fūgetsudō |
| -dōshi | 通し | all through | yodōshi | 夜通し | all night |
| -fū | 風 | style, manner | Nihon-fū | 日本風 | Japanese style |
| -gata | 方 | about (time) | yūgata | 夕方 | twilight |
| -gata | 方 | honorific form of plural | anata-gata | あなた方 | you (plural) |
| -gata | 型 | model | 1978-nen gata | 1978年型 | 1978 model |
| -gata | がた | about | sen-en gata | 千円がた | about ¥1,000 |
| -goto | 事 | matter | tadagoto | 只事 | ordinary matter |
| -han | 犯 | offense | shohan | 初犯 | the first offense |
| -hatsu | 発 | departing | Kyoto-hatsu (ressha) | 京都発 | (train) departing Kyoto |

| Suffix | Kanji | Meaning | Example | Kanji | Meaning |
|---|---|---|---|---|---|
| -hi | 費 | cost | kenchiku-hi | 建築費 | cost of construction |
| -i | 位 | rank | ichi-i | 一位 | the first in rank |
| -jaku | 弱 | a little under | yonjū-jaku | 四十弱 | a little under forty |
| -ji | 事 | matter, affair | kanshinji | 関心事 | matter of interest |
| -ji | 次 | order | dai-ni-ji | 第二次 | the second in order |
| -jin | 人 | nationality | Nihon-jin | 日本人 | Japanese |
| -jo | 所 | place | shūkaijo | 集会所 | meeting hall |
| -jō | 場 | place | undōjō | 運動場 | athletic field |
| -jū | 重 | fold | ni-jū | 二重 | two folds |
| -jū | 中 | entire | ichinichi-jū | 一日中 | all day |
| -ka | 化 | -ize | gutaika suru | 具体化する | materialize |
| -ka | 家 | professional person | geijutsu-ka | 芸術家 | artist |
| -kai | 会 | world, community | shakai | 社会 | society |
| -ke | 家 | family | Yamada-ke | 山田家 | the Yamada Family |
| -kyō | 強 | a little over | ni-mairu kyō | 二マイル強 | a little over two miles |
| -kyō | 教 | faith | kirisuto-kyō | キリスト教 | Christianity |
| -kyō | 狂 | maniac | shashin-kyō | 写真狂 | photography maniac |
| -me | 目 | ordinal | hitotsu-me | 一つ目 | the first one |
| -nai | 内 | within | kikan-nai | 期間内 | within the period |
| -ni | 似 | resemble | chichioya-ni | 父親似 | resembling father |
| -ra | 等 | plural | kodomo-ra | 子供等 | children |
| -rai | 来 | since | sakunen-rai | 昨年来 | since last year |
| -ryū | 流 | style | Furansu-ryū | フランス流 | French style |
| -sei | 性 | -ness, quality | sekkyokusei | 積極性 | positiveness |

| Suffix | Kanji | Meaning | Example | Kanji | Meaning |
|--------|-------|---------|---------|-------|---------|
| -sei | 製 | manufactured | Nihon-sei | 日本製 | manufactured in Japan |
| -sen | 選 | selections | kindai-Nihon bungakusen | 近代日本文学選 | selections from modern Japanese literature |
| -sen | 線 | transit line | Yamanote-sen | 山手線 | Yamanote line |
| -shiki | 式 | model fashion | shinshiki kyūshiki | 新式 旧式 | new model old fashion |
| -sho | 所 | place | yakusho | 役所 | government office |
| -shu | 手 | person | untenshu | 運転手 | driver |
| -sugi | 過 | past | go-ji sugi | 五時過 | after five o'clock |
| -tachi | 達 | plural | watakushi-tachi | 私達 | we |
| -tai | 帯 | zone | nettai | 熱帯 | torrid zone |
| -tan | 端 | end | sainantan | 最南端 | end furthest south |
| -tō | 等 | etc. | Beikoku, Eikoku, tō | 米国英国 等 | U.S., England, etc. |
| -tsuki | 付 | with, attached | kagu-tsuki | 家具付 | furnished (rooms, etc.) |
| -tsume =zume | 詰 | appointment (to a position, etc.) | Yokohama-zume | 横浜詰 | appointed to the Yokohama office |
| -tsuzuki | 続 | row, continuity | yane-tsuzuki | 屋根続 | rows of roofs |
| -ue | 上 | honorific for superior | chichi-ue | 父上 | venerable father |
| -usu | 薄 | lack of | temochi-usu | 手持薄 | not much on hand |
| -ya | 屋 | shop dealer | hon-ya hon-ya-san | 本屋 本屋さん | bookstore book dealer, bookstore owner |
| -yami | 病み | patient | haibyō-yami | 肺病病み | tuberculosis patient |

| Suffix | Kanji | Meaning | Example | Kanji | Meaning |
|--------|-------|---------|---------|-------|---------|
| -yoke | 除け | protection | kaze-yoke | 風除け | shelter against wind |
| -yo | 余 =amari | | | | |
| -yori | 寄り | close by | Yamanote-yori | 山手寄り | near the bluff |
| -yuki | 行き | bound for | Amerika-yuki | アメリカ行き | bound for America |
| -zuke | 付 | dated | mikka-zuke | 三日付 | dated the third |
| -zuki | 好 | lover of | yakyū-zuki | 野球好 | baseball fan |
| -zuki | 付 | attached to | taishikan-zuki | 大使館付 | attaché to an embassy |
| -zukume | ずくめ | covered with | kuro-zukume | 黒ずくめ | all in black |
| -zukushi | 尽し | enumeration | kuni-zukushi | 国尽し | enumeration of the names of countries |
| -zume | 詰 | packed | hako-zume | 箱詰 | packed in a box |
| -zumi | 積 | load | goton-zumi kasha | 五噸積貨車 | freight car with five-ton load capacity |
| -zure | ずれ | worldly-wise | seken-zure | 世間ずれ | overly wise in worldly affairs |
| -zure | づれ | company, party | futari-zure | 二人づれ | a party of two |

## COMMON PROPER NOUN-SUFFIXES

### Geographical Names

| Suffix | Kanji | Meaning | Example | Kanji | Meaning |
|--------|-------|---------|---------|-------|---------|
| -chō =machi | 町 | town, district | Eifuku-chō | 永福町 | Eifuku District |
| -dō | 道 | old province | San'in-dō | 山陰道 | San'in Province |
| -dōri =tōri | 通 | avenue, street | Ginza-dōri | 銀座通 | Ginza Street |
| -fu | 府 | metropolitan prefecture | Kyoto-fu | 京都府 | Kyoto Prefecture |
| -gawa =kawa | 川, 河 | river | Sumida-gawa | 隅田川 | Sumida River |

| Suffix | Kanji | Meaning | Example | Kanji | Meaning |
|--------|-------|---------|---------|-------|---------|
| -gun | 郡 | county, sub-prefecture | Koshi-gun | 古志郡 | Koshi County |
| -ji | 路 | road | Kiso-ji | 木曽路 | Kiso Road |
| -jima =shima | 島 | island | Iō-jima | 硫黄島 | Iwō Island |
| -kaidō | 街道 | highway | Kiso-kaidō | 木曽街道 | Kiso Highway |
| -kaidō | 海道 | highway along the sea | Tōkaidō | 東海道 | Tōkaidō Highway |
| -ken | 県 | prefecture | Chiba-ken | 千葉県 | Chiba Prefecture |
| -ko | 湖 | lake | Yamanaka-ko | 山中湖 | Lake Yamanaka |
| -ku | 区 | ward | Shinagawa-ku | 品川区 | Shinagawa Ward |
| -machi =chō | 町 | district town | Ōi-machi | 大井町 | Ōi District |
| -mura | 村 | village | Kamikumi-mura | 上組村 | Kamikumi Village |
| -rettō | 列島 | chain of islands | Chishima-rettō | 千島列島 | Kurile Islands |
| -san =yama=zan | 山 | mountain | Fuji-san | 富士山 | Mt. Fuji |
| -shi | 市 | city | Osaka-shi | 大阪市 | Osaka City |
| -shima =jima | 島 | island | Awaji-shima | 淡路島 | Awaji Island |
| -shū | 洲 | continent | Ajia-shū | アジア洲 | Asian Continent |
| -shū | 州 | U.S. state | Oregon-shū | オレゴン州 | State of Oregon |
| -to | 都 | metropolis | Tokyo-to | 東京都 | Tokyo Metropolis |
| -tō =shima=jima | 島 | island | Tonga-tō | トンガ島 | Tonga Island |
| -wan | 湾 | bay | Tokyo-wan | 東京湾 | Tokyo Bay |
| -yama =san=zan | 山 | mountain | Asama-yama | 浅間山 | Mt. Asama |
| -yō | 洋 | ocean | Taihei-yō | 太平洋 | Pacific Ocean |

| Suffix | Kanji | Meaning | Example | Kanji | Meaning |
|--------|-------|---------|---------|-------|---------|
| -zan   | 山    |         |         |       |         |

*=san=yama*

Note: In writing out a Japanese address, the largest unit comes first.

　　e.g.　*Nihon, Tokyo-to, Kodaira-shi, Suzuki-chō, 3-chōme,* 100-5
　　　　日本　東京都　小平市　　鈴木町　　3丁目　100-5
　　　　100-5, 3-chōme, Suzuki-chō, Kodaira-shi, Tokyo-to, Japan

## Personal Names

*-chan* ちゃん　(see *-san*) used affectionately to address children
　　*Tomoko-chan* 友子ちゃん　Tomoko
*-dono* 殿　Mr.; more formal than *-san*, often used in official documents
　　*Suzuki-dono* 鈴木殿　Mr. Suzuki
*-jō*　嬢　Miss; not used to address an unmarried woman directly,
　　but used to refer to her
　　*Yamada-jō* 山田嬢　Miss Yamada
*-kun*　君　Mr., Master; often used by young men and boys to address
　　their male friends
　　*Nakajima-kun* 中島君　Nakajima
*-me*　奴　expresses abuse
　　*ano Egawa-me* あの江川奴　that despicable Egawa
*-sama* 様　Mr., Mrs., Miss; more polite than *-san*, commonly used to
　　address others in letters
　　*Toda-sama* 戸田様　Mr. Toda
*-san*　さん　Mr., Mrs., Miss; most common suffix
　　*Tanaka-san* 田中さん　Mrs. Tanaka
*-shi*　氏　Mr.; honorific suffix, not used to address a man directly,
　　but used to refer to him, particularly in writing
　　*Shimizu-shi* 清水氏　Mr. Shimizu

Some of the above suffixes are used not only after proper names,
but also after some nouns.

　　e.g.　*botchan* 坊ちゃん　used to address a little boy
　　*ojō-san* お嬢さん　used to address a girl
　　*shashō-san* 車掌さん　used to address a train conductor
　　*oisha-san* (*sama*) お医者さん　used to refer to a physician
　　　　　(Usually the word *sensei* 先生　is used to address
　　　　　a physician)

Note: In writing out a person's name, the family name precedes the given name.

   e.g.  *Yamada Jirō* 山田次郎 Jirō Yamada

It should also be remembered that it is not common in Japan to call one's acquaintance (even a fairly close friend) by his/ her first name, as in the United States. *Yamada-san* (last name plus *san*) is the most common way to address Mrs. Yamada, one's acquaintance.

## Terms of Address

It is common to address persons of a certain position by their title instead of their name. This is especially true within a social structure where the ranking is apparent. In fact, it sounds almost impolite to address one's superior by his / her last name plus *-san*. It is naturally unthinkable to call your superior by just his / her first name as is often done in the United States. It should also be noted that the pronoun *anata* あなた (or *kimi* 君 for men) "you" should not be used when one talks to one's superior, that is, use of *anata* or *kimi* should be reserved only to one's equals and inferiors.

   e.g.  *Buchō*, chotto ohanashi shitai koto ga arimasu ga, ima oiso-
       gashii desu ka? 部長, 一寸お話ししたいことがありますが, 今
       お忙しいですか. "Department head, I would like to speak
       to you a minute; are you busy now?"

More examples of position traditionally addressed only by title:

| | |
|---|---|
| *kachō*(*-san*) 課長 | section chief |
| (*ken*)*chiji*(*-san*) 知事 | (prefectural) governor |
| *kōchōsensei* 校長先生 | school principal |
| *senmu*(*-san*) 専務 | managing director |
| *sensei* 先生 | most-used term for addressing a person who commands respect from the nature of his / her work such as teachers, professors, doctors, writers, Diet members, etc. Even among the colleagues of the same school, it is customary to call each other by *sensei* or so-and-so *sensei* instead of by his / her name. |
| *shachō*(*-san*) 社長 | president of a company |
| *shichō*(*-san*) 市長 | mayor |
| *chōchō*(*-san*) 町長 | mayor of a small town |
| *sonchō*(*-san*) 村長 | head of a small village |

# TERMS FOR FAMILY MEMBERS AND RELATIVES

The terms which are used to address or refer to family members or relatives come basically in pairs, the neutral one and the more polite one. The neutral form is used in writing as well as in referring to one's own family (humble form), while talking to a non-family person or persons. The polite form is used to directly address one's own family members or to refer to another person's family. This form takes a variety of suffixes, changing the level of politeness.

　e.g.　father

　　neutral:

　　　　*chichi* 父 (written)　Kare no *chichi* wa gaikōkan de aru. 彼の父は外交官である。 "His father is a diplomat."

　　　　(spoken-humble)　*Chichi* wa ima dekakete imasu. 父は今出か(掛)けています。　"Father is out now."—refers to the speaker's own father

　　　　*chichioya* 父親　more impersonal than *chichi*

　　polite:

　　　　*otōsan* (address)　*Otōsan*, kyō no gogo isogashii desu ka. お父さん，今日の午後忙しいですか。 "Dad, are you busy this afternoon?"

　　　　*Otōsan* wa donna oshigoto o shite iraremasu ka. お父さんはどんなお仕事をしていられますか. "What kind of work does your father do?"—refers to someone else's father

　　more polite:

　　　　*otōsama* お父様　used in the same way as *otōsan*, but more polite

　　affectionate:

　　　　*otōchan* (*tōchan*) お父ちゃん　used mainly by little children, addressing their father

　　　　*otōchama* お父ちゃま　used in the same way as *otōchan*, but more polite

　　rough:

　　　　*oyaji* おやじ　Not a good term, but is often used by men in informal situations to refer to their own fathers, *oyaji-san* for others'.

There are still more terms for "father," which are used in different localities in Japan, but one can easily learn them after staying there for some time.

In the following list, the terms for other family members will be given. Like the terms for "father," they have several different forms, of which the most commonly used ones will be listed.

| English equivalent | neutral | polite | more polite | children | rough |
|---|---|---|---|---|---|
| mother | haha,<br>母<br>hahaoya<br>母親 | okāsan<br>お母さん | okāsama | (o)kāchan<br>(chama) | ofukuro<br>おふくろ |
| parents | ryōshin<br>両親 | goryōshin<br>御両親 | goryōshin-<br>sama | | |
| husband | shujin<br>主人<br>otto<br>夫 | goshujin<br>御主人<br>dannasama<br>旦那様 | goshujin-<br>sama | | danna<br>旦那 |
| wife | kanai<br>家内<br>tsuma<br>妻 | okusan<br>奥さん | okusama | | kakā<br>嚊 |
| son | musuko<br>息子<br>bōya<br>坊や | musukosan<br><br>botchan<br>坊ちゃん | goshisokusama (more often used<br>御子息様　　　for a grown son)<br>obotchama (more often used for a<br>　　　　　young son) | | |
| daughter | musume<br>娘 | musumesan<br>娘さん<br>ojōsan<br>お嬢さん | ojōsama | | |
| elder brother | ani<br>兄 | oniisan<br>お兄さん | oniisama | (o)niichan<br>(chama) | aniki<br>兄貴 |
| elder sister | ane<br>姉 | onēsan<br>お姉さん | onēsama | (o)nēchan<br>(chama) | aneki<br>姉貴 |
| family | kazoku<br>家族 | gokazoku<br>御家族 | gokazokusama | | |

| English equivalent | neutral | polite | more polite | children | rough |
|---|---|---|---|---|---|
| siblings | *kyōdai* 兄弟(姉妹) | *gokyōdai* 御兄弟 | The word *kyōdai* is used for siblings, that is, for both brothers and sisters, but when one talks only about sisters, the word *shimai* 姉妹 should be used. | | |
| baby | *akanbō* 赤ん坊 | *akachan* 赤ちゃん | | | |
| grand-father | *sofu* 祖父 | *ojiisan* お祖父さん | *ojiisama* | *(o)jiichan (chama)* | *jijii* 爺 |
| grand-mother | *sobo* 祖母 | *obāsan* お祖母さん | *obāsama* | *(o)bāchan (chama)* | *babā* 婆 |
| uncle | *oji* 伯父, 叔父* | *ojisan* 伯父さん, 叔父さん | *ojisama* | *ojichan (chama)* | |
| aunt | *oba* 伯母, 叔母* | *obasan* 伯母さん, 叔母さん | *obasama* | *obachan (chama)* | |
| nephew | *oi* 甥 | *oigosan* 甥御さん | | | |
| niece | *mei* 姪 | *(o)meigosan* お姪御さん | | | |
| cousin | *itoko* いとこ | *oitokosan* おいとこさん | | | |

\* 伯父 叔父 } both uncle, but { older than one's parent / younger than one's parent

伯母 叔母 } both aunt, but { older than one's parent / younger than one's parent

# PRONOUNS 代名詞＜だいめいし＞

Japanese pronouns are a class of nouns. Thus, the rules govern‧ing the use of pronouns are the same as those of nouns as shown below:

I. Characteristics of Japanese Pronouns

1. Generally no distinction between singular and plural, except to attach plural suffixes to some personal pronouns (see Noun, p. 150)

   e.g.
   - *watakushi* 私 "I"
   - *watakushi-tachi* 私達 "we"
   - *watakushi-domo* 私共 "we"—humble plural form
   - *anata* あなた "you"—singular
   - *anata-tachi* あなた達 "you"—plural
   - *anata-gata* あなた方 "you"—honorific plural form
   - *omae* お前 "you"—used only to one's subordinate
   - *omae-ra* お前等 "you"—plural, etc.

2. No case (Particles which follow pronouns decide the case in Japanese, see Particles, pp. 93–140.)

3. Many more pronouns in Japanese than English. Many of these pronouns depend on interpersonal relationship (See below, II, 1)

II. Common Japanese Pronouns

1. Person 1st person

   *watakushi* 私 (polite), *watashi, atashi, boku* 僕 (used by men), more polite than *ore*

   2nd person

   *anata* あなた (most common), *anta* (not as polite as *anata*), *omae* お前 (to a subordinate), *kimi* (used by men)

   3rd person

   *kare* 彼 "he," *kanojo* 彼女 "she," *kono kata* この方, *sono kata* その方, *ano kata* あの方 mean "this person," "that person right there," and "that person over there," respectively. They are also used for "he," or "she." (*Kata*

megane o *kaketa*  (=kakete iru) hito  眼鏡をかけた人
"person wearing glasses"

d.  V*nakatta* (negative past)  *ikanakatta* hito 行かなかった人
"person who didn't go"

Example of a sentence with some noun modifiers

| *Watakushi no* | *tonari no* | *uchi ni* | *sunde iru* |
|---|---|---|---|
| 私の | 隣の | 家に | 住んでいる |
| (Noun+*no*) | (Noun+*no*) | (Noun+*ni*) | (V₃—relative clause) |
| (noun modifier) | (noun modifier) | (adverbial phrase) | (noun modifier) |

*Watakushi no*      *tonari no*      *uchi ni*      *sunde iru*
私の                隣の            家に            住んでいる
(Noun+*no*)        (Noun+*no*)    (Noun+*ni*)    (V₃—relative clause)
(noun modifier)   (noun modifier)  (adverbial phrase) (noun modifier)

*Kirei na*        *yasashii*      *onna no*      *hito wa* *kono*
きれい(綺麗)な     優しい         女の           人は      この
(Cop. n.+*na*)    (Adj.)         (Noun+*no*)    (Subject) (Non-conj.
                                                            adj.)
(noun modifier)  (noun modifier) (noun modifier)    (noun modifier)

*kinjo no*        *shōgakkō no*    *sensei    desu.*
近所の            小学校の          先生       です.
(Noun+*no*)      (Noun+*no*)      (Complement) (Copula—main verb)
(noun modifier) (noun modifier)

"A pretty, kind lady who lives next door to my house is a teacher at the elementary school in this neighborhood."

In the above example, the core of the sentence is *hito wa sensei desu* 人は先生です, "a person is a teacher," and the rest (*underlined* words and phrases) are mostly noun modifiers (one adverbial phrase).

# NOUN MODIFIERS
## 名詞修飾語〈めいししゅうしょくご〉

In Japanese, every noun modifier precedes the noun which it modifies whether it is a word, phrase, or clause. The following are the five most common noun modifiers.

1. Noun (or pronoun)+*no watakushi no tonari no uchi no kodomo* 私の隣の家の子供 "my neighbor's child"

2. Copular noun+*na* (positive) *kirei na* uchi きれい(綺麗)な家 "pretty house"

   Copular noun+*de wa nai* (negative) *shizuka de wa nai* tokoro 静かではない所 "place which is not quiet"

3. Adjective (positive) *ōkii* uchi 大きい家 "big house"

   (negative) *ōkikunai* heya 大きくない部屋 "room which is not big"

4. Non-conjugative adjective *konna* mono こんなもの "this kind of thing"

   *dono* hito どの人 "which person"

5. Sentence-ending verb forms—Relative clauses

   1. There is no relative pronoun in Japanese, and the verb which directly precedes the noun modifies it. (Exception, see *tokoro no*, p. 78)

   2. There is no distinction between restrictive and non-restrictive clauses in Japanese.

      a. $V_3$ (positive) *hanashite iru* hito 話している人 "talking person," that is, "person who is talking"

      b. $V_{nai}$ (negative) *hanasanai* hito 話さない人 "un-speaking person," that is, "person who doesn't speak"

      *c. $V_{ta}$ (positive past) *itta* hito 行った人 "person who went"

---

\* Sometimes $V_{ta}$ as a noun modifier, rather than being an objective modifier, implies a speaker's evaluation of the following noun.

e.g. *komatta* hito 困った人 "person with whom we are having trouble"

cf. *komatte iru* hito 困っている人 "person who is in trouble"

is more polite than *hito*. *Kata* cannot be used
without modifiers, while *hito* can be used independently without any modifiers.)

Interrogative

*dono kata* どの方 "which person," *dare* 誰 "who,"
*donata* どなた "who" (more polite than *dare*)

Note: There are many more pronouns which are used for different
occasions and in different localities in Japan.

2. Thing (demonstrative pronoun)

$\begin{cases} kore \text{ これ} \\ kochira \text{ こちら} \\ kotchi \text{ こっち} \end{cases}$ "this"  $\begin{cases} sore \text{ それ} \\ sochira \text{ そちら} \\ sotchi \text{ そっち} \end{cases}$ "that"

*dore* どれ "which of the three or more"

$\begin{cases} are \text{ あれ} \\ achira \text{ あちら} \\ atchi \text{ あっち} \end{cases}$ "that over there"

$\begin{cases} dotchi \text{ どっち} \\ dochira \text{ どちら} \end{cases}$ "which of the two"

Note: *kochira, sochira, achira* are more polite than *kore, sore, are.*
*kotchi, sotchi, atchi, dotchi* are the most colloquial.

3. Place* *koko* ここ "here," *soko* そこ "just there," *asoko*
あそこ "over there"

4. Direction   *kochira* こちら "this direction," *sochira* そち
ら "right over there," *achira* あちら "way over there,"
*dochira* どちら "which direction" (see also 2 above for
different meanings of *kochira, sochira, achira,* and
*dochira*)

For the difference of *ko, so, a* and *do,* see Non-conjugative
Adjectives, p. 92.

5. Other interrogative pronouns, see Interrogative words, p.
141.

---

* In English the place words such as "here" or "there" are always adverbs,
but in Japanese they are pronouns. Therefore, we have to add the particle
*ni* (or *de*) after these words, to use them adverbially. e.g. Sono hon wa
*koko ni* arimasu. その本はここにあります。 "The book is here."

# ADVERBS　副詞＜ふくし＞

Japanese adverbs are similar to their English counterparts in that they do not inflect, and they modify verbs, adjectives, and other adverbs. But some Japanese adverbs also modify a limited number of nouns (See Noun, II, 3, a, p. 151), as well as copular nouns plus *na*. Many Japanese adverbs have stricter limitations in their usage than English adverbs. That is, some of them are always followed by positive verbs, some only by negative verbs, and some change meanings depending on whether they are followed by positive or negative expressions. Others are always followed by tentative or tentative-negative expressions, or by expressions of comparison, and so forth. This section presents the most commonly used adverbs with these particular limitations.

In addition, there are several words which actually belong to other parts of speech, but which are sometimes used as adverbs. When used as adverbs, some of them retain their original forms, and others inflect. Examples of adverbs and words used as adverbs appear below in the following order:

I. Forms of Japanese Adverbs
    1. True adverbs
    2. Adverbs derived from other parts of speech

II. Common Adverbs and their Usage
    1. Time
    2. Quantity
    3. Degree
    4. Circumstance

III. Commonly Used Adverbs with Limitations
    1. Adverbs used only with positive expressions
    2. Adverbs used only with negative expressions or negative ideas
    3. Adverbs with meanings varying according to use with positive or negative expressions
    4. Adverbs used with conditional expressions

    5.   Adverbs used with tentative expressions

    6.   Adverbs used with negative tentative expressions

    7.   Adverbs used with expressions of comparison

I.  Forms of Japanese Adverbs

    1.   True Adverbs which modify:

        a.  Verbs, adjectives, other adverbs, copular nouns,
e.g. *mattaku* 全く "completely," *kanari* かなり
(可成) "fairly," *totemo* とても "very," etc.

        b.  Certain nouns, e.g. *zutto* mukashi ずっと昔 "long
ago," *motto* mae もっと前 "further forward," *mō*
ichido もう一度 "once more," *sukoshi* kita 少し北
"a little north," etc.

    2.   Adverbs derived from other parts of speech

        a.  Adjectives

            1.  Adj$_{ku}$ similar to English adjective+ly, e.g.
*hayaku* 早く "early," *takaku* 高く "highly,"
*ku*-form, see p. 89.

            2.  Repetition of Adj$_{stem}$, e.g. *hayabaya* 早々
"early"

            3.  Repetitition of Adj$_{ku}$, e.g. *yokuyoku* よくよく
"exceedingly"

        b.  Copular Noun+*ni*

           This adverbial phrase functions similarly to ad-
jective+*ku*, e.g. *shizuka ni* 静かに "quietly"

        c.  Nouns (See Nouns, II, 2, pp. 150-51)

            1.  Quantity words and numbers, e.g. *takusan*
沢山 "many," *sukoshi* 少し "a few," "a lit-
tle," *hitotsu* 一つ "one"

            2.  Time words, e.g. *ima* 今 "now," *kyō* 今日
"today"

            3.  Onomatopoeic words, e.g. *gatagata* がたがた
*kotsukotsu* こつこつ See pp. 202-207.

            4.  Degree words, e.g. *issō* 一層 "even more"

            5.  Circumstantial words, e.g. *mōzen* 猛然 "res-
olutely," *danko* 断固 "decisively"

        d.  Verbs

            1.  V$_{te}$ *amanjite* 甘んじて "contentedly" from
*amanjiru* 甘んじる "to be contented"

*aratamete* 改めて "again" from *aratameru* 改
める "renew"

*awasete* 合わせて "collectively" from *awaseru*
合わせる "put together"

*ayamatte* 誤って "by mistake" from *ayamaru*
誤る "err"

*kononde* 好んで "willingly" from *konomu* 好む
"like"

*kesshite* 決して "by no means" from *kessuru*
決する "determine (not) to do...," always
used with a negative verb

*hatashite* 果たして "as was expected" from
*hatasu* 果たす "accomplish"

*harete* 晴れて "openly, publicly" from *hareru*
晴れる "clear up"

*medatte* 目立って "noticeably" from *medatsu*
目立つ "be conspicuous"

*taete* 絶えて "never, not at all" from *taeru* 絶
える "cease to exist"

2. V*zu*  *taezu* 絶えず "without stopping, con-
tinuously" from *taeru* 絶える "cease to
exist"

3. V₂  *amari* あま（余）り "too..." from *amaru*
余る "remain, be left over"

4. V₂V₂ *tsugitsugi* 次々 "one by one" from *tsugu*
次ぐ "come after"

V₃V₃ *yukuyuku* 行く行く "in the future" from
*yuku* 行く "go," *kawarugawaru* かわ
るがわる "alternately" from *kawaru*
"change," *masumasu* ますます "more
and more" from *masu* 増す "increase."

5. V₃+*ni* *omouni* 思うに "in my opinion" from
*omou* 思う "think"

II. Common Adverbs and their Usage

1. Time

*futatabi* 再び "again," more literary than *mata*, e.g. *Kyonen
futatabi sono chi o lazuneta.* 去年再びその地を訪ねた。 "I
visited the place again last year."

*kanete* かねて "previously, before," e.g. *Sore ni tsuite wa*

*kanete kiite imashita.* それについてはかねて聞いていました. "I heard about it before."

*saisan* 再三 "again and again," e.g. *Saisan kikasaremashita.* 再三聞かされました. "I was told about it again and again."

*shibaraku* 暫らく "for a long time," e.g. *Ano hito ni wa shibaraku atte imasen.* あの人にはしば(暫)らく会っていません. "I haven't seen him for a long time."

*shibashiba* 屢々 "often" =*tabitabi*=*yoku yoku* is most colloquial, e.g. *Asoko e wa shibashiba ashi o hakonda.* あそこへはしばしば(屢々)足を運んだ. "I went there often."

*sugu* す(直)ぐ "immediately," e.g. *Sugu kite kudasai.* すぐ来て下さい. "Please come right away."

*tōtō* とうとう(到頭) "finally" =*yōyaku, yatto* e.g. *Tōtō dekimashita.* とうとうでき(出来)ました. "I finally finished it."

*yagate* やがて "soon" =*mamonaku* e.g. *Yagate kuru deshō.* やがて来るでしょう. "He will probably come soon."

## 2. Quantity

*chotto* ちょっと(一寸) "a little," e.g. *Chotto matte kudasai.* ちょっと待って下さい. "Please wait a minute."

*tanto* たんと "many, much," e.g. *Ano hito wa okane o tanto motte imasu.* あの人はお金をたんと持っています. "He has lots of money."

## 3. Degree

*goku* ご(極)く "exceedingly" =*totemo*=*hanahada* e.g. *Goku uchiwa no hanashi desu ga...* ごく内輪の話ですが... "It's an exceedingly personal story, but..."

*kanari* かなり(可成) "considerably, quite," e.g. *Kanari yoku dekite imasu.* かなりよくでき(出来)ています. "It is quite well done."

*mattaku* 全く "very much," e.g. *Ima mattaku komatte imasu.* 今, 全く困っています. "I am really in trouble now."

*motto* もっと "more," e.g. *Sono hō ga motto yasui desu yo.* その方がもっと安いですよ. "That is cheaper."

*mottomo* 最も "most" =*ichiban* e.g. *Sore ga mottomo jūyō da.* それが最も重要だ. "It is most important."

*taihen* 大変 "very" =*totemo* e.g. *Taihen ōkina uchi desu.* 大変大きな家です. "It is a very big house."

*yohodo* よほど(余程) "very, greatly," e.g. *Yohodo tsukareta to miete mada nete imasu.* よほど疲れたとみえてま(未)だ寝てい

ます. "Apparently he was very tired, because he is still sleeping."

*zutto* ずっと "by far, far," e.g. *Kono hō ga zutto omoshiroi.* この方がずっと面白い. "This is much more interesting."

4. Circumstance

*futo* ふと "by chance" =*gūzen*, "suddenly" =*totsuzen Ano hito no koto o futo omoidashita.* あの人のことをふと思い出した. "I happened to think of him." *Futo sonna koto o omoidashimashita.* ふとそんな事を思い出しました. "Suddenly I recalled such a thing."

*hitasura* ひたすら "earnestly," e.g. *Shikenmae na no de hitasura benkyō ni hagende imasu.* 試験前なのでひたすら勉強に励んでいます. "Because it is before his exams, he is earnestly studying hard."

*hakkiri* はっきり "clearly," e.g. *Hakkiri itte kudasai.* はっきり言って下さい. "Please say it clearly."

*zehi* 是非 "definitely, by any means," e.g. *Zehi sō shimashō.* 是非そうしましょう. "Let's do that by all means."

III. Commonly Used Adverbs with Limitations according to Use

1. **Adverbs used only with positive expressions**

*kanarazu* 必ず without fail

*Ashita wa kanarazu kimasu.* 明日は必ず来ます. "I'll come tomorrow without fail."

*karōjite* 辛うじて barely, narrowly

*Karōjite nogaremashita.* 辛うじてのがれました. "I had a narrow escape."

2. **Adverbs used only with negative expressions or negative ideas**

*anagachi* あながち (not) necessarily =*kanarazushimo*

*Anagachi uso de mo nai.* あながち嘘でもない. "It's not necessarily a lie."

*chittomo* ちっとも (not) a bit =*sukoshimo*

*Chittomo wakaranai.* ちっともわか(分)らない. "I can't understand it at all."

*ikkō* いっこう(一向) (not) in the least

*Ikkō urenai.* いっこう売れない. "I can't sell them at all."

*isasakamo* いささ(些)かも (not) in the least =*sukoshimo*

*Isasakamo odorokanai.* いささかも驚かない, "I am not surprised in the least."

*kesshite* 決して　never　*Sonna koto wa kesshite shite wa ikema-sen yo.*　そんなことは決してしてはいけませんよ.　"Don't you ever do such a thing!"

*kanarazushimo* 必ずしも (not) necessarily
*Wakai kara kanarazushimo tsukarenai to wa kagiranai.*　若いから必ずしも疲れないとは限らない. "Just because he is young, we can't say that he doesn't get tired."

*manzara* まんざら(満更)　(not) altogether
*Manzara baka de wa nai.*　まんざら馬鹿ではない. "He is not altogether a fool."

*metta ni* めった(滅多)に　rarely, seldom
*Metta ni ikimasen.*　めったに行きません. "I seldom go."

*rokuroku* ろくろく　(not) satisfactorily　=*rokuni*
*Ano ko wa rokuroku hon mo yomenai.*　あの子はろくろく本も読めない. "That child can't even read a book satisfactorily."

*sappari* さっぱり　(not) at all
*Yonde mo sappari wakarimasen.*　読んでもさっぱりわか(分)りません. "Even though I read it, I can't understand it at all."

*sukoshimo* すこしも　(not) in the least
*Sukoshimo yoki shite inakatta.*　少しも予期していなかった. "I didn't expect it at all."

*tōtei* とうてい(到底)　(not) possibly
*Sonna koto wa tōtei arienai.*　そんなことはとうていあり得ない. "Such a thing can't possibly occur."

*zenzen* 全然　(not) at all
*Zenzen dekimasen deshita.*　全然でき(出来)ませんでした. "I couldn't do it at all."

3.　**Adverbs with meanings varying according to use with positive or negative expressions**

| Adverbs | With positive expressions | With negative expressions |
|---|---|---|
| *amari*<br>あま(余)り | so Adj.... that...<br>*Amari yasui no de taku-san kaimashita.* あまり安いので沢山買いました. "It was so inexpensive that I bought a lot." | (not) very<br>*Amari takaku arimasen.* あまり高くありません. "It isn't very expensive." |
| *betsuni*<br>別に | separately<br>*Sore wa betsuni shite oite* | (not) especially<br>*Betsuni ii to mo omoi-* |

| Adverbs | With positive expressions | With negative expressions |
|---|---|---|
| | *kudasai.* それは別にして おいて下さい. "Please leave it separate." | *masen.* 別にいいとも思 いません. "I don't think it is especially good." |
| *dōmo* どうも | very much<br>*Dōmo arigatō gozai-masu.* どうも有難うござ います. "Thank you very much." | (not) very =*amari*<br>*Dōmo yoku arimasen.* どうもよくありません. "It is not very good." |
| *hotondo* ほと(殆)んど | almost<br>*Mō hotondo dekimashita.* もうほとんど出来ました. "I am almost done." | hardly<br>*Benkyō shite nakatta no de, kyō no shiken wa hotondo dekimasen de-shita.* 勉強してなかった ので今日の試験はほとん ど出来ませんでした. "Because I wasn't pre-pared, I could hardly do today's test." |
| *issai* 一切 | all =*zenbu*<br>*Uchi-jū no mono o kaji de issai yaite shimai-mashita.* 家中の物を火 事で一切焼いてしまいま した. "I lost everything in the house in a fire." | not at all =*zenzen*<br>*Sonna koto wa issai shi-rimasen deshita.* そん な事は一切知りませんで した. "I didn't know such a thing at all." |
| *mada* ま(未)だ | still<br>*Mada dekimasu.* まだで き(出来)ます. "He can still do it." | (not) yet<br>*Mada dekimasen.* まだ でき(出来)ません. "I haven't finished it yet." |
| *mō* もう | already<br>*Mō gohan o tabemashita.* もうごはん(御飯)を食べ ました. "I have eaten dinner already." | (not) any longer<br>*Mō konna koto wa shi-masen.* もうこんな事は しまん. "We won't do this kind of thing any longer." |
| *nakanaka* なかなか (中々) | considerably, quite (with Adj.)<br>*Nakanaka yoku deki-* | hardly (usually taking time to do something)<br>*Nakanaka dekimasen.* |

| Adverbs | With *positive* expressions | With *negative* expressions |
|---|---|---|
| | *mashita.* なかなかよくでき(出来)ました. "You have done it quite well." | なかなかでき(出来)ません. "It's taking some time to do it." |
| *totemo* とても | very (with Adj.) *Totemo kawaii onna no ko desu ne.* とても可愛い女の子ですね. "She is a very cute girl, isn't she?" | not at all, can't possibly *Ano hito ni wa totemo kanawanai.* あの人にはとてもかなわない. "I am no match for him, really." |
| *zenzen* 全然 | wholly, entirely *Sono koto wa zenzen himitsu ni shite oite kudasai.* その事は全然秘密にしておいて下さい. "Keep that matter an absolute secret, will you?" | not at all *Sonna koto wa zenzen shirimasen deshita.* そんな事は全然知りませんでした. "I didn't know such a thing at all." |

## 4. Adverbs used with conditional expressions

*mangaichi* 万が一   by any chance   =*man'ichi*
> *Mangaichi shippai shitara, sore koso taihen desu.* 万が一失敗したら，それこそ大変です. "If by any chance we fail, it will be catastrophic."

*moshi* もし   if
> *Moshi ame ga futtara ikimasen.* もし雨が降ったら行きません. "If it rains, I won't go."

*moshi* もし   even if=*tatoe*   =*yoshi*
> *Moshi ame de mo ikimasu.* もし雨でも行きます. "Even if it rains, I'll go."

*tatoe* たとえ   even if   =*moshi*=*yoshi*
> *Tatoe ame de mo ikimasu ka.* たとえ雨でも行きますか. "Even if it rains, will you go?"

## 5. Adverbs used with tentative expressions

*aruiwa* ある(或)いは   perhaps
> *Aruiwa sō ka mo shirenai desu.* あるいはそうかもしれないです. "Perhaps it might be so."

*ōmune* おおむ(概)ね   probably, perhaps   =*taigai*

*Ōmune sonna koto darō to omotte imashita.* おおむねそんなことだろうと思っていました. "I thought that it would perhaps be like that."

*ōyoso* おおよそ(大凡) roughly, nearly
*Ōyoso sō naru no de wa nai ka to omotte imashita.* おおよそそうなるのではないかと思っていました. "I was thinking it would probably turn out like that."

*sadameshi* 定めし presumably
*Sadameshi otsukare deshō.* 定めしお疲れでしょう. "I am sure you are very tired."

*sazo* さぞ(嘸) no doubt, surely
*Sazo kirei datta deshō.* さぞきれい(綺麗)だったでしょう. "I am sure it was beautiful."

*tabun* 多分 probably
*Tabun ashita wa irassharu deshō.* 多分明日はいらっしゃるでしょう. "Probably he will come tomorrow."

*osoraku* おそ(恐)らく probably
*Kyō wa osoraku konai deshō.* 今日はおそらく来ないでしょう. "He will probably not come today."

## 6. Adverbs used with negative-tentative expressions

*masaka* まさか surely (not) =*yomoya*
*Masaka (Yomoya) kyō wa konai darō to omoimasu.* まさか今日は来ないだろうと思います. "I surely don't think he will come today."

## 7. Adverbs used with expressions of comparison

*atakamo* あたか(恰)も as if
*Atakamo kanemochi no yō ni furumau.* あたかも金持のように振舞う. "He behaves as if he were a rich man."

*chōdo* 丁度 as if, like =*marude*
*Chōdo hiruma no yō ni akarui desu.* 丁度昼間のように明るいです. "It's as bright as day."

*mushiro* むし(寧)ろ rather
*Watakushi wa mushiro sono hō ga suki desu.* 私はむしろその方が好きです. "I rather like it better."

*samo* さも as if
*Samo benkyōka no yō ni itte imashita.* さも勉強家のように言っていました. "He was talking as if he were a very diligent man."

# ONOMATOPOEIC WORDS
## (*GISEIGO* 擬声語＜ぎせいご＞ *GITAIGO* 擬態語＜ぎたいご＞)

In English, onomatopoeic words are those which imitate natural sounds. In Japanese, however, these words not only imitate natural sounds, but also describe or give an image of a certain action. There are literally hundreds of these words. The words which represent sound are called *giseigo* (sound-imitating words), while the words which describe actions are *gitaigo* (action-imitating words). Some words can be used as both *giseigo* and *gitaigo*. These words can be used as adverbs as they are, or sometimes with the particle *to* (occasionally *ni*) added. They are very important in Japanese, because often the use of *giseigo* or *gitaigo* is the only way to describe accurately a certain action or condition. For example, the verb *warau* can be "to smile" or "to laugh" depending on which *giseigo* (or *gitaigo*) is used with it.

| | |
|---|---|
| *nikoniko warau* にこにこ笑う | "smile" |
| *niyaniya warau* にやにや笑う | "grin" |
| *geragera warau* げらげら笑う | "laugh boisterously" |
| *kusukusu warau* くすくす笑う | "giggle," "chuckle" |
| *herahera warau* へらへら笑う | "laugh condescendingly," etc. |

Common Onomatopoeic Words and Examples of their Usages

| Onomatopoeic words | Used as *giseigo* (sound-imitating w.) | Used as *gitaigo* (action-describing w.) |
|---|---|---|
| *batabata* ばたばた | footstep or flapping sound, e.g. *batabata hashiru* | hurry-scurry |
| *bechabecha* べちゃべちゃ | chattering, tattling, e.g. *bechabecha shaberu* | |
| *berabera* べらべら | talking glibly, e.g. *berabera shaberu* | |
| *biribiri* びりびり | sound of tearing up (paper, thin cloths, etc.), e.g. *biribiri yaburu* | |
| *bishobisho* びしょびしょ | | drip, soak to the skin, e.g. *bishobisho ni nureru* (*naru*) |
| *boribori* ぼりぼり | munch, crunch, e.g. *boribori taberu* | (scratch oneself) violently, e.g. *boribori kaku* |

| Onomatopoeic words | Used as *giseigo* (sound-imitating w.) | Used as *gitaigo* (action-describing w.) |
|---|---|---|
| *boroboro* ぼろぼろ | | crumble into decay, e.g. *boroboro ni naru* |
| *botabota* ぼたぼた | drip drip | |
| *boyaboya* ぼやぼや | | absent-minded, e.g. *boyaboya shite iru* |
| *bukubuku* ぶくぶく | bubbling | fat, baggy, e.g. *bukubuku futotte iru* |
| *burabura* ぶらぶら | | dangling, e.g. *burabura sagaru* at leisure, e.g. *burabura suru* |
| *buruburu* ぶるぶる | | shaking, e.g. *buruburu furueru* |
| *buyobuyo* ぶよぶよ | | soft and flabby, e.g. *buyobuyo suru* |
| *chakichaki* ちゃきちゃき | | efficient, e.g. *chakichaki suru* |
| *chanchan* ちゃんちゃん | | regularly, promptly, e.g. *chanchan harau* |
| *chinchin* ちんちん | boiling sound of hot water, e.g. *chinchin waku* | |
| *chokochoko* ちょこちょこ | | toddling walk, e.g. *chokochoko aruku* |
| *dabudabu* だぶだぶ | | loose garment, e.g. *dabudabu da* |
| *dokidoki* どきどき | sound of heart throbbing | nervous, e.g. *dokidoki suru* |
| *dondon* どんどん | boom boom boom (sound of a drum) bang bang (sound of a gun) | walk briskly, e.g. *dondon aruku* |
| *doyadoya* どやどや | sound of many footsteps, e.g. *doyadoya haitte kuru* | |
| *fūfū* ふうふう | sound of hard breathing or blowing | being exhausted, working hard, e.g. *fūfū iu (da)* |

| Onomatopoeic words | Used as *giseigo* (sound-imitating w.) | Used as *gitaigo* (action-describing w.) |
|---|---|---|
| *furafura* ふらふら | | being dizzy, being exhausted, e.g. *furafura suru* |
| *gabugabu* がぶがぶ | drink liquid thirstily e.g. *gabugabu nomu* | |
| *gamigami* がみがみ | speak crossly e.g. *gamigami okoru* | |
| *gatagata* がたがた | rattling noise | trembling, e.g. *gatagata furueru* rickety, e.g. *gatagata da* |
| *gayagaya* がやがや | talk noisily | |
| *geragera* げらげら | laugh loudly | |
| *gobogobo* ごぼごぼ | sound of gushing water | |
| *gubugubu* ぐぶぐぶ | sound of rinsing one's mouth | |
| *gungun* ぐんぐん | | walk briskly, e.g. *gungun aruku* |
| *guruguru* ぐるぐる | | turn around and around, e.g. *guruguru mawaru* |
| *gūgū* ぐうぐう | sound of deep sleeping sound of hungry stomach, e.g. *i ga gūgū naru* | |
| *hakihaki* はきはき | | speak clearly, e.g. *hakihaki shite iru (hanasu)* |
| *herahera* へらへら | | laugh condescendingly |
| *hokahoka* ほかほか | | warm, e.g. *hokahoka suru* |
| *hyokohyoko* ひょこひょこ | | unsteady steps, e.g. *hyokohyoko aruku* |
| *hyorohyoro* ひょろひょろ | | tall and skinny, e.g. *hyorohyoro sei ga takai* |
| *jirojiro* じろじろ | | staring at something, e.g. *jirojiro miru* |
| *jimejime* じめじめ | | damp and humid, e.g. *jimejime suru* |

| Onomatopoeic words | Used as *giseigo* (sound-imitating w.) | Used as *gitaigo* (action-describing w.) |
|---|---|---|
| *jūjū* じゅうじゅう | sizzling sound | |
| *kachikachi* かちかち | sound of two hard objects touching | |
| *kankan* かんかん | sound of bell | being very angry, e.g. *kankan okoru* |
| | | strong heat, e.g. *kankan hi ga teru* |
| *kasakasa* かさかさ | sound of dry objects touching | being very dry, e.g. *kasakasa suru* |
| *kerokero* けろけろ | | nonchalant, e.g. *kerokero suru* |
| *kirakira* きらきら | | shiny, e.g. *kirakira hikaru* |
| *korokoro* ころころ | | round object rolling, e.g. *korokoro korogaru* |
| *kotokoto* ことこと | sound of rapping | |
| *kotsukotsu* こつこつ | sound of knocking | industrious, e.g. *kotsukotsu hataraku* |
| *kuchakucha* くちゃくちゃ | | messed up, wrinkled up, e.g. *kuchakucha ni marumeru* |
| *kyorokyoro* きょろきょろ | | goggle, e.g. *kyorokyoro miru* |
| *magomago* まごまご | | confused, e.g. *magomago suru* |
| *mojimoji* もじもじ | | hesitate, e.g. *mojimoji suru* |
| *monyamonya* もにゃもにゃ | | mumble, e.g. *monyamonya iu* |
| *nichanicha* にちゃにちゃ | | soft and sticky, slimy, e.g. *nichanicha suru* (*kuttsuku*) |
| *nikoniko* にこにこ | | smile, e.g. *nikoniko warau* |
| *niyaniya* にやにや | | grin, e.g. *niyaniya warau* |

| Onomatopoeic words | Used as *giseigo* (sound-imitating w.) | Used as *gitaigo* (action-describing w.) |
|---|---|---|
| *pachipachi* ぱちぱち | sound of applause and fire crackling | |
| *pasapasa* ぱさぱさ | | dry, e.g. *pasapasa suru* |
| *pekopeko* ぺこぺこ | | hungry stomach, e.g. *onaka ga pekopeko da*, servile behavior, e.g. *pekopeko ojigi suru* |
| *perapera* ぺらぺら | | fluent in language, e.g. *eigo ga perapera da* |
| *pikapika* ぴかぴか | | shiny, e.g. *pikapika hikaru* |
| *pinpin* ぴんぴん | | very healthy, e.g. *pinpin shite iru (da)* |
| *pokapoka* ぽかぽか | | very warm, e.g. *pokapoka atatakai* |
| *poripori* ぽりぽり | crunch crunch | |
| *poroporo* ぼろぼろ | | shedding copious tears, crumble, e.g. *poroporo namida o nagasu* |
| *potsupotsu* ぽつぽつ | fall in big drops | little by little, e.g. *potsupotsu hanasu* |
| *puripuri* ぷりぷり | | being mad, e.g. *puripuri okoru* |
| *sarasara* さらさら | sound of clear stream, rustling | feel of dry and smooth touch, e.g. *sarasara shite iru* |
| *sekaseka* せかせか | | restless, e.g. *sekaseka suru (aruku)* |
| *shikushiku* しくしく | | cry sorrowfully, e.g. *shikushiku naku* |
| *shimijimi* しみじみ | | keenly, deeply, e.g. *shimijimi kanjiru* |
| *shinshin* しんしん | | quiet and cold, e.g. *shinshin to yo ga fukeru* |
| *shitoshito* しとしと | | raining quietly, e.g. *shitoshito ame ga furu* |

| Onomatopoeic words | Used as *giseigo* (sound-imitating w.) | Used as *gitaigo* (action-describing w.) |
|---|---|---|
| *supasupa* すぱすぱ | | smoke, puff, e.g. *supasupa tabako o fukasu* |
| *sutasuta* すたすた | | briskly, e.g. *sutasuta aruku* |
| *suyasuya* すやすや | | sleeping peacefully, e.g. *suyasuya nemuru* |
| *tekateka* てかてか | | bright, shiny, e.g. *tekateka hikaru* |
| *tobotobo* とぼとぼ | | trudgingly, e.g. *tobotobo aruku* |
| *tonton* とんとん | sound of knocking | move quickly, e.g. *tonton hashiru* |
| *wakuwaku* わくわく | | be excited, e.g. *mune ga wakuwaku suru* |
| *yochiyochi* よちよち | | totteringly, e.g. *yochiyochi aruku* |
| *yoroyoro* よろよろ | | staggeringly, e.g. *yoroyoro aruku* |
| *yūyū* ゆうゆう | | self-composed, e.g. *yūyū shite iru* |
| *zāzā* ざあざあ | sound of pouring rain | |
| *zakuzaku* ざくざく | jingle, e.g. *okane ga zakuzaku aru* | |
| *zawazawa* ざわざわ | rustling | noisy with movement of many people, e.g. *zawazawa suru* |
| *zutazuta* ずたずた | | cut or tear into shreds, e.g. *zutazuta ni kiru* |
| *zunzun* ずんずん | | without a moment's delay, e.g. *zunzun susumu* |

# CONJUNCTIONS　接続詞＜せつぞくし＞

A conjunction is a word used to connect sentences, words, phrases, or clauses.　There are two kinds of conjunctions in Japanese: sentence-beginning conjunctions and conjunctions between words, phrases, or clauses.

I.　Common sentence-beginning conjunctions (many of them are a combination of two or more words, and sometimes it is not easy to recognize them as conjunctions).

| | | |
|---|---|---|
| *aruiwa*<br>ある(或)いは<br>＝*matawa* | or | |
| *daga* だが<br>＝*desuga* | but, however | *desuga* is more polite |
| *dakara* だから<br>＝*desukara* | so, therefore | *desukara* is more polite |
| *dakedo* だけど<br>＝*dakeredomo* | but | *dakedo* is more colloquial<br>than *dakeredomo* |
| *danoni* だのに | but | very colloquial |
| *dattara* だったら<br>＝*deshitara* | if so | *deshitara* is more polite |
| *datte* だって | but, yet | very colloquial |
| *de* で | and so | |
| *dewa* では<br>＝*ja* | well then | *ja* is more colloquial |
| *demo* でも | but | colloquial |
| *hatashite*<br>果たして | as expected | |
| *kakushite*<br>か(斯)くして | in this way | literary expression |
| *katsu* か(且)つ | moreover | literary expression |
| *keredo(mo)* けれど | but | |
| *mata* 又 | and, moreover | |
| *matawa* 又は<br>＝*aruiwa* | or | |
| *mottomo*<br>もっと(尤)も | however, of course | |

| | | |
|---|---|---|
| *nao* なお(尚) | further | |
| *sarani* 更に | further | literary expression |
| *sate* さて | well | |
| *shikaruni* しかるに | however | literary expression |
| *shikashi* しか(併)し | but | |
| *shikashinagara* しかしながら | however | literary expression |
| *shitagatte* 従って | therefore | |
| *shitemiruto* して見ると | then | |
| *sōkatoitte* そうかと言って | even so | |
| *sokode* そこで | thereupon, accordingly | |
| *somosomo* そもそも | in the first place | |
| *sonoue* その上 | moreover | |
| *soredakara* それだから | therefore, accordingly | |
| *sorede* それで | therefore, thereupon | |
| *soredemo* それでも | but, even that | |
| *soredewa* それでは | well then | |
| *soredokoroka* それどころか | far from it | |
| *sorekara* それから | and then | |
| *soremo* それも | and that | |
| *sorenara* それなら | if so | |
| *soreni* それに | besides | |
| *soretomo* それとも | or | |
| *sorewasōto* それはそうと | by the way | |
| *soreyueni* それ故に | so | literary expression |
| *sōshitara* そうしたら | and then | |

*sōshite* そうして　and
　=*soshite*
*sōsuruto*　　　　then, if so
そうすると
*sōsureba*　　　　then
そうすれば
*tada* ただ(唯)　　only, but
*tadashi* 但し　　but　　　　　　literary expression
*toitte* と言って　and yet, but even so
*tokorode* ところで by the way
*tokoroga* ところが but
*towaie* とは言え　however
*tsuitewa* ついては in this connection
*yueni* 故に　　　so, therefore　　literary expression
*yotte* よ(依)って　therefore　　　literary expression

II.　Conjunctions between:
　　1.　Nouns
　　　　a.　"and"　*oyobi* 及び, *narabini* 並びに, both more
　　　　　　　　　　literary than:
　　　　　　　　　*dano* だの See Particles, p. 99
　　　　　　　　　*nari* なり See Particles, p. 120
　　　　　　　　　*to* と　　See Particles, p. 134
　　　　　　　　　*toka* とか See Particles, p. 135
　　　　　　　　　*ya* や　　See Particles, p. 138
　　　　　　　　　*yara* やら See Particles, p. 139

　　　　b.　"or"　*matawa* 又は *aruiwa* ある(或)いは, both more
　　　　　　　　literary than *ka* か See Particles, p. 110
　　　　c.　"both...and..."　*mo* も　See Particles, p. 116
　　2.　Adjectives
　　　　a.　"and"　Adj*kute* adj くて See Verb-following Expres-
　　　　　　　　　sions, p. 84
　　　　　　　　*dano* だの　See Particles, p. 100
　　　　b.　"or" *ka* か See Particles, p. 110
　　3.　Copular nouns
　　　　a.　"and" *de* で　See Particles, p. 102
　　　　b.　"or"　*ka* か See Particles, p. 110
　　4.　Clauses
　　　　a.　Co-ordinating conjunctions

1. "and" $V_2$ See Function of Second Base of the Verb, pp. 5–6

   $V_{te}$ V て See Verb-following Expressions, p. 54

   $V_3$ *shi* $V_3$ し See Verb-following Expressions, p. 74

   $V_{tari}$ $V_{tari}$ V たり V たり See Verb-following Expressions, p. 54

2. "but" $V_3$ *ga* $V_3$ が See Verb-following Expressions, p. 62

   $V_3$ *keredomo* $V_3$ けれども See Verb-following Expressions, p. 65

3. "or" $V_3$ *ka*... $V_3$ *ka* $V_3$ か... $V_3$ か See Particle *ka*, p. 110

b. Subordinating conjunctions

   1. Conditional verb-endings

      a. "if" $V_3$ *to* $V_3$ と See Conditionals, p. 30

         $V_{ba}$ V ば See conditionals, p. 30

         $V_{tara}$ V たら See Conditionals, p. 31

         $V_3$ *nara* V なら See Conditionals, pp. 31–32

      b. "even if" $V_{te}$ *mo* V ても See Verb-following Expressions, p. 57

      c. "if not" $V_{nai}$ *to* V ないと See Verb-following Expressions, p. 41

         $V_{nakattara}$ V なかったら See Verb-following Expressions, p. 42

         $V_{nakereba}$ V なければ See Verb-following Expressions, p. 42

         $V_{nai}$ *nara* V ないなら See Verb-following Expressions, p. 41

      b. "even if not" $V_{nakute}$ *mo* V なくても See Verb-following Expressions, p. 43

   2. Particles as conjunctions

      a. "because..." $V_3$ *kara* $V_3$ から See Verb-following Expressions, p. 64

$V_3$ *no de*　$V_3$ ので　See Verb-following Expressions, p. 72

  b.　"in order to..." $V_3$ *no ni*　$V_3$ のに　See Verb-following Expressions, p. 73

  c.　"although..." $V_3$ *no ni*　$V_3$ のに　See Verb-following Expressions, p. 73

  d.　"while..." $V_2$ *nagara* $V_2$ ながら See Verb-following Expressions, pp. 49–50

  e.　"than..." $V_3$ *yori*　$V_3$ より　See Verb-following Expressions, p. 81

**3.** Nouns used as conjunctions

  a.　"while..." $V_3$ *aida* [*ni*] $V_3$ 間 See Verb-following Expressions, p. 60

  b.　"after..." $V_{ta}$ *ato* [*de*] V た後 See Verb-following Expressions, p. 51

  c.　"before" $V_3$ *mae* [*ni*]　$V_3$ 前　See Verb-following Expressions, p. 67

  d.　"in order to..." $V_3$ *tame* [*ni*] $V_3$ ため (為) See Verb-following Expressions, p. 74

  e.　"when..." $V_3$ *toki* [*ni*] $V_3$ 時 See Verb-following Expressions, p. 77

# INTERJECTIONS
## 感動詞＜かんどうし＞, 間投詞＜かんとうし＞

An interjection is an independent word which expresses such things as surprise, lamentation or address. Interjections become neither subject nor predicate, and never modify other words. Some of the common interjections are as follows:

   I.  Surprise *a'* あっ *ara* あら *oya* おや *mā* まあ
              e.g. *Ara, shibaraku deshita wa ne.* あら, しば(暫)らくでしたわね. "Well, I haven't seen you for a long time!"

  II.  Distress *ā* ああ *ō* おう *yareyare* やれやれ *oyaoya* おやおや
              e.g. *Ā, zannen deshita ne.* ああ, 残念でしたね. "Ah, it was too bad."

 III.  Address *oi* おい *kora* こら *kore* これ *yai* やい
              e.g. *Oi, sonna koto wa suru na.* おい, そんな事はするな. "Hey, don't do such a thing!"

\*IV.  Answer *hai* はい *iie* いいえ *ē* ええ (*hai* is more polite than *ē*)
              e.g. *Ano hon o yomimashita ka. Hai, yomimashita.* あの本を読みましたか. はい, 読みました. "Did you read that book?" "Yes, I read it."

   V.  Doubt *hate* はて *hatena* はてな
              e.g. *Hate, are o doko ni oita ka na.* はて, あれをどこ(何処)においたかな. "Let me see, where did I put it?"

  VI.  Resolving doubt *naruhodo* なるほど(成程)
              e.g. *Naruhodo, yoku wakarimashita.* なるほど, よくわか(分)りました. "Oh, I see, I got it (understood it well)."

 VII.  Admiration *hē* へー *fūmu* ふーむ

---

\* Care should be taken when one answers a negatively posed question, because *hai* "yes" and *iie* "no" are reversed.
    e.g. *Ashita irasshaimasen ka.* 明日いらっしゃいませんか. "Won't you go tomorrow?"
    *Hai, mairimasen.* はい, 参りません. "No, I won't go."
    *Iie, mairimasu.* いいえ, 参ります. "Yes, I'll go."

e.g. *Hē, taishita mono desu ne.* へー，大し
たものですね. "Well, that is something!"

VIII. Urging *sora* そら *hora* ほら etc.

e.g. Sora, sonna ni bonyari shite nai de...
そら，そんなにぼんやりしてないで...
"There, don't be so absent-minded."

# FORMAL LEVEL OF WORDS AND EXPRESSIONS
敬語＜けいご＞

## LEVELS OF FORMALITY OF VERBS

One of the important aspects of Japanese verbs is the level of formality. That is, the same verb can be presented in various ending forms, even though the meaning is EXACTLY THE SAME. These different endings are used on different occasions. For example, written Japanese and spoken Japanese have, more often than not, different endings. Moreover, even in written Japanese, several different endings can be found according to the style of writing chosen by the author. The verb endings ordinarily found in most books, articles, and lectures are very likely not found in children's stories, because these verb endings are the more literary endings (dictionary form endings), while those in children's stories are the colloquial endings (2nd base verb form plus the suffix *masu*, or the *desu* form of the copula).

In spoken Japanese, too, verb forms often change depending upon placement within the sentence: whether they appear in the middle or at the end of the sentence; whether the speaker is superior, inferior, or equal, to the listener according to Japanese tradition; or, frequently, whether the speaker and listener are male or female.

Thus the array of endings is complex, especially if we include verbs plus sentence-ending particles. It is not necessary to be familiar with all these endings, but one should familiarize oneself with the common endings presented in I, II and III below.

For convenience, endings are divided roughly into four categories in this book:

I. Informal level (dictionary form or 3rd base [$V_{ta}$ for the perfective tense] of the verb and adjective)

　　This is the verb-ending form most commonly used in written Japanese, but in spoken Japanese, too, it appears frequently in the middle of the sentence, followed by a noun which it modifies, or with conjunctions.

　　　　e.g. Sakubun o *kaku*. 作文を書く. "I write a composition."
　　　　(sentence-ending)

Nani ka *taberu* mono ga arimasu ka. 何か食べるもの
がありますか. "Is there anything to eat?" (noun
modifier)

Igirisu ni wa *itta* keredomo, Furansu ni wa ikimasen
deshita. イギリスには行ったけれども，フランスには
行きませんでした. (before a conjunction) "I went to
England, but I did not go to France."

As a verb-ending form, this level is also used in conver-
sations among men, but not among women, since it sounds
very rough.

   e.g. Ashita *iku* ka. 明日行くか. "Will you go tomorrow?"
        (sentence ending.)

   Ā, ashita *iku*. ああ，明日行く. "Yeah, I'll go tomorrow." (sentence ending)

II. Polite level (2nd base verb plus *masu* [*mashita*], dictionary
form of adjectives plus *desu* [*deshita*], and copula *desu* [*deshita*], as sentence ending)

   This is the form most commonly used in spoken Japanese.
   However, perhaps because this ending sounds softer than
   the dictionary form, children's stories are often written in
   this form rather than in informal endings.

   e.g. Watakushi wa kyō gakkō ni *ikimasu*. 私は今日学
        校に行きます. "I am going to school today."

   Mukashi mukashi ojiisan to obāsan ga *arimashita*.
   昔々おじいさんとおばあさんがありました.     "Long
   long ago there lived an old man and an old
   woman." In fairy tales, it is common to use the
   verb *arimashita* for people who lived.

III. Formal level

   This is the most formal level of speech. The details
   of the use of this level are found in the succeeding
   pages, pp. 216–30.

IV. Very familiar level

   These endings are very colloquial and need not be
   learned in the beginning. However, when at the stage of
   reading modern Japanese fiction, or when visiting Japan,
   one will begin to meet them frequently, and should be
   able to recognize them. Often, from the tone of the
   endings, the reader (listener) can determine such things as
   the age, sex, and social class of the speaker.

e.g.   Women's speech

Kyō wa *ikanai wa*. 今日は行かないわ. "I won't go today."

Kinō itta no [yo]. 昨日行ったの. "I went yesterday."

Ashita *kite ne*. 明日来てね. "Please come tomorrow, OK?" etc.

Men's speech

Ashita wa kitto *yomu yo*. 明日はきっと読むよ. "I'll read it tomorrow for sure."

Kore o *suru ne*. これをするね. "I'll do it, OK?" etc.

## HONORIFIC AND HUMBLE VERB FORMS

Formal speech which requires honorific and humble verbs (nouns, adjectives, etc.) is one of the most characteristic features of the Japanese language. It is therefore imperative to learn both the honorific and humble verb forms, if one wishes to read and speak proper Japanese fluently.

I.   Honorific Forms Borrowed from Other Verb Forms

1.   Passive voice form (more often used by men than women)

a.   Vowel-stem verbs ($V_1$+*rareru*) Sensei ga okashi o *taberaremashita*. 先生がお菓子を食べられました. "The teacher ate a cake."

b.   Consonant-stem verbs ($V_1$+*reru*) Anata ga sore o *kakaremashita* ka. あなたがそれを書かれましたか. "Did you write it?"

c.   Irregular verbs

*suru—sareru* Mō ano oshigoto o *saremashita* ka. もうあのお仕事をされましたか. "Have you done that work already?"

*kuru—korareru* Myōnichi mata koko e *koraremasu* ka. 明日又ここへ来られますか. "Are you coming back here again tomorrow?"

Note: "*Ashita*" is read "*myōnichi*" to keep it in harmony with the honorific verb.

2.   Causative-passive form

   a.  Vowel-stem verb ($V_1$ + *saserareru*)   Tennō-Heika ga sore o *tsuzukesaserareta.* 天皇陛下がそれを続けさせられた. "The Emperor deigned to continue it."

   b.  Consonant-stem ($V_1$ + *serareru*)   Denka ga kono hon o *kakaserareta.* 殿下がこの本を書かせられた. "His Highness wrote this book."

   c.  Irregular verbs

      *suru—saserareru*   Kōtaishi ga Yōroppa ni ryokō *saserareta.* 皇太子がヨーロッパに旅行させられた. "The Crown Prince traveled to Europe."

      *kuru—kosaserareru*   Kōtaishi Hidenka mo goissho ni hikōjō made *kosaserareta.* 皇太子妃殿下も御一緒に飛行場まで来させられた.   "The Crown Princess came to the air:ort, also."

> Note: This is the highest form of honorific. It is seldom used now, because the Japanese language has become much more informal in recent years. But one might come across these expressions in reading articles written before World War II.

## II. Regular Honorific and Humble Forms

   1.  Honorific (*o* $V_2$ *ni naru*)  *Osuwari ni narimasen* ka. お坐りになりませんか. "Won't you sit down?"

   2.  Humble (*o* $V_2$ *suru*)  Kinō denwa o *okake shimashita.* 昨日電話をおかけしました. "I called you yesterday."

      Humble (*o* $V_2$ *itasu*)  Sakujitsu odenwa o *okake itashimashita.* (more polite) 昨日お電話をおかけ致しました. "I called you yesterday."

> Note: Special care should be taken when using this humble form, because its use is limited to occasions when the speaker's action involves the listener. So such a sentence as *Watakushi ga osuwari itashimasu,* 私がお坐り致します. does not make any sense in Japanese, even though the speaker who is not used to the correct humble form might think he/she is saying, "I will sit down," in a polite humble form.

There are more formal honorific and humble forms, but they are omitted in this section, since they are not used as commonly as the ones listed. (e.g. *o* $V_2$ *asobasu* for honorific, *o* $V_2$ *mōshiageru* for humble, etc.)

## III.  Irregular Honorific and Humble Verb Forms

Some of the most common verbs have irregular honorific and humble forms, as well as regular honorific and humble forms. These irregular forms are shown in the next pages.

Note:  Regular (including passive) and irregular honorific verb forms are mostly used interchangeably, that is, one can use whichever the form one prefers. However, in the Tokyo area it may be that the use of the honorific forms made from passive verbs is more often preferred by men, while irregular forms by women.

  e.g.  Itsu Sendai e *ikaremasu* ka? "When are you going to Sendai?" may carry a more masculine tone than: Itsu Sendai e *irasshaimasu* ka?

## IRREGULAR HONORIFIC AND HUMBLE VERB FORMS

| Verb | IRREGULAR | |
| --- | --- | --- |
| | Honorific | Humble |
| ageru 上げる "to give" | | sashiageru 差し上げる |
| aru ある "to be" "to have" | gozaimasu (neuter) ございます | |
| au 会う "to meet" | | ome ni kakaru お目にかかる |
| da だ "to be"-copula de aru である | de irassharu でいらっしゃる | de gozaimasu でございます |
| (kaze o) hiku 風邪をひく "to catch a cold" | (okaze o) mesu お風邪を召す | |
| iku 行く "to go" | irassharu いらっしゃる | mairu 参る |
| iru いる "to be" | irassharu いらっしゃる orareru おられる oide ni naru おいでになる | oru おる |
| iu 言う "to say" | ossharu おっしゃる | mōsu 申す mōshiageru 申し上げる |
| kariru 借りる "to borrow" | | haishaku suru 拝借する haishaku itasu 拝借致す |
| kiku 聞く "to hear" "to ask" | | ukagau 伺う oukagai suru お伺いする oukagai itasu お伺い致す |
| kiru 着る "to wear" | omeshi ni naru お召しになる | |
| kuru 来る "to come" | irassharu いらっしゃる oide ni naru おいでになる okoshi ni naru おこしになる | mairu 参る |

| REGULAR | | |
| --- | --- | --- |
| Honorific 1 (Passive form) | Honorific 2 (*o* $V_2$ *ni naru*) | Humble (*o* $V_2$ *suru*) (*o* $V_2$ *itasu*) |
| agerareru 上げられる | oage ni naru お上げになる | oage suru お上げする oage itasu お上げ致す |
| | oari ni naru おありになる oari da おありだ | |
| awareru 会われる | oai ni naru お会いになる | oai suru お会いする oai itasu お会い致す |
| | | |
| (okaze o) hikareru お風邪をひかれる | (okaze o) ohiki ni naru お風邪をおひきになる | |
| ikareru 行かれる | | |
| irareru いられる | | |
| | | |
| iwareru 言われる | | |
| karirareru 借りられる | okari ni naru お借りになる | okari suru お借りする okari itasu お借り致す |
| kikareru 聞かれる | okiki ni naru お聞きになる | okiki suru お聞きする okiki itasu お聞き致す |
| kirareru 着られる | | |
| korareru 来られる | | |

| Verb | IRREGULAR | |
| --- | --- | --- |
| | Honorific | Humble |
| ukagau 伺う<br>"to go calling" | | oukagai suru お伺いする<br>oukagai itasu お伺い致す<br>oukagai mōshiageru<br>お伺い申し上げる<br>agaru 上がる |
| miru 見る "to see" | goran ni naru<br>御覧になる | haiken suru 拝見する<br>haiken itasu 拝見致す |
| miseru 見せる<br>"to show" | | ome ni kakeru<br>お目にかける |
| neru 寝る "to sleep" | oyasumi ni naru<br>お休みになる | |
| nomu 飲む "to drink" | oagari ni naru<br>おあがりになる | itadaku 戴く |
| omou 思う "to think" | | zonjiru 存じる |
| omotte iru 思っている<br>"to be thinking" | | omotte oru 思っておる |
| shinu 死ぬ "to die" | okakure ni naru<br>お隠れになる<br>onakunari ni naru<br>お亡くなりになる | |
| shiru 知る "to know" | | *zonjiru 存じる<br>zonjiageru 存じ上げる |
| shitte iru 知っている<br>"to know," "to be<br>acquainted with" | gozonji da 御存じだ<br>gozonji de irassharu<br>御存じでいらっしゃる<br>shitte irassharu<br>知っていらっしゃる | zonjite oru 存じておる<br>shitte oru 知っておる<br>zonjiagete oru<br>存じ上げておる |
| suru する "to do" | nasaru なさる | itasu 致す |
| taberu 食べる<br>"to eat" | meshiagaru 召し上がる<br>oagari ni naru<br>おあがりになる | itadaku 戴く |
| tazuneru<br>"to ask" 尋ねる<br>"to visit" 訪ねる | | ukagau 伺う |
| (toshi o) toru 年をとる<br>"to become older" | (otoshi o) mesu<br>お年を召す | |

* used only in negative form (See the verb *shiru*, p. 107)
    e.g.   Zonjimasen. 存じません. "I don't know."
        Zonjiagemasen. 存じ上げません. "I don't know."

| REGULAR | | |
|---|---|---|
| Honorific 1<br>(Passive form) | Honorific 2<br>(*o* V₂ *ni naru*) | Humble<br>(*o* V₂ *suru*)<br>(*o* V₂ *itasu*) |
| | | |
| mirareru 見られる | | |
| miserareru 見せられる | omise ni naru<br>お見せになる | omise suru お見せする<br>omise itasu お見せ致す |
| yasumareru 休まれる | | |
| nomareru 飲まれる | onomi ni naru<br>お飲みになる | |
| omowareru 思われる | ōmoi ni naru<br>お思いになる | |
| | ōmoi ni natte iru<br>お思いになっている | |
| shinareru 死なれる | | |
| | | |
| | | |
| sareru される | | |
| taberareru 食べられる | otabe ni naru<br>お食べになる | |
| tazunerareru<br>尋(訪)ねられる | otazune ni naru<br>お尋(訪)ねになる | otazune suru<br>お尋(訪)ねする |
| (otoshi o) torareru<br>お年をとられる | (otoshi) o otori ni naru<br>お年をおとりになる | |

## FORMAL LEVEL OF ADJECTIVES

The combination of an adjective plus *gozaimasu* is the formal level of the adjectives.  The stems of the adjectives make the following change before *gozaimasu*.

I.  Adjective, stem ending in *o*: lengthen *o*, and add *gozaimasu*.

| Informal level or dict. form | Stem | Polite level | Formal level |
|---|---|---|---|
| *omoshiroi* | *omoshiro* | *Omoshiroi desu.* | *Omoshirō gozaimasu.* |
| 面白い | 面白 | 面白いです | 面白うございます. |
| "interesting" | | "It is interesting." | |
| *yoi (ii)* | *yo* | *yo (ii) desu.* | *Yō gozaimasu.* |
| よい（いい） | よ | よい（いい）です. | ようございます. |
| "good" | | "It is good." | |

Note:  Exception in this category—Adjective, ending with *ōi*: simply add *gozaimasu* directly after the stem *ō*.

| | | | |
|---|---|---|---|
| *ōi* | *ō* | *Ōi desu.* | *Ō gozaimasu.* |
| 多い | 多 | 多いです | 多ございます. |
| "many" | | "There are many." | |
| *tōi* | *tō* | *Tōi desu.* | *(o) Tō gozaimasu.* |
| 遠い | 遠 | 遠いです. | （お）遠ございます. |
| "far" | | "It is far away." | |

II.  Adjective, stem ending in *a*: change *a* to *ō*, and add *gozaimasu*.

| | | | |
|---|---|---|---|
| *takai* | *taka* | *Takai desu.* | *(o) Takō gozaimasu.* |
| 高い | 高 | 高いです. | （お）高うございます. |
| "high" | | "It is high." | |
| "expensive" | | "It is expensive." | |
| *nagai* | *naga* | *Nagai desu.* | *(o) Nagō gozaimasu.* |
| 長い | 長 | 長いです. | （お）長うございます. |
| "long" | | "It is long." | |

III.  Adjective, stem ending in *u*: lengthen *u*, and add *gozaimasu*.

| | | | |
|---|---|---|---|
| *yasui* | *yasu* | *Yasui desu.* | *(o) Yasū gozaimasu.* |
| 安い | 安 | 安いです. | （お）安うございます. |
| "cheap" | | "It is cheap." | |

| samui | samu | Samui desu. | (o)Samū |
|-------|------|-------------|---------|
| 寒い | 寒 | 寒いです. | gozaimasu. |
| "cold" | | "It is cold." | (お)寒うございます. |

IV. Adjective, stem ending in *i*: change *i* to *ū*, and add *gozai-masu*.

| muzukashii | muzukashi | Muzukashii desu. | (o)Muzukashū gozaimasu. |
|------------|-----------|------------------|-------------------------|
| 難しい | 難し | 難しいです. | (お)難しゅうござい |
| "difficult" | | "It is difficult." | ます. |
| yasashii | yasashi | Yasashii desu. | (o)Yasashū gozaimasu. |
| 易(優)しい | 易(優)し | 易(優)しいです. | (お)易(優)しゅうご |
| "easy" | | "It is easy." | ざいます. |
| "gentle" | | "She is gentle." | |

Note: Exception in this category:

| ōkii | ōki | Ōkii desu. | Ōkyu gozaimasu. |
|------|-----|-----------|-----------------|
| 大きい | 大き | 大きいです, | 大きゅうございます. |
| | | "It is big." | (*y* is inserted between *k* and *u*) |

## FORMAL LEVEL OF SOME COMMON EXPRESSIONS

| Polite | Formal | English equivalent |
|--------|--------|--------------------|
| *Sumimasen* | *Mōshiwake gozaimasen.* | I am sorry. |
| 済みません. | 申し訳ございません. | |
| *\*Sumimasen deshita.* | *\*Mōshiwake gozaimasen deshita.* | I am sorry. I was sorry. |
| 済みませんでした. | 申し訳ございませんでした. | |
| *Sumimasen.* | *Osoreirimasu.* | Excuse me. |
| 済みません. | 恐れ入ります. | |
| *Arigatō.* | *Arigatō gozaimasu.* | Thank you. |
| 有難う. | 有難うございます. | |
| | *\*Arigatō gozaimashita.* | |
| | 有難うございました. | |
| | *Arigatō zonjimasu.* | Thank you. |
| | 有難う存じます. | |

---

\* The perfective forms (*ta*-forms) are used when the action for which one is apologizing, thanking, or congratulating, occurred in the past.

*Arigatō zonjimashita.
有難う存じました。
Osoreirimasu.              Thank you.
恐れ入ります。               I am much obliged.
*Osoreirimashita.
恐れ入りました。

Omedetō.     Omedetō gozaimasu.        Congratulations.
おめでとう.   おめでとうございます。
             *Omedetō gozaimashita.
             おめでとうございました。
             Omedetō zonjimasu.        Congratulations.
             おめでとう存じます。
             *Omedetō zonjimashita.
             おめでとう存じました。

* The perfective forms (ta-forms) are used when the action for which one
is apologizing, thanking, or congratulating occurred in the past.

## THREE LEVELS OF IMPERATIVE

| Levels | | Example | English equivalent |
|---|---|---|---|
| Informal | $V_5$ (imperative) see p. 6 | Kake. 書け. | Write! |
| | $V_{te}$ kure | Kaite kure. 書いてくれ. | Write (it) for me. |

The above two forms are very abrupt, so their use should be avoided.

| | | | |
|---|---|---|---|
| Polite | $V_2$ nasai | Kakinasai. 書きなさい. | Write. |
| | o $V_2$ nasai | Okakinasai. お書きなさい. | Write. |
| | $V_{te}$ kudasai | Kaite kudasai. 書いて下さい. | Please write. |
| Formal | o $V_2$ kudasai | Okaki kudasai. お書き下さい. | Please write. |
| | o $V_2$ kudasaimase | Okaki kudasai- mase. お書き下さいませ. | Please write. |

The above examples are the most common imperative forms.
There are several other forms, some more informal, and others
more formal.

## HONORIFIC NOUN-PREFIXES, *O* AND *GO*

There are two honorific prefixes used with nouns, *o* and *go*. Because both of them are often written with the same Chinese character, 御, one has to establish which reading is correct for each case. Fortunately, however, it seems that in recent years *o* is more often written with *hiragana* お, while 御 is still used for *go*. There is no definite rule governing when a noun takes *o* and when a noun takes *go* as an honorific prefix, except that words which originate from Chinese may more often take *go*, while Japanese words may usually take *o*. It should probably be mentioned briefly that the character 御 is sometimes read *on*, *mi*, or *gyo*. These are also honorific prefixes, but they are much less common than *o* or *go* (e.g. *onmi* 御身 "your body," *kami no mikokoro* 神の御心 "God's will," *gyoi* 御意 "your wishes," etc.).

The function of the honorific prefix is roughly divided into the following categories:

1. Idiomatic—Attached to some nouns when they sound more idiomatic if they are used with *o* or *go*. In this case these prefixes do not signify any particular politeness.

    e.g. *gohan* ごはん(御飯) "cooked rice," "meal," *ocha* お茶 "tea"

2. Respect for others—Attached when one talks about the objects or actions of others in order to show a feeling of respect.

    e.g. *goshujin* 御主人 "your husband" *okarada* お体 "your body"

3. Politeness—Attached when one wants to show politeness in formal speech. This prefix is often excessively used by some women, particularly in the Tokyo area, but too much use of this prefix could sound affected. In ladies' conversation, it may not be uncommon to hear *ohitotsu*, *ofutatsu*, etc., for "one" and "two." Even more extreme examples are *opan* or *okōhī* for such foreign words as bread or coffee. Also, in high-class Japanese inns, one may hear the maids use these honorific prefixes when they speak to the customers, because

they are trained to be very polite to them.

One should also remember that an honorific word can imply respect in one instance, and politeness in another. Therefore, one has to decide from the context which meaning is intended in each case. That is, if the speaker is talking about the object or action of others, the honorific prefix is very likely intended to show respect, but if the prefix is used for the speaker's action, it is to show politeness in formal speech.

    e.g. *Gokyōryoku* itashimasu.　御協力致します.　"I'll cooperate."
      —politeness
      *Gokyōryoku* onegai itashimasu.　御協力お願い致します.　"We'll request your (honorable) cooperation."—respect

The following is a sample list of nouns which often appear with honorific prefixes. Honorific prefixes are often combined with honorific and humble verb endings to raise the level of formality.

## NOUNS WITH HONORIFIC PREFIXES *O* OR *GO*

| Noun | Meaning | Honorific form | | Function of honorific |
|---|---|---|---|---|
| *anshin* | peace of mind | *goanshin* | 御安心 | respect |
| *benkyō* | study | *obenkyō* | お勉強 | respect |
| | | or | | |
| | | *gobenkyō* | 御勉強 | |
| *bon* | tray | *obon* | お盆 | idiomatic |
| *bon* | Festival of the Dead | *obon* | お盆 | idiomatic |
| *byōki* | sickness | *gobyōki* | 御病気 | respect |
| *cha* | tea | *ocha* | お茶 | idiomatic |
| *daiji* | precious | *odaiji* | お大事 | respect |
| *denwa* | telephone | *odenwa* | お電話 | politeness |
| *enryo* | restraint | *goenryo* | 御遠慮 | respect |
| *genki* | good health | *ogenki* | お元気 | respect |
| *meshi* (*han*) | cooked rice | *gohan* | 御飯 | idiomatic |
| *hima* | leisure hours | *ohima* | お暇 | respect |
| *hon* | book | *gohon* | 御本 | respect |
| *iken* | opinion | *goiken* | 御意見 | respect |
| *jikan* | time | *ojikan* | お時間 | respect |
| *kage* | patronage | *okage* | お陰 | idiomatic |

| Noun | Meaning | Honorific form | | Function of honorific |
|------|---------|----------------|---|----------------------|
| kanemochi | rich person | okanemochi | お金持 | idiomatic/ politeness |
| karada | body | okarada | お体 | respect |
| kashi | cake | okashi | お菓子 | idiomatic |
| keiko | lesson | okeiko | お稽古 | politeness |
| kekkon | marriage | gokekkon | 御結婚 | respect |
| kenkyū | research | gokenkyū | 御研究 | respect |
| kome | uncooked rice | okome | お米 | idiomatic |
| kōi | favor | gokōi | 御好意 | respect |
| kyaku | customer, guest | okyaku(san) | お客(さん) | idiomatic |
| manzoku | satisfaction | gomanzoku | 御満足 | respect |
| miyage | present, souvenir | omiyage | お土産 | idiomatic |
| mizu | water | omizu | お水 | idiomatic |
| on | debt of gratitude to a superior | goon | 御恩 | respect |
| rikai | understanding | gorikai | 御理解 | respect |
| ryokō | travel | goryokō | 御旅行 | respect |
| ryōshin | parents | goryōshin | 御両親 | respect |
| shigoto | work | oshigoto | お仕事 | respect |
| shinpai | worry | goshinpai | 御心配 | respect |
| shokuji | meal | oshokuji | お食事 | politeness/ idiomatic |
| shujin | husband | goshujin | 御主人 | respect |
| taku | house, family | otaku | お宅 | respect |
| teinei | politeness | goteinei | 御丁寧 | respect |
| tomodachi | friend | otomodachi | お友達 | politeness |
| yakusoku | promise | oyakusoku | お約束 | politeness |
| yūshoku | supper | oyūshoku or goyūshoku | お夕食 御夕食 | politeness |

## NOUNS OF TIME IN FORMAL SPEECH

Some very commonly used nouns of time, such as *kyō* and *ashita*, have more formal equivalents. The following is a short list of these words with examples showing how they are used.

| English | Colloquial | More formal | Example |
|---|---|---|---|
| today | *kyō*<br>今日 | *honjitsu*<br>本日<br>*konnichi*<br>今日 | *Kyō* wa ii tenki desu. 今日はいい天気です. "It's fine weather today."<br><br>*Honjitsu* wa ii otenki de gozaimasu. 本日はいいお天気でございます. "It's fine weather today." |
| tomorrow | *ashita*<br>明日 | *myōnichi*<br>明日 | *Ashita* ikimasu. 明日行きます. "I'll go tomorrow."<br><br>*Myōnichi* mairimasu. 明日参ります. "I'll go tomorrow." |
| yesterday | *kinō*<br>昨日 | *sakujitsu*<br>昨日 | *Kinō* wa isogashii deshita. 昨日は忙しいでした. "I was busy yesterday."<br><br>*Sakujitsu* wa isogashū gozaimashita. 昨日は忙しゅうございました. "I was busy yesterday." |
| this year | *kotoshi*<br>今年 | *konnen*<br>今年<br>*honnen*<br>本年 | *Kotoshi* wa ame ga ōi desu. 今年は雨が多いです. "We have had lots of rain this year."<br><br>*Honnen* wa ame ga ō gozaimasu. 本年は雨が多うございます. "We have had lots of rain this year." |
| last year | *kyonen*<br>去年 | *sakunen*<br>昨年 | *Kyonen* Nihon ni ikimashita. 去年日本に行きました. "I went to Japan last year."<br><br>*Sakunen* Nihon ni mairimashita. 昨年日本に参りました. "I went to Japan last year." |
| this time<br>or<br>next time<br>depending on<br>the case | *kondo*<br>今度 | *kono tabi*<br>この度 | *Kondo* wa hikōki de kimashita. 今度は飛行機で来ました. "This time I came by plane."<br><br>*Kono tabi* wa hikōki de mairimashita. この度は飛行機で参りました. "This time I came by plane." |

| time | *toki*<br>時 | *ori* or<br>折<br>*setsu*<br>節 | *Ano toki* wa arigatō gozai-mashita. あの時は有難うご ざいました. "Thank you for your kindness at that time." *Ano ori* wa arigatō zonjima-shita. あの折は有難う存じま した. "Thank you for your kindness at that time." |
|------|-------------|----------------------------------|------------------------------------------------------------------------------|

Note: When one uses formal time words, it is more common to use formal verb and adjective endings also, as shown above.

## EXTREMELY COLLOQUIAL EXPRESSIONS

The following expressions might be called "extremely colloquial." They often contain contractions and ellipses, and are based on the spoken language. Because their number is countless, liberty has been taken to include only a few examples, which may serve as suggestions in dealing with similar expressions.

*aitsu* あいつ =*are, ano yatsu Aitsu wa hontō ni baka da na.* あいつは本当に馬鹿だな. "That guy is really stupid."

*arya* ありゃ =*are wa Arya ittai nan' dai?* ありゃ一体何だい. "What on earth is it?"

*arya shinai* ありゃしない =*ari wa shinai=nai* (emphatic) *Nihon hodo konde iru tokoro wa arya shinai.* 日本程混んでいる所はあり ゃしない. "There is no country which is more crowded than Japan."

*cha* ちゃ =*te wa Itcha ikemasen yo.* 行っちゃいけませんよ. "You mustn't go, you know."

*chau* ちゃう =*te shimau Kyō warui koto [o] shichatta.* 今日悪い 事しちゃった. "I did a bad thing today."

Note: In colloquial speech, particles are often omitted. *Chau* is more often used by women.

*chimau* ちまう =*te shimau Shinkeisuijaku ni natchimai sō da.* 神経衰弱になっちまいそうだ. "I feel as if I am going to have a nervous breakdown." *chimau* is more often used by men.

*dai* だい =*desu ka Kore nan' dai.* これ何だい. "What is this?"

*datte* だって

1. =*de atte mo=de mo Ikura binbō datte anna kitanai uchi ni*

*sumanakutemo yosasō na mon' da.* いくら貧乏だってあんな汚い家に住まなくてもよさそうなもんだ. "Even if they are poor, it seems they don't have to live in such a dirty house."

2.　=*da to (iu) Nan' datte?* 何だって. "What did you say?"

*ja* じゃ　=*de wa Sō ja nai.* そうじゃない. "It's not that."

*koitsu* こいつ　=*kore Koitsu wa yokunai na.* こいつはよくないな. "This is no good."

*korya* こりゃ　=*kore wa Korya komatta koto ni natta.* こりゃ困ったことになった. "This turned out to be a lot of trouble."

*n'* ん　=*no Doko e iku n' deshō.* 何処へ行くんでしょう. "I wonder where he is going."

*nakucha* なくちゃ　=*nakute wa* =*nakereba Konna muzukashii mondai wa anta de nakucha tokenai deshō.* こんな難しい問題はあんたでなくちゃ解けないでしょう. "I suppose you're the only one who can solve such a difficult problem."

*nando* なんど　=*nanka*=*nado Sonna hon nando yomu no mo iya da.* そんな本なんど読むのもいやだ. "I would hate to read such a book."

*nya* にゃ　=*ni wa Ano ko nya komatta.* あの子にゃ困った. "I had so much trouble with that kid."

*soitsu* そいつ　=*sore Soitsu wa okashii.* そいつはおかしい. "That's funny."

*sorya* そりゃ　=*sore wa Sorya bakagete iru na.* そりゃ馬鹿げている. "That's idiotic."

*surya* すりゃ　=*sureba Kō surya yoku naru darō.* こうすりゃよくなるだろう. "If you do this, it'll probably improve."

*tatte* たって　=*te mo Boku ga nani o shitatte kamawanai darō.* 僕が何をしたって構わないだろう. "No matter what I do, you don't care, do you?"

*te ya shinai* てやしない　=*te [wa] inai Jibun no koto shika kangaete ya shinai.* 自分のことしか考えてやしない. "He thinks of nothing but himself."

*tottemo* とっても　=*totemo Tottemo tsukareta wa.* とっても疲れたわ. "I am so tired."

*yappari* やっぱり　=*yappashi*=*yahari Yappari kite yokatta.* やっぱり来てよかった. "As I thought, it was a good thing that I came."

# APPENDIX I

# COUNTING SYSTEM

## NUMBERS 数詞

There are two ways of counting in Japanese: one is the native Japanese system which goes only as far as ten, and the other is borrowed from the Chinese and will go as high as one chooses.

*Original Japanese counting system*

Used when 1. counting objects by the piece.
2. counting a person's age (equivalent to *is-sai, ni-sai,* etc. [see p. 239], but *is-sai, ni-sai* sound more formal than *hitotsu, futatsu*).

| | | | | | | |
|---|---|---|---|---|---|---|
| *hitotsu* | 一つ | one | *muttsu* | 六つ | six |
| *futatsu* | 二つ | two | *nanatsu* | 七つ | seven |
| *mittsu* | 三つ | three | *yattsu* | 八つ | eight |
| *yottsu* | 四つ | four | *kokonotsu* | 九つ | nine |
| *itsutsu* | 五つ | five | *tō* | 十 | ten |

*Hatachi* 二十 twenty—*hatachi* is used for a person's age, "twenty years old," equivalent to *nijus-sai.*

*System borrowed from the Chinese*

| | | | | | | |
|---|---|---|---|---|---|---|
| *ichi* | 一 | one | *hachi* | 八 | eight |
| *ni* | 二 | two | *ku (kyū)* | 九 | nine |
| *san* | 三 | three | *jū* | 十 | ten |
| *shi* | 四 | four | *jū-ichi* | 十一 | eleven |
| *go* | 五 | five | *jū-ni* | 十二 | twelve |
| *roku* | 六 | six | *jū-san* | 十三 | thirteen |
| *shichi* | 七 | seven | *jū-shi* | 十四 | fourteen, etc. |
| *nijū* | 二十 | twenty | *gojū* | 五十 | fifty |
| *nijū-ichi* | 二十一 | twenty-one | *rokujū* | 六十 | sixty |
| *nijū-ni* | 二十二 | twenty-two | *shichijū* | 七十 | seventy |
| *sanjū* | 三十 | thirty | *hachijū* | 八十 | eighty |
| *yonjū* | 四十 | forty | *kyūjū* | 九十 | ninety |
| | | | *\*hyaku* | 百 | one hundred |

---

\* Japanese always omit one in one hundred: never *ichi-hyaku,* but always just *hyaku.*

| | | | | |
|---|---|---|---|---|
| *hyaku-ichi* 百一 | one hundred one | *nisen* | 二千 | two thousand |
| *hyaku-jū* 百十 | one hundred ten | *sanzen* | 三千 | three thousand |
| | | *yonsen* | 四千 | four thousand |
| | | *gosen* | 五千 | five thousand |
| *nihyaku* 二百 | two hundred | *rokusen* | 六千 | six thousand |
| *sanbyaku* 三百 | three hundred | *nanasen* | 七千 | seven thousand |
| *yonhyaku* 四百 | four hundred | *hassen* | 八千 | eight thousand |
| *gohyaku* 五百 | five hundred | *kyūsen* | 九千 | nine thousand |
| *roppyaku* 六百 | six hundred | *ichiman* | 一万 | ten thousand |
| *nanahyaku* 七百 | seven hundred | *hyakuman* | 百万 | one million |
| *happyaku* 八百 | eight hundred | **ichioku* | 一億 | one hundred million |
| *kyūhyaku* 九百 | nine hundred | *itchō* | 一兆 | one trillion |
| **sen* (or *issen*) 千 | one thousand | | | |
| *sen-hyaku* 千百 | one thousand one hundred | | | |

## ORDINAL NUMBERS

| first | *ichi-ban* 一番 | *dai-ichi* 第一 | *hitotsu-me* 一つ目 | *ichi-ban-me* 一番目 |
|---|---|---|---|---|
| second | *ni-ban* 二番 | *dai-ni* 第二 | *futatsu-me* 二つ目 | *ni-ban-me* 二番目 |
| third | *san-ban* 三番 | *dai-san* 第三 | *mittsu-me* 三つ目 | *san-ban-me* 三番目 |
| fourth | *yo-ban* 四番 (*yon-ban*) | *dai-yon* 第四 | *yottsu-me* 四つ目 | *yo-ban-me* 四番目 |
| fifth | *go-ban* 五番 | *dai-go* 第五 | *itsutsu-me* 五つ目 | *go-ban-me* 五番目 |
| sixth | *roku-ban* 六番 | *dai-roku* 第六 | *muttsu-me* 六つ目 | *roku-ban-me* 六番目 |
| seventh | *nana-ban* 七番 (*shichi-ban*) | *dai-shichi* 第七 | *nanatsu-me* 七つ目 | *nana-ban-me* 七番目 |
| eighth | *hachi-ban* 八番 | *dai-hachi* 第八 | *yattsu-me* 八つ目 | *hachi-ban-me* 八番目 |
| ninth | *ku-ban* 九番 | *dai-ku* 第九 | *kokonotsu-me* 九つ目 | *ku-ban-me* 九番目 |

* For one thousand, one hears both *sen* and *issen*.
** *Oku* and *chō* are always preceded by *ichi*: *ichioku* and *itchō*, and never *oku* or *chō*.

| tenth | *jū-ban* | *dai-jū* | —— | *jū-ban-me* |
|---|---|---|---|---|
|  | 十番 | 第十 |  | 十番目 |

Note: The above ordinal numbers are nouns. They should be followed by *no* if they are used as noun modifiers.

　　　e.g.　Ano hito wa kono *kurasu* de *ichi-ban* desu. (noun) あの人は
　　　　　　このクラスで一番です．"He is the first (top) in this class."
　　　　　　Yamada-san wa ano *mittsu-me no* isu ni suwatte iru hito
　　　　　　desu. (attributive)　山田さんはあの三つ目の椅子に坐ってい
　　　　　　る人です．"Mr. Yamada is the person who is sitting on
　　　　　　that third chair."

　　The suffix *me* is used after number+counter (see pp. 236–41).

　　　e.g.　Ano *gonin-me no* hito wa dare desu ka. あの五人目の人は誰
　　　　　　ですか．"Who is that fifth person?"
　　　　　　Mō *nihai-me* no kōhī o nonde imasu. もう二杯目のコーヒー
　　　　　　を飲んでいます．"I am already drinking a second cup of
　　　　　　coffee."

## JAPANESE NUMBERS AND ENGLISH NUMBERS

As the use of commas shows, the division of the unit in the English number system comes between every three digits. In Japanese, the division is made every four digits, as shown below.

| | | | | | |
|---|---|---|---|---|---|
| o | one | o | ichi | 一 | |
| o | ten | o | jū | 十 | |
| o | hundred | o | hyaku | 百 | |
| o, | thousand | o | sen | 千 | |
| o | ten thousand | o, | man | 万 | |
| o | hundred thousand | o | jūman | 十万 | |
| o, | million | o | hyakuman | 百万 | |
| o | ten million | o | senman | 千万 | |
| o | hundred million | o, | oku | 億 | |
| o, | billion | o | jūoku | 十億 | |
| o | ten billion | o | hyakuoku | 百億 | |
| o | hundred billion | o | sen'oku | 千億 | |
| o, | trillion | o, | chō | 兆 | |
| ⊣ | ten trillion | ⊣ | jutchō | 十兆 | |

## COUNTERS　助数詞

Japanese uses many different counters to count objects, depending on the type of thing being counted. This tradition is similar to such English phrases as "three *slices* of bread," "three *pairs* of socks," "three *cups* of coffee."

In Japanese, for example, *mai* is used for counting thin objects, *hon* is used for long objects, and so forth.

It should also be remembered that in grouping objects in Japanese the divisions are based on groups of fives and tens, instead of sixes and twelves as in the West. Traditionally, Japanese has no such group as the dozen (dāsu ダース is the Japanese rendering of the English dozen). For example, sets of Japanese dishes or bowls are sold in units of five.

The following is a partial list of common counters. A sample counting up to ten is given once for each new beginning letter, and occasional examples showing how to use the suffix are also included. Exceptions are shown by the use of parentheses.

**b-** **bai** 倍 (multiplicative) times
*ichi-bai* "one time"
*ni-bai* "double," "twice"
*san-bai* "triple," "three times"
*yon-bai*
*go-bai*
*roku-bai*
*nana-bai*
*hachi-bai*
*kyū (ku)-bai*
*jū-bai*

　　e.g. *Tochi no nedan ga kyonen no ni-bai ni natta.*
土地の値段が去年の二倍になっ
た.　"The price of the land has doubled since last year."

**-ban** 番　See Ordinal Numbers, pp. 234–35

**-bun** 分　part, fraction
*ni-bun no ichi* 1/2
*yon-bun no san* 3/4
　↓

**c-** **-chaku** 着　clothes
*it-chaku* "one dress"
*ni-chaku* "two suits"

*san-chaku*
*yon-chaku*
*go-chaku*
*roku-chaku*
*nana-chaku*
*hat-chaku*
*kyū-chaku*
*jut-chaku*
　↓

**-chō** 丁　*tōfu* "beancurd"
*it-chō* "one *tōfu*"
　↓

**-chō** 挺　a pair of scissors
*it-chō* "one pair" of scissors
　↓

**d-** **-dai** 台　vehicle
*ichi-dai* "one car"
*ni-dai* "two trucks"
*san-dai*
*yo-dai*
*go-dai*
*roku-dai*
*shichi-dai*
*hachi-dai*
*ku-dai*
*jū-dai*

**-do** 度 (occurrence) time
*ichi-do* "one time"
↓

e- **-en** 円 yen
*ichi-en* "one yen"
*ni-en*
*san-en*
*yo-en*
*go-en*
*roku-en*
*shichi-en*
*hachi-en*
*kyū-en*
*jū-en*

f- **-fuku** 服  puff of tobacco smoke, packet of powdered medicine, cup of green tea
*ip-puku*
*ni-fuku*
*san-puku*
*yon-fuku* ⎫
*go-fuku* ⎪
*rop-puku* ⎪
*nana-fuku* ⎬ not common
*hap-puku* ⎪
*kyū-fuku* ⎪
*jup-puku* ⎭
    e.g.  *Tabako o ip-puku ikaga desu ka.* タバコ(煙草)を一服いかが(如何)ですか. "Will you have a cigarette?"

**-fuku** 幅 *kakemono* "hanging scroll"
*ip-puku* "one kakemono"
↓

h- **-hai** 杯 cup
*ip-pai* "one cup" of tea
*ni-hai* "two cups" of coffee

*san-bai*
*yon-hai*
*go-hai*
*rop-pai, roku-hai*
*nana-hai*
*hap-pai*
*kyū-hai*
*jup-pai*

**-hatsu** 発 round of ammunition
*ip-patsu* "one shot"
*ni-hatsu*
*(san-patsu)*
    e.g.  Kare wa *san-patsu* utta. 彼は三発打った. "He fired three shots."

**-hen** 遍 (occurrence) time = *do*
*ip-pen* "one time," "once"
*ni-hen*
↓

**-hen** 篇 chapter, canto, volume, etc.
*ip-pen* "one chapter"
*ni-hen*
↓

**-hiki** 匹 small animal
*ip-piki* "one dog"
*ni-hiki* "two cats"
↓

**-hon** 本 long object
*ip-pon* "one pencil"
*ni-hon* "two umbrellas"

j- **-jō** *tatami* "straw mat"
*ichi-jō* "one *tatami*"
*ni-jō*
*san-jō*
*yo-jō*
*go-jō*

k-

*roku-jō*
*shichi-jō*
*hachi-jō*
*kyū-jo*
*jū-jō*
**-jō** 帖  ream of paper
*ichi-jō* "one ream"
↓
**-jō** 条 article of documents
*ichi-jō Dai ichi-jō* "Article I"
↓

**k-**   **-ka** 課  lesson
*ik-ka* "one lesson"
*ni-ka*
*san-ka*
*yon-ka*
*go-ka*
*rok-ka*
*shichi (nana)-ka*
*hak-ka*
*kyū-ka*
*juk-ka*
**-kai** 回 (repetitive) time
*ik-kai* "one time"
↓
**-kan** 巻 volume
*ik-kan* "one volume"
↓
**-ken** 軒 house
*ik-ken* "one house"
↓
**-ko** 個 piece
*ik-ko* "one piece"
↓
**-kyaku** 脚 chair
*ik-kyaku* "one chair"
↓

**m-**   **-ma** 間 room
*(hito-ma)* "one room"
*(futa-ma)*
*(mi-ma)*
*yo-ma*
*go-ma*
*roku-ma*
*nana-ma*
*hachi-ma*
*(kokono-ma)* ⎫
*(jū-ma)* ⎭ not common
**-mai** 枚 thin object
*ichi-mai* "one sheet" of paper
*ni-mai* "two slices" of toast
*san-mai*
*yo (yon)-mai*
↓
*shichi (nana)-mai*
*hachi-mai*
*kyū (ku)-mai*
*jū-mai*
**-maki** 巻 roll
*(hito-maki)* "one roll"
*(futa-maki)*
*(mi-maki)*
*yo-maki*
**-mei** 名 people—more formal
   than *-nin*
*ichi-mei* "one person"
↓
*yo (yon)-mei*

**n-**   **-nin** 人 people
*(hitori)* "one person"
*(futari)*
*san-nin*
*yo-nin*
*go-nin*
*roku-nin*

*shichi-nin*
*hachi-nin*
*ku-nin*
*jū-nin*

**r-**  **-retsu** 列 row
*ichi-retsu* "one row"
*ni-retsu*
*san-retsu*
*yon* (*yo*)-*retsu*
*go-retsu*
*roku-retsu*
*shichi*(*nana*)-*retsu*
*hachi-retsu*
*kyū-retsu*
*jū-retsu*

**-rin** 輪 flower
*ichi-rin* "one flower with
  ↓         stem"
**-ryo** 両(輛) carriage
*ichi-ryō* "one car"
  ↓

**s-**  **-sai** 歳(才) age
*is-sai* "one year old"
*ni-sai*
*san-sai*
*yon-sai*
*go-sai*
*roku-sai*
*nana-sai*
*has-sai*
*kyū-sai*
*jus-sai*

**-sao** 棹 *tansu* "chest of
  drawers"
(*hito-sao*) "one *tansu*"
(*futa-sao*)
(*mi-sao*)
(*yo-sao*)
(*itsu-sao*)

**-satsu** 冊 books
*is-satsu* "one book"
  ↓

**-sho** 章 chapter
*is-shō* "one chapter"
  ↓

**-shu** 首 poem
*is-shu* "one poem"
  e.g. *is-shu yomu.* 一首よむ.
  "to compose a poem."
  ↓

**-soku** 足 footwear
*is-soku* "a pair" of socks
*ni-soku* "two pairs" of shoes
  ↓

**-sō** 艘 boat
*is-sō* "one boat"

**t-**  **-tan** 反 roll of kimono material
*it-tan* "one *tan*"
*ni-tan*
*san-tan*
*yon-tan*
*go-tan*
*roku-tan*
*nana-tan*
*hat-tan*
*kyū-tan*
*jut-tan*

**-tan** 反 land, .245 acres
*it-tan* "one *tan*"
  ↓

**-teki** 滴 drop of liquid
*it-teki* "one drop"
  ↓

**-ten** 点 point
*it-ten* "one point"

↓

**-tō** 頭 big animal
*it-tō* "one cow"
*ni-tō* "two horses"
↓

**tsu-** **-tsui** 対 a pair
*it-tsui* "one pair"
*ni-tsui*
*san-tsui*
*yon-tsui*
*go-tsui*
*roku-tsui*
*nana-tsui*
*hat-tsui*
*kyū-tsui*
*jut-tsui*

**-tsū** 通 letter
*it-tsū* "one letter"
↓

**w-** **-wa** 羽 bird
*ichi-wa, ip-pa* "one bird"
*ni-wa*
*san-ba*
*yon-wa*
*go-wa*
*roku-wa, rop-pa*
*shichi-wa*
*hachi-wa, hap-pa*

*kyū-wa*
*jū-wa, jup-pa*

**-wa** 把 bunch, bundle
*ichi-wa, ip-pa* "one bundle"
↓

**-wari** 割 10%
*ichi-wari* "10%"
↓

*roku wari*
*shichi-wari, nana-wari*
*hachi-wari*
*kyū-wari*
*jū-wari*

**z-** **-zen** 膳 a pair of chopsticks
*ichi-zen* "one pair" of
                    chopsticks
*ni-zen*
*san-zen*
*yo-zen*
*go-zen*
*roku-zen*
*shichi-zen*
*hachi-zen*
*ku (kyū)-zen*
*jū-zen*

**-zen** 膳 bowl of rice
*ichi-zen* "one bowl" of rice
↓

Note: 1.   It is not common in Japanese to use the expression corresponding to "a cup of tea," *ip-pai no ocha* 一杯のお茶, or "a sheet of
paper," *ichi-mai no kami* 一枚の紙, etc. As shown in the examples below, the particle follows the noun, not the number
plus the counter.

    e.g.   *Ocha o ip-pai (ip-pai ocha o) nomimashita.* お茶を一杯飲
みました. "I drank a cup of tea."
*Kami ga san-mai (San-mai kami ga) arimasu.* 紙が三枚
あります. "There are three sheets of paper."

2. *Han* 半 "half" is always used after the counter.

    e. g.  *san-bai han* 三杯半 "three-and-a-half cups," "three cups and a half"

        *ni-sai han* 二歳半 "two-and-a-half years old"

# DATES

## Japanese Years

From ancient times Japan has kept track of time by grouping years into periods, or eras, as they are sometimes called. Some periods lasted for a long time, while others lasted only for a very short time. The changes of the periods often depended on superstitions.

Since 1872 the Western calendar has been used, while at the same time the old idea of period names has been retained, except that they now coincide with the reign of each successive Emperor. Thus we have:

the Meiji period 明治     1868–1912
the Taishō period 大正     1912–1926
the Shōwa period 昭和     1926–to the present

One frequently sees the Japanese year used alone. For example, the dates of historical events are more often given in Japanese period names. Or, trying to find the publishing date for a book, one may encounter the Japanese year at the end of the book, though of late the Western dates are frequently used. When one asks a Japanese person about his date of birth, the answer may be given in the Japanese year. It is, therefore, essential to know how to convert the Japanese date into the Western year as quickly and correctly as possible. The following is a simple method for it.

25th year of Meiji   明治二十五年     1868+25−1    1892
3rd year of Taishō   大正三年         1912+3−1     1914
54th year of Shōwa  昭和五十四年    1926+54−1   1979 etc.

The reason for subtracting one is that the first year is not to be counted. When an Emperor dies, the year is changed immediately. In 1912, for example, up to the 30th of July belongs to the Meiji period, while the 31st belongs to Taishō, because Emperor Meij died on the 30th of July and his son, Emperor Taishō, then became Emperor. The year 1912, then, is the 45th year of Meiji as well as the 1st of Taishō. For the same reason, 1926 is the 15th year of Taishō as well as the 1st of Shōwa (See the chart, p. 242).

## Conversion Table

| Jap. Year | Christ. Year | Jap. Year | Christ. Year | Jap. Year | Christ. Year |
|---|---|---|---|---|---|
| Meiji 1 | 1868 | Taishō 4 | 1915 | Shōwa 37 | 1962 |
| 明治 2 | 1869 | 大正 5 | 1916 | 昭和 38 | 1963 |
| 3 | 1870 | 6 | 1917 | 39 | 1964 |
| 4 | 1871 | 7 | 1918 | 40 | 1965 |
| 5 | 1872 | 8 | 1919 | 41 | 1966 |
| 6 | 1873 | 9 | 1920 | 42 | 1967 |
| 7 | 1874 | 10 | 1921 | 43 | 1968 |
| 8 | 1875 | 11 | 1922 | 44 | 1969 |
| 9 | 1876 | 12 | 1923 | 45 | 1970 |
| 10 | 1877 | 13 | 1924 | 46 | 1971 |
| 11 | 1878 | 14 | 1925 | 47 | 1972 |
| 12 | 1889 | 15 | 1926 | 48 | 1973 |
| 13 | 1880 | Shōwa 1 | 1926 | 49 | 1974 |
| 14 | 1881 | 昭和 2 | 1927 | 50 | 1975 |
| 15 | 1882 | 3 | 1928 | 51 | 1976 |
| 16 | 1883 | 4 | 1929 | 52 | 1977 |
| 17 | 1884 | 5 | 1930 | 53 | 1978 |
| 18 | 1885 | 6 | 1931 | 54 | 1979 |
| 19 | 1886 | 7 | 1932 | 55 | 1980 |
| 20 | 1887 | 8 | 1933 | 56 | 1981 |
| 21 | 1888 | 9 | 1934 | 57 | 1982 |
| 22 | 1889 | 10 | 1935 | 58 | 1983 |
| 23 | 1890 | 11 | 1936 | 59 | 1984 |
| 24 | 1891 | 12 | 1937 | 60 | 1985 |
| 25 | 1892 | 13 | 1938 | 61 | 1986 |
| 26 | 1893 | 14 | 1939 | 62 | 1987 |
| 27 | 1894 | 15 | 1940 | 63 | 1988 |
| 28 | 1895 | 16 | 1941 | 64 | 1989 |
| 29 | 1896 | 17 | 1942 | Heisei 1 | 1989 |
| 30 | 1897 | 18 | 1943 | 平成 2 | 1990 |
| 31 | 1898 | 19 | 1944 | 3 | 1991 |
| 32 | 1899 | 20 | 1945 | 4 | 1992 |
| 33 | 1900 | 21 | 1946 | 5 | 1993 |
| 34 | 1901 | 22 | 1947 | 6 | 1994 |
| 35 | 1902 | 23 | 1948 | 7 | 1995 |
| 36 | 1903 | 24 | 1949 | 8 | 1996 |
| 37 | 1904 | 25 | 1950 | 9 | 1997 |
| 38 | 1905 | 26 | 1951 | 10 | 1998 |
| 39 | 1906 | 27 | 1952 | 11 | 1999 |
| 40 | 1907 | 28 | 1953 | 12 | 2000 |
| 41 | 1908 | 29 | 1954 | | |
| 42 | 1909 | 30 | 1955 | | |
| 43 | 1910 | 31 | 1956 | | |
| 44 | 1911 | 32 | 1957 | | |
| 45 | 1912 | 33 | 1958 | | |
| Taishō 1 | 1912 | 34 | 1959 | | |
| 大正 2 | 1913 | 35 | 1960 | | |
| 3 | 1914 | 36 | 1961 | | |

It is also important to remember that the Japanese always count out the full number in the Western year, e.g. (*is*) *sen-kyūhyaku-shichijūku-nen* 1979 千九百七十九年 (one thousand nine hundred and seventy-nine years). To say *jūku-shichijūku-nen* (nineteen seventy-nine) does not make any sense in Japanese.

## Months of the Year

| | | | | | | |
|---|---|---|---|---|---|---|
| Ichigatsu | 一月 | January | Shichigatsu | 七月 | July |
| Nigatsu | 二月 | February | Hachigatsu | 八月 | August |
| Sangatsu | 三月 | March | Kugatsu | 九月 | September |
| Shigatsu | 四月 | April | Jūgatsu | 十月 | October |
| Gogatsu | 五月 | May | Jūichigatsu | 十一月 | November |
| Rokugatsu | 六月 | June | Jūnigatsu | 十二月 | December |

## Days of the Week

Getsuyōbi (Moon day)
　月曜日　Monday
Kayōbi (Fire [Mars] day)
　火曜日　Tuesday
Suiyōbi (Water [Mercury] day)
　水曜日　Wednesday
Mokuyōbi (Wood [Jupiter] day)
　木曜日　Thursday

Kinyōbi (Metal [Venus] day)
　金曜日　Friday
Doyōbi (Earth [Saturn] day)
　土曜日　Saturday
Nichiyōbi (Sun day)
　日曜日　Sunday

## Days of the Month

This list is used both for the day of the month and for the duration, except *tsuitachi*, the 1st day of the month (*ichinichi* means one day long). Most of the numbers are followed by *nichi*, and a few are followed by *ka* as indicated; *tsuitachi* and *hatsuka* are exceptions.

| | | | | | | | |
|---|---|---|---|---|---|---|---|
| | *tsuitachi* | 一日 | 1st | | *jūni-nichi* | 十二日 | 12th |
| | *futsu-ka* | 二日 | 2nd | | *jūsan-nichi* | 十三日 | 13th |
| | *mik-ka* | 三日 | 3rd | -*ka* | *jūyok-ka* | 十四日 | 14th |
| | *yok-ka* | 四日 | 4th | | *jūgo-nichi* | 十五日 | 15th |
| | *itsu-ka* | 五日 | 5th | | *jūroku-nichi* | 十六日 | 16th |
| -*ka* | *mui-ka* | 六日 | 6th | | *jūshichi-nichi* | 十七日 | 17th |
| | *nano-ka* | 七日 | 7th | | *jūhachi-nichi* | 十八日 | 18th |
| | *yō-ka* | 八日 | 8th | | *jūku-nichi* | 十九日 | 19th |
| | *kokono-ka* | 九日 | 9th | -*ka* | *hatsu-ka* | 二十日 | 20th |
| | *tō-ka* | 十日 | 10th | | *nijūichi-nichi* | 二十一日 | 21st |
| | *jūichi-nichi* | 十一日 | 11th | | *nijūni-nichi* | 二十二日 | 22nd |

| *nijūsan-nichi* | 二十三日 | 23rd | | *nijūhachi-nichi* | 二十八日 | 28th |
|---|---|---|---|---|---|---|
| *-ka nijūyok-ka* | 二十四日 | 24th | | *nijūku-nichi* | 二十九日 | 29th |
| *nijūgo-nichi* | 二十五日 | 25th | | *sanjū-nichi* | 三十日 | 30th |
| *nijūroku-nichi* | 二十六日 | 26th | | *sanjūichi-nichi* | 三十一日 | 31st |
| *nijūshichi-nichi* | 二十七日 | 27th | | | | |

misoka 晦日  last day of the month
ōmisoka 大晦日  last day of the year

## Lunar Months  陰暦〈いんれき〉

Of the twelve months, *Yayoi, Satsuki,* and *Shiwasu* are still quite frequently used. *Yayoi no sora* 弥生の空 "spring sky," *Satsuki ame* (*samidare*) 早月雨 "early summer rain," *Shiwasu no machi* 師走の町 "busy year-end streets," etc.

| Mutsuki | 睦月 | 1st month | Fumizuki (Fuzuki) | | |
|---|---|---|---|---|---|
| Kisaragi | 如月 | 2nd month | | 文月 | 7th month |
| Yayoi | 弥生 | 3rd month | Hazuki | 葉月 | 8th month |
| Uzuki | 卯月 | 4th month | Nagatsuki | 長月 | 9th month |
| Satsuki | 早(皐)月 | 5th month | Kannazuki | 神無月 | 10th month |
| Minazuki | 水無月 | 6th month | Shimotsuki | 霜月 | 11th month |
| | | | Shiwasu | 師走 | 12th month |

# THE CHINESE ZODIAC

## Twelve Chinese Horary Characters and Symbolic Animals  十二支 〈じゅうにし〉

Japanese are still fond of using the traditional symbolic animals of the Chinese zodiac. This is particularly true at the beginning of a new year, or for a person's year of birth. It is not uncommon to hear a person ask, *Anata wa nanidoshi desu ka.* あなたは何年ですか. "In what animal year were you born?" As shown below, this is a twelve-year cycle.

| Horary Characters | | Corresponding Hours | Symbolic Animals | | Corresponding Years | | | |
|---|---|---|---|---|---|---|---|---|
| Ne | 子 | 11 p.m.— 1 a.m. | Rat | 鼠 | 1936 | 1948 | 1960 | 1972 |
| Ushi | 丑 | 1 a.m.— 3 a.m. | Ox | 牛 | 1937 | 1949 | 1961 | 1973 |
| Tora | 寅 | 3 a.m.— 5 a.m. | Tiger | 虎 | 1938 | 1950 | 1962 | 1974 |
| U | 卯 | 5 a.m.— 7 a.m. | Hare | 兎 | 1939 | 1951 | 1963 | 1975 |
| Tatsu | 辰 | 7 a.m.— 9 a.m. | Dragon | 龍 | 1940 | 1952 | 1964 | 1976 |

| Horary Characters | | Corresponding Hours | Symbolic Animals | | Corresponding Years | | | |
|---|---|---|---|---|---|---|---|---|
| Mi | 巳 | 9 a.m.—11 a.m. | Snake | 蛇 | 1941 | 1953 | 1965 | 1977 |
| Uma | 午 | 11 a.m.— 1 p.m. | Horse | 馬 | 1942 | 1954 | 1966 | 1978 |
| Hitsuji | 未 | 1 p.m.— 3 p.m. | Sheep | 羊 | 1943 | 1955 | 1967 | 1979 |
| Saru | 申 | 3 p.m.— 5 p.m. | Monkey | 猿 | 1944 | 1956 | 1968 | 1980 |
| Tori | 酉 | 5 p.m.— 7 p.m. | Cock | 鶏 | 1945 | 1957 | 1969 | 1981 |
| Inu | 戌 | 7 p.m.— 9 p.m. | Dog | 犬 | 1946 | 1958 | 1970 | 1982 |
| I | 亥 | 9 p.m.—11 p.m. | Boar | 猪 | 1947 | 1959 | 1971 | 1983 |

## HOUR OF THE DAY

| a.m./p.m. | *ji* 時 o'clock | *fun* 分 minute | *byō* 秒 second |
|---|---|---|---|
| *gozen* 午前 | *ichi-ji* | *ip-pun* | *ichi-byō* |
| | (one o'clock) | (one minute) | (one second) |
| (a.m.) | *ni-ji* | *ni-fun* | *ni-byō* |
| | *san-ji* | *san-pun* | *san-byō* |
| | *yo-ji* | *yon-fun* (*yon-pun*) | *yon-byō* |
| | *go-ji* | *go-fun* | *go-byō* |
| | *roku-ji* | *rop-pun* | *roku-byō* |
| | *shichi-ji* | *nana-fun* | *nana-byō* |
| | | (*shichi-fun*) | |
| | *hachi-ji* | *hap-pun* | *hachi-byō* |
| | | (*hachi-fun*) | |
| | *ku-ji* | *kyū-fun* | *kyū-byō* |
| | *jū-ji* | *jup-pun* | *jū-byō* |
| | *jūichi-ji* | *jūip-pun* | *jūichi-byō* |
| | *jūni-ji* | *nijup-pun* | *nijū-byō* |
| *gogo* 午後 | *ichi-ji* (*jūsan-ji*)* | *nijūip-pun* | *nijūichi-byō* |
| | *ni-ji* (*jūyo-ji*)* | *sanjup-pun* | *sanjū-byō* |
| (p.m.) | | *sanjūip-pun* | *sanjūichi-byō* |
| | | *yonjup-pun* | *yonjū-byō* |
| | | *yonjūip-pun* | *yonjūichi-byō* |
| | | *gojup-pun* | *gojū-byō* |
| | | *gojūip-pun* | *gojūichi-byō* |
| | *jūni-ji* (*nijūyo-ji*)* | *rokujup-pun* | |

Note: 1. Words to remember in stating time in Japanese

    *sugi* 過 past (often omitted)

    *mae* 前 before

    *han* 半 half

---

\* Used for timetables.

2. There is no equivalent Japanese time word to the English "quarter." The "quarter" is always expressed in Japanese *jūgo-fun* 十五分.

3. In stating date and time in Japanese, the largest unit comes first.

> e.g.   *sen-kyuhyaku-shichijūku-nen Shigatsu tōka gozen jū-ji san-jup-pun nijūgo-byō (sugi)* 一九七九年四月十日午前十時三十分二十五秒（過）"thirty minutes, twenty-five seconds, after ten o'clock, a.m., April 10, 1979."
>
> *Shōwa gojūyo-nen Gogatsu tsuitachi gogo san-ji jup-pun mae* 昭和五十四年五月一日午後三時十分前 "ten minutes before three o'clock, p.m., May 1, 54th year of Shōwa."

# DURATION OF TIME

In English the duration of time is usually expressed by placing the preposition "for" before the time: for a year, for two months, for three weeks, etc. In Japanese the common way to express duration is to add the suffix *-kan* 間 meaning "duration." Care has to be taken, however, because of some irregularities in the use of *-kan*. The following illustrates proper use of time-duration terms.

I. Time units which always take *-kan* to show duration

| | | | |
|---|---|---|---|
| Week | *is-shū-kan* | 一週間 | "for one week" |
| | *ni-shū-kan* | 二週間 | "for two weeks,"  etc. |
| Hour | *ichi-ji-kan* | 一時間 | "for one hour" |
| | *ni-ji-kan* | 二時間 | "for two hours,"  etc. |

II. Time units which sometimes take *-kan* to show duration

Year    *ichi-nen-kan* (or *ichi-nen*) 一年（間）"for one year"
           *ni-nen-kan* (*or ni-nen*) 二年（間）"for two years"
           (Both expressions are common.)

Month    *ik-kagetsu-kan* (or *ik-kagetsu, hito-tsuki*) "for one
       一ケ月間        一ケ月       一月      month"
         *ni-kagetsu-kan* (or *ni-kagetsu, futa-tsuki*) "for two
       二ケ月間        二ケ月       二月      months"
         *san-kagetsu-kan* (or *san-kagetsu, mi-tsuki*) "for three
       三ケ月間        三ケ月       三月      months"
         (Of the three expressions, the two in the parentheses are more common, but for four months

or more, only the *-kagetsu-kan* or *-kagetsu* is
used.)

| | | | |
|---|---|---|---|
| | *yon-kagetsu-kan* (or *yon-kagetsu*) | | "for four |
| | 四ケ月間　　　　　　四ケ月 | | months" |
| | *go-kagetsu-kan* (or *go-kagetsu*) | | "for five |
| | 五ケ月間　　　　　　五ケ月 | | months," etc. |
| Day | —　　　　　　*ichi-nichi* 一日 | | "for one day" |
| | *futsu-ka-kan* (or *futsu-ka*) 二日 (間) | | "for two days" |
| | *mik-ka-kan* (or *mik-ka*) 三日 (間) | | "for three days," etc. |

(*ichi-nichi* "one day" is the only exception, and
takes no *-kan*. For four days or more, see pp.
243–44.)

| | | | |
|---|---|---|---|
| Minute | *ip-pun-kan* (or *ip-pun*) | 一分 (間) | "for one minute" |
| | *ni-fun-kan* (or *ni-fun*) | 二分 (間) | "for two minutes," etc. |
| Second | *ichi-byō-kan* (or *ichi-byō*) | 一秒 (間) | "for one second" |
| | *ni-byō-kan* (or *ni-byō*) | 二秒 (間) | "for two seconds," etc. |

# APPENDIX II

## PUNCTUATION

There are several marks which correspond to English punc-
tuation: *tōten* 読点、 (a comma, literally reading point), *kuten* 句点。
(a period, literally phrase or clause point), *kakko* 括弧 「 」 (quotation
marks), ( ) (parentheses), [ ] (brackets), etc., but rules for their
use seem to be less rigid than in English. For example, the use
of *tōten*, or comma, seems to be quite arbitrary. (For question mark,
see p. 63, *-ka*, Note.)

## APPENDIX III

# HOW TO READ A JAPANESE SENTENCE
## (SIMPLE STEPS TO FOLLOW)

Many Japanese sentences seem long, but if one knows how to read them, they will not seem as impossible to handle as one may have thought. Try the following steps:

I. Find all conjunctions between clauses in the sentence.

    e.g. $V_2$ *nagara* ながら    $V_3$ *shi* し

         $V_3$ *ga* が         $V_3$ *to* と

         $V_3$ *kara* から       $V_{ba}$ ば

         $V_3$ *keredo(mo)* けれど   $V_{tara}$ たら

         $V_3$ *no de* ので     $V_{te}$ て

         $V_3$ *no ni* のに     $V_{te}$ *mo* ても etc.

    (For more conjunctions, see p. 210–12.)

    If there are no conjunctions, simply follow the steps after III below.

II. Divide the sentence into separate short clauses after each conjunction.

III. In each clause:

1. Find the sentence-ending expression, if there is any. Most of the Japanese sentence-ending expressions can be translated at the beginning of an English sentence.

    e.g. *koto ga aru* ことがある    *sō da* そうだ

         *koto ni naru* ことになる  *yō da* ようだ

         *koto ni suru* ことにする   *to iu* という

         *no (n') da* のだ       *to omou* と思う

         *rashii* らしい         *wake da* わけだ etc.

    (For more sentence-ending expressions, see Verb-following Expressions, pp. 39–86.)

2. Find the main verb.

    a. If there is a sentence-ending expression, the main verb should directly precede the sentence-ending expression.

    b. If there is no sentence-ending expression, the main verb should directly precede the conjunction.

    c. The main verb could be any one of the following:

1. Copula
2. Verb ⎰Transitive
          ⎱Intransitive
3. Adjective

> Note: Be alert to all the different verb forms; present, perfective, positive, negative, tentative, potential, honorific, passive, causative, causative-passive, etc.

IV. Find the subject for the verb

1. If there is a subject, it will be marked with such particles as *wa, ga, mo, shika,* and *dake.* Also one should remember that the grammatical subject may be a simple word like *no,* because *no* is often used as a noun.

> e.g. Soko ni iru *no* wa Yamada-san desu.　そこにいるの は山田さんです.　"The one who is there is Mr. Yamada."

(For more *no* as nouns, see p. 128.)

2. If there is no subject, one will have to supply it, guessing from the context. One of the difficulties in reading Japanese is that each clause may have a different subject, yet the subjects may still be omitted.

> e.g. Mō gofun mo sureba ame ga agaru kara mate to itta ga, matazu ni dete shimatta.　もう五分もすれ ば雨が上るから待てと言ったが待たずに出てしまっ た.　"He said to wait, because it might stop rain- ing in five minutes or so, but I left without wait- ing." Or, depending on the context, it can also be translated, "I said to wait, because it might stop raining in five minutes or so, but he left without waiting."

V. Once one finds the main verb and its subject (existent or supplied), they will become the core of the sentence.

VI. The rest will merely be the additions to the core of the sentence.
　They may be some of the following elements:

1. Sentence-beginning conjunctions (See pp. 208–210)
2. Adverbs
   Adverbial phrases ⎰how, when, where, how many (much), etc.

3.   Noun-modifiers $\left\{\begin{array}{l}\text{Other noun} + no \\ \text{Copular noun} + na \\ \text{Adjectives} \\ \text{Non-conjugative adjectives} \\ V_3 \\ V_{ta}\end{array}\right\}$ See pp. 189-90

4.   Direct object (See the particle *o*, pp. 129-30)
     Indirect object (See the particle *ni*, p. 122)

*EXAMPLES*

*Senkichi wa   Kanda no   aru hakariya no mise ni hōkō shite iru.*
仙吉　は　　神田　の　或る 秤 屋　の　店　に　奉公して いる.
*Sore wa   aki rashii   yawaraka na   sunda hizashi ga   kon no daibu*
それ は　　秋 らしい　柔 ら か　な　澄んだ 陽ざし が　紺　の　大分
*hageochita   noren no   shita kara shizuka ni   misesaki ni sashikonde*
はげ落ちた 暖簾　の　下 か ら　静 か に　店　先　に　差し込んで
*iru toki datta.   Chōbagōshi no   naka ni   suwatte   taikutsusō   ni*
いる時だった.　　　帳 場 格 子　の　中 に　　坐 っ て　　退屈そう　に
*makitabako o   fukashite ita bantō ga   hibachi no soba de shinbun o*
巻 煙 草　を　ふかして いた 番頭　が　火 鉢　の　傍　で　新　聞　を
*yonde iru wakai bantō ni konna fū ni hanashikaketa.*
読んでいる 若い 番頭　に　こんな風 に 話しかけた.

The above excerpt from Shiga Naoya's 志賀直哉 *Kozō no kami-sama* 小僧の神様   may look complex at the first glance, but if one looks at it carefully, it consists of three sentences which are not basically so complex.   In each sentence, once the core of the sentence (subject and main verb) is located, the remaining parts are all modifiers (noun modifiers, adverbial phrases, etc.).

1.   *Senkichi wa* $\left\{\begin{array}{l}\textit{Kanda no} \\ \textit{aru} \\ \textit{hakariya no}\end{array}\right\}$ <u>*mise* ni *hōkō shite iru.*</u>

"Senkichi is employed at a certain scale shop in Kanda."
   *Core of the sentence*:
      *Senkichi wa   hōkō shite iru.*   "Senkichi is employed."
      (subject)         (main verb)

*Remaining parts*:

noun modifiers $\begin{cases} Kanda\ no & (\text{Noun}+no) \\ aru & (\text{Non-con-} \\ & \text{jugative adj.}) \\ hakariya\ no & (\text{Noun}+no) \end{cases}$ $\begin{cases} mise\ \text{ni} \\ (\text{adv. phrase—} \\ \text{where}) \end{cases}$

2.  *Sore wa* $\begin{cases} aki\ rashii \\ yawaraka\ na \\ sunda \end{cases}$ $\underline{hizashi}\ ga$ $\begin{cases} kon\ no \\ daibu \\ hageochita \end{cases}$ $\begin{matrix} \underline{noren}\ no \\ shita\ \ kara \end{matrix}$

$\begin{cases} shizuka\ ni \\ misesaki\ ni \end{cases}$ *sashikonde iru   toki datta.*

"It was the time when the fall-like, soft, clear sun's rays were quietly pouring into the store front from under the mostly faded blue *noren* curtains."

*Core of the sentence*:

Sore wa   toki                datta.          "It was the time."

(subject)  (complement)   (main verb)

*Remaining parts*:

noun modifiers: $\begin{cases} aki\ rashii & (\text{Noun}+rashii) \\ yawaraka\ na & (\text{Cop.}+na) \\ sunda & (\text{V}_{ta}) \end{cases}$ $hizashi$

relative clauses: $\begin{cases} kon\ no & (\text{subject of relative} \\ & \text{clause}) \\ daibu & (\text{adv.—degree}) \\ hageochita & (\text{V}_{ta}\text{—noun modifier}) \end{cases}$ $noren$

$\begin{cases} hizashi\ ga & (\text{subject of rela-} \\ & \text{tive clause}) \\ sashikonde\ iru & (\text{V}_3\text{—noun modifier}) \end{cases}$ $toki$

adverbial phrases:  *noren no shita kara* (from where)

*shizuka ni* (how)

*misesaki ni* (to where)

3.  $\begin{cases} Ch\bar{o}bag\bar{o}shi\ no\ naka\ ni \\ suwatte \\ taikutsus\bar{o}\ ni \\ makitabako\ o\ fukashite\ ita \end{cases}$ *bantō* ga $\begin{cases} hibachi\ no\ soba\ de \\ shinbun\ o\ yonde\ iru \\ wakai \end{cases}$ $\begin{matrix} bant\bar{o} \\ \text{ni} \end{matrix}$

*konna fū ni hanashikaketa.*

"The clerk, who was sitting inside the latticed counter with a bored look, smoking a cigarette, talked in the following manner to the young clerk, who was reading a newspaper beside a brazier."

*Core of the sentence*:

　*bantō ga hanashikaketa.*　"The clerk talked (to the clerk)."
　(subject)　(main verb)

*Remaining parts*:

　relative clauses: *chōbagōshi no naka ni* (adv.—where)

　　　　　　　　　*suwatte* (V*te*—conjunction, "and")

　　　　　　　　　*taikutsusō ni* (adv.—how)　　　　　*bantō*

　　　　　　　　　*makitabako o fukashite ita*

　　　　　　　　　　　　(V*ta*—noun modifier)

　　　　　　　　　*hibachi no soba de* (adv.—where)　*bantō* ni

　　　　　　　　　*shinbun o yonde iru* (V₃—noun　　(indirect

　　　　　　　　　　　　　　　　　modifier)　　obj.)

　　　　　　　　　*wakai* (adj.—noun modifier)

　adverbial phrase: *konna fū ni* (how)

# INDEX I
## VERB-FOLLOWING EXPRESSIONS AND NOUN-FOLLOWING EXPRESSIONS
Verb-following expressions in lower case
### NOUN-FOLLOWING EXPRESSIONS IN UPPER CASE

(See also alphabetical lists of Common Noun-suffixes, pp. 179–82,
Counters, pp. 235–41 and Particles, pp. 93–140)
In order to extend its usefulness as a reading aid, the following list includes
many Chinese characters, even though some of them may not appear frequently in contemporary writings.

agaru あ(上)がる, 47
ageru あ(上)げる, 47
aida 間, 60
asaru あさ(漁)る, 47
o V₂ asobasu お遊ばす, 47

ba V₃ dake ば V₃ だけ(丈), 81
  = ba V₃ hodo
ba V₃ hodo ば V₃ ほど(程), 81
ba ii n' desu ga...ばいいんですが, 81
(Interrog. w.)＋ ba ii no ka ばいい
  のか, 81
ba ii no ni ばいいのに, 82
ba koso ばこそ, 82
baai 場合, 60
Vta baai, 51
bae ば(栄)え, 47
bakari ばかり, 60
Vta bakari, 51
bakari de wa nai ばかりではない,
60
  nai bakari de wa nai, 40
BAKARI DE WA NAKU...MO ば
  かりではなく…も, 156
BAKARI KA...MO ばかりか…も,
156
BAMU ばむ, 156
bekarazaru べからざる, 61
bekarazu べからず, 61
beki べき, 61
BIRU びる, 156
BURU ぶる, 156

da だ, 51 = ta
o V₂ da お V₂ だ, 47
da ato de だ後で, 51 = ta ata de
da baai [wa] だ場合, 51
  = ta baai [wa]
da bakari だばかり, 51
  = ta bakari
da bakari ni だばかりに, 51
  = ta bakari ni
da ga saigo だが最後, 52
  = ta ga saigo
da koto ga aru だことがある, 52
  = ta koto ga aru
da koto ga atta だことがあった,
  52 = ta koto ga atta
da koto ni suru だことにする, 52
  = ta koto ni suru
da mama だまま(儘), 52
  = ta mama
da mono da だものだ, 52
  = ta mono da
da oboe ga aru だ覚えがある, 52
  = ta oboe ga aru
da tameshi ga nai だ例がない, 52
  = ta tameshi ga nai
da tokoro da だところだ, 52
  = ta tokoro da
da tokoro de だところで, 52
  = ta tokoro de
da tokoro ga だところが, 52
  = ta tokoro ga
da tsumori da だつ(積)もりだ, 53

# INDEX II
# GRAMMAR

Handbook of
Modern Japanese Grammar
口語日本文法便覧

1981年7月10日　初版発行　　　1991年11月25日　16刷発行

検印省略

著　者　Yoko M. McClain

発行者　株式 北星堂書店
　　　　会社

代表者　山 本 雅 三

〒113 東京都文京区本駒込 3-32-4
Tel (03) 3827-0511　Fax (03) 3827-0567

**THE HOKUSEIDO PRESS**
32-4, Honkomagome 3-chome, Bunkyo-ku, Tokyo 113 Japan

❖落丁・乱丁本はお取替いたします。